Race Relations in the United States, 1940–1960

Race Relations in the United States, 1940–1960

THOMAS J. DAVIS

Race Relations in the United States
Ronald H. Bayor, General Editor

GREENWOOD PRESS
Westport, Connecticut • London

Library of Congress Cataloging-in-Publication Data

Davis, Thomas J. (Thomas Joseph)
    Race relations in the United States, 1940–1960 / Thomas J. Davis.
        p. cm. — (Race relations in the United States)
    Includes bibliographical references and index.
    ISBN-13: 978–0–313–34276–9 (v : alk. paper)
    ISBN-13: 978–0–313–33717–8 (set : alk. paper)
    1. United States—Race relations—History—20th century.   I. Title.
    E184.A1D284   2008
    305.800973—dc22   2007050305

British Library Cataloguing in Publication Data is available.

Library of Congress Catalog Card Number: 2007050305
ISBN-13: 978–0–313–34276–9 (vol.)
          978–0–313–33717–8 (set)

First published in 2008

Greenwood Press, 88 Post Road West, Westport, CT 06881
An imprint of Greenwood Publishing Group, Inc.
www.greenwood.com

Printed in the United States of America

The paper used in this book complies with the
Permanent Paper Standard issued by the National
Information Standards Organization (Z39.48–1984).

10 9 8 7 6 5 4 3 2 1

To
All those of faith and hope and quiet strength
who have practiced and are practicing their principles in lives filled with the
humanity and humility of charity,
who give with no concern of getting,
who do their duties
as God gives them
to understand their duties,
and especially to
Duke Davis, Newton Francis Davis, their brothers and sisters,
and
Ada Sterling Johnson and Joseph Johnson Sr., their sons and daughters,
especially Lula, and their grandchildren and great-grandchildren
and
Ida M. Brock and Edward Elmore Brock III, and especially their daughter,
Brenda

Contents

Series Foreword

W.E.B. Du Bois, an influential African American civil rights activist, educator, and scholar, wrote in 1903 that "the problem of the twentieth century is the problem of the color line." Although Du Bois spoke only of the situation affecting African Americans, we now know that the twentieth century brought issues to the fore that affected all of America's racial and ethnic groups. It was a century that started with vicious attacks on blacks and other minority Americans, as evident in the 1906 Atlanta race riot, and included within its years substantial civil rights gains in legislation and public attitudes as revealed by the Civil Rights Act of 1964 and the Voting Rights Act of 1965. Everything that occurred took place during the time of two world wars, the Great Depression, the Cold War, the turbulent 1960s, the Civil Rights and Women's movements, the rise of the Conservative movement, and the Persian Gulf and Iraqi wars.

The first volumes in the *Race Relations in the United States* series include coverage of significant events, influential voices, race relations history, legislation, media influences, culture, and theories of intergroup interactions that have been evident in the twentieth century and related to race. Each volume covers two decades and encapsulates the state of race relations by decade. A standard format is followed per decade, allowing comparison of topics through the century. Historians have written the topical essays in an encyclopedic style, to give students and general readers a concise, yet authoritative overview of race relations for the decade studied.

Coverage per decade includes a Timeline, Overview, Key Events, Voices of the Decade, Race Relations by Group, Law and Government, Media and Mass Communications, Cultural Scene, Influential Theories and Views on Race, and a Resource Guide. Furthermore, each volume contains an introduction for the two decades and a selected bibliography and index. Historical photos complement the set.

The volumes not only deal with African Americans, Native Americans, Latinos, and Asian Americans but also with religious entities such as Jewish Americans. The history is a fascinating story that deals with such personalities as Henry Ford,

Marcus Garvey, Martin Luther King Jr., Cesar Chavez and Dolores Huerta, Russell Means, and George Wallace; defining events such as the imprisonment of Japanese Americans during World War II, the 1943 Zoot suit riots in California against Mexican Americans, the Selma to Montgomery Civil Rights march in 1965, and the American Indian Movement's occupation of Wounded Knee, South Dakota in 1973; and legislation and court cases deciding who could enter the country and who could become a citizen. The 1960s as a decade of new civil rights acts, immigration laws, and cultural changes are covered along with the increase in new immigration that marked the 1980s and 1990s. The volumes familiarize readers with the role of the Ku Klux Klan, the fear of a "Yellow Peril," and the stereotypes that impeded the attainment of equality for many minorities.

The books' focus will enable readers to understand the progress that has been made in the face of relentless persecution and oppression. As the year 2000 approached and passed, the United States was a different country than it had been in 1900. Many problems remained in relation to immigration and civil rights, but the days of lynching, racially discriminatory laws, and culturally negative stereotypes have largely faded. The story is a positive one of growth and change, but one that provides lessons on the present and future role of race relations.

One of the enduring changes that can be seen is on TV where the human landscape has evolved from ugly images of racial and ethnic groups to more multicultural and accepting views. When television first appeared, African Americans, Native Americans, Asian Americans, and Hispanic Americans were portrayed in negative ways. Blacks were often portrayed as ignorant servants and Native Americans as savages. "Stepin Fetchit," Charlie Chan, wild Indians, and the "Frito Bandito" are gone. These negative images evident in the 1950s would not find a place in today's media. By itself, that represents a significant change in attitudes and indicates the progress that has been made in intergroup relations. How this happened is what students and general readers will find in these volumes.

Ronald H. Bayor
Series Editor

Preface

The diversity of race relations in the United States challenges any attempt to capture the subject comprehensively. It necessarily spills over any spatial or temporal confines, for the subject traverses locality, region, and nation. And it neither starts nor stops with calendar dates. Race relations run in multiple currents, overlapping in their ebbing and flowing. Even focusing on a limited number of years, such as the decades of the 1940s and 1950s, in a single work of very limited pages provides scant opportunity to reach any full measure of the lived experience of the millions of individuals whose behavior and beliefs constituted the reality of intergroup and interpersonal race relations. A legion of untold stories lies beneath the sweep of the survey offered in this book. Those stories collectively supplied a continually shifting American identity. Their recorded and unrecorded events, their details of love and hate, their ordinary and extraordinary conduct shaped the content and character of all American relations.

Complexity necessarily shaped U.S. race relations in the 1940s and 1950s, and not then alone. This book collapses much of that complexity. Sketching cultural, political, and social dynamics during the two decades, it suggests cohesion and continuity of action more apparent in hindsight than during the unfolding times. It is episodic and illustrative rather than comprehensive. It addresses selected, signal obstacles and achievements in tracing the central development of race relations during the two decades—the successful cumulative confrontation that collapsed the legal structure of segregation white supremacy imposed throughout the United States. It accents racism's clash with democratic values. It also emphasizes the power concerned people organizing at the grassroots developed and deployed to reform national and local politics and society. The decades displayed varied interplay of conflicting ideologies, popular culture, and political and social radicalism, reaction, and resistance.

The plan of the series in which this book appears called for treating the complexity of U.S. race relations within discussions of five distinct groupings identified by ancestral geographic origins in Africa, America, Asia, or Europe, and also by Hispanic and Latino heritage. Such clusterings emphasize imposed identities.

They are not intended here as personally exclusive. Instead, they serve to high-light realities of public policies and practices that shaped U.S. race relations as culturally and socially constructed power relations of exclusion and inclusion.

In the context of power, the book treats the often self-centered efforts of various nonwhite and Hispanic and Latino groups working to reconfigure their separate relations with whites. Race relations were not, however, an exclusive encounter between nonwhites and whites. They developed among nonwhites, including Latinos, who competed against each other for access and opportunity. Maneu-vering for advantage against one another, they developed their own angry and hateful race relations within the structure of white supremacy. Those stories are not treated here. This book does not treat those spoken and unspoken conflicts, which lay expansively as rich terrain beckoning further scholarly exploration. Nor does the book develop class, gender, and international dimensions of U.S. race relations. It acknowledges the movement for civil rights during the 1940s and 1950s as a major development not only in U.S. history but in international history. America's domestic race relations very much entered the dynamics of international affairs and foreign policy.

This historical synthesis traces part of an ongoing evolution in U.S. history and identity. It seeks to contribute to understanding a slice of the sequential developments and processes Americans in their endless varieties have undergone to come together and stand apart as living images of the U.S. motto *e pluribus unum*. There is, of course, much more to say on the subject. The brief selected bibliography offers some of the most general works for continued thinking. The notes and sources for the included documents also offer more specific studies, and the resource guides point to more specific readings.

Acknowledgments

I thank the many who made this work a reality. Special thanks go to general editor Ronald H. Bayor for inviting me to do the book. Similarly, I thank editor Wendi Schnaufer at Greenwood Press for her work. My thanks go also to the Arizona State University Libraries, the Library of Congress, the U.S. National Archives and Records Administration, and the Center for Oral and Public History (COPH) at California State University, Fullerton.

I thank my students for continuing to teach me about U.S. history, law, and life. For general and specific advice, counsel, and friendship that helped sustain me and thus this project, I thank Mary Francis Berry, Lula Johnson Davis, Moses N. Moore, Wilson Jeremiah Moses, and Mary Magdalene Mendoza Staten. Brenda M. Brock contributed significantly from her amazing knowledge of popular American culture and literature, particularly film and fiction. Her hopefully soon forthcoming study, *Hidden Images: Nation, Race and Gender in Pulitzer Prize Novels*, should further enlighten us all with her insights to the importance of race and gender and their interaction in shaping twentieth-century America.

Introduction

The 1940s and 1950s were pivotal decades in U.S. race relations. Few other consecutive decades witnessed more significant shifts in the traditional race-based foundations and frameworks of white Anglo American domination and nonwhite subordination. Under increasing pressure during the two decades, the seemingly settled state of affairs reflected in race-based segregation collapsed. Government, law, public policy, and popular opinion eroded acceptance of apartheid practices. Legal sanctions fell away from separate and unequal treatment of nonwhites. Fresh demands insisted the United States put fully into practice its long espoused principles guaranteeing every person under its jurisdiction equal protection of the laws—regardless of race, color, culture, or other heritage.

The 1940s and 1950s escalated constructive dissatisfaction throughout the range and reach of U.S. race relations. How individuals and institutions in the United States saw and treated race became more and more central personal and political issues. The Carnegie Corporation of New York's 1944, near 1,500-page, landmark study *An American Dilemma: The Negro Problem and Modern Democracy*, directed by Swedish political economist Gunnar Myrdal, detailed the disquieting condition of U.S. race relations and pointed the way toward immediate fixes and long-term improvements. Neither the problems nor the solutions, however, were simply black-and-white. The "Negro problem" was illustrative, not all inclusive. The spectrum of race in U.S. law and life colored the American population broadly in a nonwhite/white dichotomy. Both sides of the divide contained multiplicities of peoples with various identities. Race relations reached them all.

For all its diversity, U.S. race relations always turned on one primary color and culture. Whites of Anglo European heritage stood atop the dichotomy. Blacks stood at the bottom. Stereotyped African Americans epitomized the despised nonwhite *Other* in U.S. law, life, and society. Other nonwhites filled out the race mix. American Indians, Asian Americans, and Mexican Americans and other Hispanic and Latino Americans figured prominently in the structure and substance of changing U.S. race relations. Developments and events during the

1940s and 1950s pushed Americans of whatever color or background to think deeply and differently about the concept of race and how their nation and they, personally, constructed and deployed race.

President Franklin D. Roosevelt illustrated the decades' introduction of change with his June 1941 Executive Order 8802. It decreed that "there shall be no discrimination in the employment of workers in defense industries or government because of race, creed, color, or national origin."[1] FDR's proclaiming principles of fair employment practices came only under threat of a massive demonstration in the nation's capital. The president and many of the nation's other officials saw the prospect of a planned, black-led protest march on Washington, D.C., in July 1941 as fraught with possibilities for national embarrassment. They conceded to head it off with the executive order's pledge of nondiscrimination.

Much change accumulated during the 1940s and 1950s from insistent, relentless demands for respect of personal, individual, and civil rights, such as the threatened 1941 march on Washington displayed. As America's largest and most visible minority, blacks pushed in the forefront to remove racial barriers to political and social freedom. They aimed to change living conditions and standards. They were not so much interested in promises as in practices. They were hardly alone. In their own ways, almost every nonwhite population in the United States mounted protests against stifling segregation. Asian Americans, for example, gained voices in state legislatures and in the U.S. Congress. Hispanic Americans also stood tall in the parade of protests. Although technically categorized as "whites," they too were relegated in Anglo-American apartheid.

The National Association for the Advancement of Colored People (NAACP) and its Legal Defense Fund (LDF) relentlessly confronted constitutional inconsistencies in segregation. The NAACP and LDF pressed anti-segregation cases to the highest levels, appealing to the U.S. Supreme Court and to the courts of national and world opinion. The League of United Latin American Citizens (LULAC), the American G. I. Forum, and other Hispanic groups challenged discrimination that also treated them as virtual non-Americans. Their victories in cases against public school segregation in *Mendez v. Westminster School District* (1946–1947), anti-miscegenation laws in *Perez v. Sharp* (1948), and racialized discrimination in *Hernandez v. Texas* (1954) set landmarks. The National Congress of American Indians (NCAI) and other Indian groups beat their own drums against persisting injustices. Indeed, American Indians in the 1940s and 1950s found themselves again fighting to sustain their very existence and recognized cultural identity and independence.

The interning of virtually the entire U.S. mainland Japanese American population in concentration camps for the duration of World War II (1939–1945) after Japan's December 1941 attack on America at Pearl Harbor epitomized for many boundless race-based U.S. injustices in the 1940s. It exposed vicious, old, racist, anti-Asian and anti-immigrant hatreds. Its imagined "yellow peril" replenished the backlashes of the 1800s that excluded first the Chinese and by the

1920s all other Asians from immigrating to the United States or becoming naturalized U.S. citizens.

Like Japanese American internment, most of what happened in U.S. race relations in the 1940s centered on World War II. It was, after all, the crucial episode of the twentieth century. Its onset, unfolding, and aftermath dominated most aspects of American life during the decade. Nazi leader Adolf Hitler's directing Germany to invade Poland in September 1939 changed the world. The ensuing war altered much of the map of Europe, Asia, and Africa. It shifted much in America, too. It strained old barriers of race relations. Massive demands for troops and workers opened previously white-only places and positions in the segregated United States.

World War II snared U.S. society in a predicament. Its accepted segregation shared much ideologically and institutionally with its vilified Nazi enemy. Versions of white supremacy dominated America as well as Germany. Indeed, Hitler's Nazis were not without a significant American following. U.S. interning of Japanese Americans also filled concentration camps. The black press particularly pilloried U.S. hypocrisy. African American newspapers mocked U.S. propaganda that pitched war against Germany and Japan as struggles for democracy. America's real struggle for democracy was domestic as well as foreign, the black *Pittsburgh Courier* insisted. In February 1942, the newspaper launched a "Double V Campaign" for democracy abroad *and* at home.

Nazi crimes against humanity altered accepted racial attitudes in America and around the globe. Horror at the race-based human slaughter memorialized as the Holocaust and other atrocities revolted world opinion. It turned away even the appearance of any acceptance of principles or practices of race-based dominance or subordination akin to the Nazi propaganda about naturally degraded human groups or a super race based on white supremacy. Revulsion at the ideology of racial superiority and inferiority further transformed thinking about race, culture, and human biology.

More than ideology shifted during World War II. Mobilizing for defense drew Americans into unprecedented contact. Geographic, occupational, and residential movement trampled old boundaries. Nonwhites and whites shared work and social spaces as seldom before. For many the closeness was unwelcome. It also proved volatile. Race riots erupted across America in the spring and summer of 1943. It reached from Mobile, Alabama, to Detroit, Michigan, and from Los Angeles, California, to New York City. America's vaunted melting pot proved not so accommodating, even amid vaunted wartime pressures for unity.

The home front underwent rapid and far-reaching change during the war. Nonwhites and women grabbed jobs previously denied them. "Whites-only" and "men-only" work gave way to the performance of able hands of whatever color or gender. Shifts in sexuality and family life accompanied the changes. Popular culture vibrated with nontraditional images, perceptions, and understandings. Movies, music, and popular magazines edged into more pluralistic demographics. The white predominant old mainstream had to accommodate new sights, sounds, and steps. Drastic change was afoot, and with it a fresh era of race relations edged into U.S. society.

Physical changes were prominent and widespread. Where and how Americans lived shifted. Technology swept the nation headlong into transformed areas and opportunities. With automobiles, television, and so much more, Americans found themselves in different places, doing different things in and with their lives. Post-1945 suburbs stamped much of the nation's shifting demographic character and direction. Manners and tastes took fresh turns. Indeed, rampant change challenged old ways. That provoked strong reactions. Renewed battles broke out afresh in America's seemingly unending culture wars. Race relations served as a primary battleground.

The 1940s mobilized forces for changing race relations. Calls for democracy and human rights summoned Americans from various perspectives to organize against racial discrimination and segregation. The interracial and interfaith Committee (later Congress) of Racial Equality (CORE) founded in Chicago, Illinois, in 1942 exemplified the broadening movement to end American apartheid. Rising above his own personal bias and native, old slave-state background, Missourian Harry S Truman elevated equality to a national issue in postwar America.

As president, Truman articulated domestic and global contexts for changing race relations. Beginning in 1947, he launched a campaign to better establish and enforce civil rights as a matter of fundamental fairness. He made it also a matter that reached national and international security in the climate of the intensifying Cold War between the United States as self-styled champion of democracy and the Union of Soviet Socialist Republics (USSR) as champion of communism. Truman ordered the desegregation of the U.S. Armed Forces and with other executive action pushed federal nondiscrimination policies. Congress thwarted most of his broader anti-segregation proposals.

Courts at the federal and state level hearkened to complaints against segregation. In *Mendez v. Westminster School District* (1946–1947), for instance, federal courts in California upheld Mexican Americans' challenges against their children's being segregated in public schools. The California Supreme Court in *Perez v. Sharp* (1948) outlawed the state ban on interracial marriage. The U.S. Supreme Court's 1954 ruling in *Brown v. Board of Education* became a desegregation landmark. Such school decisions cast the Court in the 1950s as a major, and much vilified, force against segregation. The rulings also energized both sides in the battle over changing race relations.

The anti-segregation struggle enveloped more than public schools. Race relations reached every fiber in the fabric of American life. It was no stray thread to be simply snipped. It required more than patchwork. Tugging at it threatened to unravel America's traditional white topcoat. Particularly some white Americans feared such unraveling would strip them of their long developed and customary identity, for traditional race relations had defined much about how they saw themselves. It supplied the shape and substance of who they thought they were and what they thought America was. It also supplied the standards for their color-coded social values.

More than a few whites worried that if nonwhites came to share goods and services with them, that would devalue the goods and services and the lifestyles whites had previously enjoyed when such goods and services were racially restricted. Such shifting would erase important distinctions between being white and being nonwhite, such persons feared. Elements of white exclusivity played large in such perceptions and stamped race relations. Among some whites, discrimination persisted as an impetus not simply to keep up with the proverbial Joneses but to keep ahead and certainly to stay ahead of nonwhites. It was part of the prejudice of a conspicuous consumption society. And consumerism was soaring in post-1945 America. That made it the best of times for some and the worst of times for others.

American nonwhites' material conditions generally improved in the 1940s and 1950s. Yet they persistently lagged general U.S. standards. The discrepancies continued to incite their insistence on sharing in the hallowed American promises of equal access and equal opportunity. And they demanded more than mere promises; they demanded results. Yet committing to change to improve nonwhites' conditions threatened the positions of whites who viewed themselves as engaged in a zero-sum game where nonwhites' gains necessarily meant whites' losses. Such views perpetuated a tricky politics of race relations.

The campaign to improve race relations garnered considerable conservative resistance in the 1940s and 1950s. More radical changes produced recalcitrance and more reactionary resistance. Deeply ingrained perceptions of self and society were at issue. An overwhelming and unrelenting majority of white Americans during the decades rejected any suggestion they were racist or contributed to racism. They tended to believe firmly that their own advantages and status, like economic and social outcomes in America generally, reflected personal behavior, not systemic discrimination.

Demonstrations in the streets and the glare of television more and more in the 1950s exposed structural barriers nonwhites faced in America. Blacks' bus boycotts in Baton Rouge, Louisiana; Montgomery, Alabama; and Tallahassee, Florida, for instance, concentrated national and global attention on segregation. Confronted with raw evidence of blatant inequities and injustices, many white Americans yielded to the sense that de jure segregation should be outlawed and stopped. Congress reluctantly reached that position in part in September 1957. Passing the first federal civil rights act since 1875, the national legislature confirmed the increasingly popular conclusion that Jim Crow segregation should die, at least in regard to voting rights. The act established a Commission on Civil Rights to examine conditions and recommend changes in other areas.

Eliminating sanctions for racial discrimination required more than a single piece of federal legislation or isolated federal action. Securing the 1957 statute, as well as winning the line of federal and state court decisions against segregation, had been no top-down success. The public policy changes followed constructive dissatisfaction demonstrated on sidewalks and streets. It was not the result of any elite politics. It resulted from growing, mass-based popular politics. It resulted from grassroots insurgency spreading weed-like to choke the carefully tended and long cultivated racist growths that customarily covered over nonwhites as unequal and inessential parts of the American landscape.

More and more, the 1940s and 1950s evidenced people, particularly nonwhites, empowering themselves and each other in moving toward a shared purpose of realizing the ideals America declared as its foundation. By the close of the 1950s, the Reverend Dr. Martin Luther King Jr. had come to articulate a public morality of equality in a language resonating in American values. His voice echoed the marching footfalls of impatient millions. That broadening, radical movement marked the closing of two decades that truly transformed race relations in the United States.

NOTE

1. Exec. Order No. 8802, 6 Fed. Reg. 3109 (June 25, 1941).

1940s

TIMELINE

1939–1945 World War II

1940

Civil rights advocate and educator George I. Sánchez publishes his study of public educational neglect, *Forgotten People: A Study of New Mexicans*, highlighting discrimination against Hispanics.

Richard Wright publishes his novel, *Native Son*, and essay, *How "Bigger" Was Born: The Story of Native Son*.

June 29 The Alien Registration Act requires all aliens 14 years and older to register with the U.S. government.

1941

George I. Sánchez becomes president of the League of United Latin American Citizens (LULAC).

Richard Wright publishes *12 Million Black Voices: A Folk History of the Negro in the United States*.

January A. Philip Randolph and other black leaders form the March on Washington Movement, threatening a mass demonstration on July 1, 1941, to protest blacks' being excluded from jobs in national defense industries and being segregated in the U.S. Armed Forces.

U.S. War Department announces formation of the 99th Pursuit Squadron, the first black fliers in the U.S. Army Air Corps and part of what becomes the all-black 332nd Fighter Group collectively known as the Tuskegee airmen because they trained at Tuskegee Institute in Alabama.

June 25   President Franklin D. Roosevelt issues Executive Order 8802, creating the federal Fair Employment Practices Committee (FEPC), in response to pressure from the March on Washington Movement.

July 30   President Roosevelt establishes the Office of Inter-American Affairs to improve relations with Latin America.

December 7   Japan attacks the U.S. Navy Pacific Fleet Headquarters at Pearl Harbor, Hawaii, plunging America into World War II against Japan, Italy, and Germany, and prompting President Roosevelt to proclaim U.S.-resident German, Italian, and Japanese nationals to be enemy aliens; U.S. agents arrest 2,000 Japanese American community leaders.

1942

With black James Farmer and white George Houser as co-leaders, an interracial group of students in Chicago founds the Committee (later Congress) of Racial Equality (CORE); many in the group are also members of the pacifist Fellowship of Reconciliation (FOR) inspired by journalist and popular writer Krishnalal Shridharani's 1939 book *War Without Violence*, which outlines India's "Mahatma" Gandhi's nonviolent campaigns. Protesting segregation in public accommodations, the group adapts the industrial labor tactic of sit-ins and begins to expand nationwide.

William Faulkner publishes his novel *Go Down, Moses*, treating the influence of slavery and race on the contemporary South.

January 12   The U.S. Supreme Court in *Taylor v. Georgia* further outlaws debt peonage as a form of slavery or involuntary servitude.

February 19   President Roosevelt issues Executive Order 9066, the basis for U.S. war-time interning of Japanese Americans, some until June 1946.

March 21   Congress enacts criminal penalties to reinforce President Roosevelt's Executive Order 9066.

June 1   The U.S. Supreme Court in *Hill v. Texas* reiterates the law against racial discrimination in selecting grand jurors.

July 23   United States and Mexico agree to the Bracero temporary laborers program.

| August 4 | Congress confirms and funds Braceros under the title "Mexican Farm Labor Supply Program." |

1943

	Race riots rock the United States in the midst of World War II.
April	Japanese Americans interned at Topaz Relocation Center in Utah protest conditions and treatment, including guards shooting and killing 62-year-old former San Francisco resident James Hatsuki Wakasa in an alleged escape attempt on April 11. The protest leads to U.S. authorities isolating so-called hard cases at Tule Lake Relocation Center in Northern California.
May 25	Race riot occurs in Mobile, Alabama.
May 31	Race riots, called the zoot suit riots, begin in Los Angeles and continue until June 7.
June	Japanese American volunteers in Hawaii organize as the segregated U.S. Army's 100th Infantry Battalion and the 442nd Regimental Combat Team for service in the European Theater of Operations (ETO). Beginning in North Africa, the 100th's distinguished service earned it the nickname "Purple Heart Battalion." One of its members was future Congressman Daniel Inouye. The 1951 movie *Go For Broke*, titled from the battalion's motto, depicts some of its exploits.
June 15–16	Race riot occurs in Beaumont, Texas.
June 20–22	Race riot occurs in Detroit, Michigan.
June 21	The U.S. Supreme Court in *Hirabayashi v. United States* upholds internment of Japanese Americans.
August 1	Race riot occurs in New York City
November 5	U.S. Army troops quell protest among Japanese Americans interned at Tule Lake Relocation Center in Northern California, placing it under martial law until January 14, 1944.
December 17	Congress repeals U.S. immigration exclusion of Chinese immigrants.

1944

Swedish political economist Gunnar Myrdal publishes six-year-long Carnegie Corporation-funded study, *An American Dilemma: The Negro Problem and American Democracy*.

Yankton Sioux Ella Deloria, an anthropologist and ethnologist who studied with Franz Boas and Margaret Mead at Columbia

University in New York City, publishes *Speaking of Indians*, with insights to how Indians can come to participate fully in American life.

The *National Congress of American Indians* (NCAI) organizes to oppose federal termination policies.

February   Japanese Americans protest being subjected to the draft while also being interned. Noted resistance occurs at the Heart Mountain War Relocation Center in Wyoming and also at the Poston War Relocation Center in Arizona, where the FBI on February 21 jailed 28-year-old George S. Fugii for urging other draftable *Neisi* (U.S.-born children of Japanese) to refuse to report for preinduction physical examinations.

April 3   The U.S. Supreme Court in *Smith v. Allwright* rules unconstitutional Texas's all-white primary elections.

April 10   The U.S. Supreme Court in *Pollock v. Williams* reiterates that state criminal statutes enforcing labor for debt create illegal peonage under the Thirteenth Amendment.

November 7   New York City's Harlem congressional district elects Adam Clayton Powell Jr. to Congress, where he becomes one of two blacks in the U.S. House of Representatives.

December 17   The U.S. War Department revokes its directive excluding all persons of Japanese ancestry from the West Coast under Executive Order 9066.

December 18   The U.S. Supreme Court in *Korematsu v. United States* reiterates legality of Japanese internment, but the same day draws a line in *Ex parte Endo*, pronouncing it unconstitutional for the U.S. government to hold loyal citizens without probable cause and due process.

1945

Osage writer John Joseph Mathews publishes *Talking to the Moon*; Richard Wright publishes his novel *Black Boy*.

April 12   Harry S Truman becomes U.S. president upon Roosevelt's death.

May 7   Germany surrenders, ending the war in Europe.

August 6, 9   U.S. atomic bombs devastate Japanese cities of Hiroshima and Nagasaki.

August 15   Japan surrenders.

September 2   World War II officially ends.

October 24   Signatories ratify the United Nations (UN) charter.

November 1	John H. Johnson launches monthly *Ebony* magazine, the start of the largest black-owned U.S. publishing company.
December 28	War Brides Act allows foreign-born wives of U.S. citizens who served in the U.S. Armed Forces to immigrate to the United States

1946

February 18	In *Mendez v. Westminster School District*, federal courts in California uphold Mexican Americans' challenge to being segregated in public schools; it is upheld on appeal April 14, 1947.
June 3	U.S. Supreme Court in *Morgan v. Commonwealth of Virginia* outlaws racial segregation on interstate buses.
July 2	Congress passes the Luce-Celler Act, opening immigration to persons from India and the Philippines with small quotas and allowing such persons to become naturalized U.S. citizens.
July 4	U.S. recognizes the independence of the Philippines.
July 28	President Truman appoints Jesús T. Piñero as Puerto Rico's first native-born governor.
August	The color line falls in the National Football League (NFL) as the Los Angeles Rams, just moved from Cleveland, Ohio, sign Kenny Washington and Woody Strode and the Cleveland Browns sign Marion Motley and Bill Willis, the first blacks to play in the league.
August 13	Congress creates the Indian Claims Commission to settle Indians' claims against the United States for seized land and other losses.
November 5	Phoenix, Arizona, district elects Chinese American immigrant Wing F. Ong to the state legislature, making him the first Asian American elected to a U.S. state office.
December 5	President Truman's Executive Order 9808 creates a committee to recommend ways to make civil rights more effective.

1947

The National Association for the Advancement of Colored People (NAACP) petitions the United Nations to examine U.S. racism.

"Operation Bootstrap" helps push laborers from Puerto Rico to the United States, and major airlines initiate direct service

	between San Juan, Puerto Rico, and Miami, Florida, and New York City, facilitating migration.
March	Don Barksdale of the University of California at Los Angeles (UCLA) becomes the first black named a college basketball All-American and later becomes the first black to play for the U.S. Olympic basketball team (1948) and the first black to play in the National Basketball Association (NBA)'s All-Star game (1953).
April 10	CORE sponsors a two-week Journey of Reconciliation with eight white and eight black men riding public transportation together to end segregation in interstate travel. The planned travel through Virginia, North Carolina, Tennessee, and Kentucky falls short as police at various points repeatedly arrest and jail group members. The trip foreshadows later events called "Freedom Rides."
April 15	Jackie Robinson breaks Major League Baseball (MLB)'s color barrier in the National League as he joins the Brooklyn Dodgers and goes on to win MLB Rookie of the Year.
July 5	Larry Doby breaks MLB's color barrier in the American League as he joins the Cleveland Indians.
October 29	The President's Committee on Civil Rights issues its report, *To Secure These Rights*.

1948

	William Faulkner publishes his novel *Intruder in the Dust*, focusing on racial justice (movie adaptation appears in 1949).
January 12	The U.S. Supreme Court in *Sipuel v. Oklahoma State Board of Regents* rules constitutional equal protection requires states to admit qualified blacks to previously all-white graduate or professional state schools when the state maintains no comparable black institutions.
February 2	President Truman urges Congress to adopt civil rights initiatives.
May	Southern Democrats protest federal interference with states' rights and eventually form the States Rights Party, popularly known as the Dixiecrats, to run a presidential ticket in the November 1948 election.
May 3	The U.S. Supreme Court in *Shelley v. Kraemer* rules racially restrictive housing covenants constitutionally unenforceable.
July 23	Displaced Persons Act opens U.S. immigration.
July 26	President Truman's Executive Order 9981 directs the U.S. Armed Forces to desegregate.

August	Alice Coachman becomes the first African American woman to win an Olympic gold medal (high jump), and Japanese American Harold Sakata wins a silver medal (weight-lifting) at the Olympic Games in London.
October 28	The California Supreme Court in *Perez v. Sharp* outlaws state ban on interracial marriage.
November	Puerto Rico votes in Luis Muñoz Marín as its first elected governor (he serves until 1964).

1949

	Congress directs the Bureau of Indian Affairs (BIA) to begin relocation of Indians from tribal reservations to cities.
May 4	Advancing the developing theme of termination, the newly appointed commissioner of the Bureau of Indian Affairs announces the time would soon come when all Indian tribal designations and treaty restrictions would be set aside.
September 12	Jackie Robinson named MLB National League Most Valuable Player, the first nonwhite to win.
October	Television airs entire MLB World Series for the first time.
October 1	People's Republic of China declares itself established, and Congress in treaty with the Republic of China (Taiwan) opens U.S. entry to Chinese fleeing communists.

OVERVIEW

The 1940s was a decade of far-reaching change in U.S. race relations. Emerging from the Great Depression of the 1930s and entering into World War II (1939–1945), Americans of every race, color, and background faced wrenching developments from the nation's mobilizing to become what President Franklin D. Roosevelt in his December 29, 1940, radio address in his series of Fireside Chats described as "the arsenal of democracy."

The war shifted the U.S. population, physically and psychologically. Millions of men left home for service in the U.S. Armed Forces. Hundreds of thousands of women joined them. By 1945, the U.S. military had 12.1 million persons on active duty.[1] That was about one in every nine Americans, and among them were 265,006 women. Hundreds of thousands of those who went off to war never returned to live in the places they left, and almost all who did return home to live came with different perspectives of themselves, their nation, and their world.

The war altered American life. It changed life for those who fought on the front lines in Africa, Europe, and the Pacific. It affected all who served. It reached those they left behind, too. Their absence changed the communities they left. Others moved into their old jobs. Indeed, widespread demand for workers opened opportunities for many, particularly nonwhites and women, previously segregated from the better paying positions of white men. Intense demand for increased production also created new jobs, expanding employment. Wartime demands outstripped the workforce almost everywhere.

The war transformed the United States from an economically depressed nation of too few jobs and lingering, double-digit unemployment into a nation of jobs begging for workers. The relative scarcity of labor boosted wages and beckoned workers to move to improve their position. The first of what would become 5 million blacks swelled what was called the Great Black Migration that had started at the beginning of the 1900s to shift blacks from the rural South to urban areas, especially northern industrial centers. Other nonwhites joined the flow.

Tens of thousands of workers from Mexico and Puerto Rico also moved from their homes to fill needs at U.S. worksites. Mexicans came largely in and around the Bracero program of so-called guest workers that began in 1942. Puerto Ricans migrated largely after 1945. The influx of Spanish speakers enlarged lines of migration, with significant long-range impact. An immediate consequence of the large-scale population movement pushed and pulled many previously isolated and marginalized persons and places into broader contact with others.

Closer contacts created new, and not always welcome, interaction among groups. Anger and frustration erupted in spots, especially as whites sensed nonwhites, particularly blacks, encroaching on previously all-white preserves. In Detroit, Michigan, for example, white auto workers during the early days of World War II went on wildcat "hate-strikes" to protest plants' hiring and upgrading blacks. Strikers snubbed union discipline and solidarity. United Auto Workers (UAW) union president Roland Jay "R. J." Thomas found little leverage to bridge the gap between his black and white members, even on vital war production lines. He virtually begged for federal intervention. Seeking a shield from white workers' wrath while maintaining a friendly front toward blacks, Thomas surreptitiously maneuvered for "government agencies to take decisive, even punitive actions [against wildcat strikers], which he could then vigorously support," analysts later revealed.[2]

Racial violence drew mobs into U.S. streets in the midst of the war. A rash of race riots rocked the nation in 1943. Clashes over naval and dockyard work prompted whites to attack blacks in Mobile, Alabama, in May. In Los Angeles, California, in early June, local whites and at-liberty white sailors, soldiers, and Marines attacked young Hispanics in the so-called zoot suit riots. Whites spread their attacks also into the city's black Watts section. Beaumont, Texas, had a racial blow-up in mid-June. Detroit had a race riot in late June. New York City's Harlem erupted in racial fighting in early August.

The fighting over contested turf or aggrieved sensibilities signaled something of the profound changes many Americans found unsettling. They were being forced to face race. For many whites it was their first personal encounter. They were used to ignoring nonwhites. Much of American culture strove to make nonwhites invisible. If it could not hide the persons themselves, it could and did hide their problems from significant public attention. Much during the 1940s shattered that invisibility, and the big changes started during the war.

At almost every turn, nonwhites were appearing in the American public eye as the 1940s progressed. Often insistently so. Asian Americans, for example, decried the wholesale U.S. internment of Japanese Americans. They protested U.S. immigration exclusions. Filipino Americans and Puerto Ricans also protested U.S. colonialism. Mexican Americans battled being relegated in fact as a despised race, even though U.S. law labeled them "white." American Indians battled, too, against being treated as a subjected people segregated from the opportunities of mainstream America. Foremost in protesting the obscenity of U.S. race relations in the 1940s were the poster people in the degradation of American apartheid—blacks.

Public attention on race relations mounted during the decade. Nazi atrocities early provoked questioning of race theories. Unfolding horrors from the Holocaust later heightened sensitivities Americans themselves had developed. Academic studies and popular literature throughout the 1940s advanced fresh views of nonwhites, Hispanics, and U.S. race relations. Books such as Richard Wright's *Native Son* (1940) and William Faulkner's *Go Down, Moses* (1942) and *Intruder in the Dust* (1948) cut into old racial stereotypes.

Mainstream audiences opened for black voices such as Wright's. Black poet Gwendolyn Brooks would, by the end of the decade, become the first African American to win a coveted Pulitzer prize, signifying critical acclaim and a measure of public acceptance. White writers worthy of note also emerged in the 1940s to criticize the racial status quo. Particularly in the South, writers beyond Faulkner, such as Wilbur Cash, Carson McCullers, William Percy, and Lillian Smith, for example, challenged the traditional racial structures of their region.

Postwar America appeared to brim with possibilities for new openness in racial discourse. The postwar world with its destroyed European empires, old colonies demanding independence, repugnance to genocidal, race-based slaughter, and announced dedication to human rights in the fledgling United Nations' charter appeared to demand that the United States put its house in order in regard to its racial policies and practices.

President Harry S Truman embraced the fresh vision with remarkable initiatives. His special message to Congress on civil rights in February 1948 outlined a legislative program that proved to be more than a decade before its time. With its strong cadre of southern Democrats and segregation sympathizers, Congress generally rebuffed the president. He did succeed in securing the 1948 Japanese-American Evacuation Claims Act to partially redress internment outrages. And exercising his executive authority, he managed significant advances. His 1948 order for the U.S. Armed Forces to desegregate became a landmark.

If he was out of step with the nation's legislature, President Truman proved very much in line with the nation's courts. Prompted by a series of suits the National Association for the Advancement of Colored People's (NAACP) Legal Defense and Education Fund (LDF), the League of United Latin American Citizens (LULAC), other groups, and individuals across the nation launched, federal and state courts were whittling away segregation's structure. In *Mendez v. Westminster School District*, for example, federal courts in 1946 and 1947 outlawed public school segregation against "Spanish-speaking children" in California.

In *Perez v. Sharp* in 1948, the California Supreme Court struck down the state's anti-miscegenation statutes. Also in 1948, the U.S. Supreme Court in *Sipuel v. Board of Regents of the University of Oklahoma* reiterated that a state must provide the same educational opportunities to blacks as it provides to whites. And in *Shelley v. Kraemer*, the nation's highest court struck a blow against residential segregation, prohibiting legal enforcement of covenants restricting nonwhites from buying or renting homes in certain areas.

So as the 1940s drew to a close, the legal segregation that served as the foundation of U.S. race relations was not what it was when the decade began.

KEY EVENTS

THE MARCH ON WASHINGTON, 1941

In January 1941, the international president of the Brotherhood of Sleeping Car Porters and Maids, A. Philip Randolph, called for a nationwide protest against black employment exclusion, particularly in defense industries then beginning to boom with the growing demands of World War II (1939–1945). Randolph saw good jobs as the primary means to improve blacks' lives. The head of the first black-led union chartered in the American Federation of Labor (AFL) also knew too well the pernicious practices that excluded blacks from the promises of American life and left them perennially impoverished.

As the 1940s opened from the dark days of the 1930s Great Depression, improving employment for most blacks started with simply getting employment. Widely excluded from industrial jobs by employers and erstwhile fellow employees, the bulk of blacks in 1940 sat unemployed or woefully underemployed. When they found work, it was usually in the most menial positions and with the most meager pay. Blacks were the proverbial last hired and first fired. By official count, black unemployment topped 40 percent during the 1930s. Unofficially it seldom dipped below 50 percent. It was always significantly higher than white unemployment.

Randolph well understood that to bargain for jobs, blacks needed leverage with which to work. Shut out from industrial unions for the most part, blacks had little leverage there. Woefully marginalized, they had mostly their numbers and the political and public pressure their numbers could bring to bear. So Randolph boldly sought to put blacks' numbers to work.

To impress black demands on the nation and its public leaders, Randolph exhorted blacks to march by the tens of thousands on the U.S. capital on the advent of the nation's 1941 July 4th celebration. He worked with Dutch-born minister A. J. Muste, executive director of the Fellowship of Reconciliation (FOR), an organization of religious affiliates promoting nonviolent reform. With his principal lieutenant, 28-year-old social justice activist Bayard Rustin, and others, Randolph organized the March on Washington Movement (MOWM). The planned protest captured the spirit of many of the nation's more than 13 million blacks. It garnered support also among many whites. Yet many vociferously denounced MOWM.

Walter White, executive director of the National Association for the Advancement of Colored People (NAACP), suggested to President Franklin D. Roosevelt that at least 100,000 blacks might descend on the capital. The logistics for such a showing were hardly improbable. The District of Columbia itself contained 187,266 blacks, according to the 1940 federal census. Its neighbors Virginia (656,168) and Maryland (301,931) added almost a million more blacks. Together the three held about 1 in 11 of the nation's African Americans. A strong turnout of local blacks would by itself bring tens of thousands to the capital.

The image worried President Roosevelt and other federal officials. Many decried any such display as MOWM planned. They vividly recalled the ugly public humiliation when 20,000 World War I veterans and their families descended on Washington, D.C., in the spring and summer of 1932. The so-called Bonus Army camped on the muddy Flats across the Anacostia River from the capital's governmental core. The protesters named their swamp shanty "Hooverville," mocking President Herbert Hoover whom they excoriated for doing too little to provide relief from the Depression. They rallied to receive immediately the bonus Congress in 1924 had promised to pay veterans in 1945 for their 1917–1919 war service. The U.S. Senate spurned the unemployed marchers' pleas that they needed the money then, not later.

Violence erupted when D.C. police tried to clear the shantytown, and it escalated when President Hoover acceded to calls for U.S. troops to restore order. General Douglas MacArthur commanded the clear out, assisted by his aide Dwight D. Eisenhower. Major George S. Patton's 3rd Cavalry Regiment from Fort Myer, Virginia, and the 12th Infantry Regiment from Fort Howard, Maryland, used tear gas and unsheathed bayonets to clear the Bonus Army camp. Untallied deaths followed and casualties reached the hundreds. Pictures and reports of the confrontation shocked the nation. No one wanted a repeat.

To head off the possibility of any frightful confrontations with blacks massed at the Capitol, a reluctant President Roosevelt negotiated with MOWM leaders. The largest of his concessions was Executive Order 8802 issued on June 25, 1941.

With characteristically timid commitment to equal rights, Roosevelt declared grandly that it was "the policy of the United States to encourage full participation in the national defense program by all citizens of the United States, regardless of race, creed, color, or national origin." He directed all federal agencies and departments to "take special measures appropriate to assure" their vocational and training programs had no "discrimination because of race, creed, color, or national origin." And he required the same nondiscrimination from all federal contractors. To oversee compliance he established a five-person Committee on Fair Employment Practices (FEPC)—a forerunner of the Equal Employment Opportunity Commission (EEOC) President John F. Kennedy would create in his 1961 Executive Order 10925.

Yielding to conciliation rather than insisting on confrontation, MOWM persisted as a behind-the-scenes persuader for expanded black opportunities throughout World War II. It dissipated in 1947. MOWM's jobs-thrust distinguished it from other leading black organizations of the day. It shared with the National Urban League (NUL) a vision of better living conditions for blacks, but housing and community structures were not MOWM's focus. It offered none of the heritage-based uplift of Marcus Garvey's Universal Negro Improvement Association (UNIA). MOWM veered also from the NAACP's focus on litigation to vindicate blacks' legal rights. MOWM's push for economic freedom based on solid and sustained earnings reflected a bit of Tuskegee Institute founder Booker T. Washington's vision of blacks' advancing through vocational improvement.

MOWM wedged open opportunities that made an immediate difference. Its vision proved even more important over time. It planted and nurtured seeds later generations harvested. Its coalition-building broadened the base of effective civil rights agitation as illustrated in the 1942 creation of the Congress of Racial Equality (CORE). The 1963 March on Washington for Jobs and Freedom was a direct MOWM offshoot. Its demands to further economic justice and to focus black expectations and frustrations on dramatic, direct action displayed strategic and tactical insights that strengthened the basis for transforming the segregated structure of U.S. race relations.

INTERNING OF JAPANESE AMERICANS, 1942

Japan's devastating attack on the U.S. Navy Pacific Fleet headquarters and base at Pearl Harbor, Hawaii, on Sunday, December 7, 1941, plunged the United States into World War II (1939–1945) as a combatant. The war underway in Europe since September 1939 and Japan's prior forays in the Far East had earlier put Americans on edge. Fears of subversive activities by foreign agents and of foreigners themselves turned official and popular suspicions on aliens and on Americans whose looks or language marked them apart from conventional all-American images.

Almost as soon as news of the Pearl Harbor attack reached President Franklin D. Roosevelt, he issued Proclamation 2525. Identifying Japanese nationals as "alien enemies," FDR limited their travel, restricted their property rights, and authorized their internment. On December 8, he issued Presidential Proclamations 2526 and 2527 similarly targeting German and Italian nationals, although Congress did not declare war on Germany and Italy until December 11. FBI raids immediately arrested thousands of German American and Italian American suspects. Some spent six or seven years interned. The last were not released until August 1948, and then only on swearing under penalty of imprisonment not to publicly disclose their ordeal. It was Japanese Americans, however, who suffered the most massive U.S. wartime internment.

Old racial animus against Japanese agitated attack hysteria on the Pacific coast. About 120,000 Japanese Americans lived there in 1940. In fact, 75.9 percent of the mainland's 254,718 Americans of Asian or Pacific Islander heritage lived in the three West Coast states of California (65.8%), Oregon, and Washington. The relatively large number of Asians in the region stirred friction as early as the 1840s, starting with Chinese arriving in the California Gold Rush. Focus shifted to Japanese in the early 1900s. Beginning with California in 1913, states enacted Alien Land Laws to keep Japanese and other Asian immigrants from owning

Japanese Americans wait in line for their assigned housing at an interment camp in Manzanar, California, March 24, 1942. Many were forced from their homes in Los Angeles by the U.S. Army. AP Photo.

farms and other real property. Similar discrimination hounded Asian Americans in jobs, housing, and schools.

Federal law from the 1880s on steadily shut immigration to Asians and denied those already landed from becoming naturalized U.S. citizens. No *Issei*—immigrants born in Japan—were American citizens, for example. Only their American-born children, the *Nisei*, were U.S. citizens. Many white Americans refused to accept *Nisei*, any more than *Issei*, as Americans. They held special suspicion for *Nisei* known as *Kibei* because their parents sent them to Japan for schooling. Suspicions fixed on their ethnic heritage. More simply, their physical features marked them in many minds as enemies.

On February 19, 1942, FDR issued Executive Order 9066 authorizing the secretary of war and designated commanders "to prescribe military areas . . . from which any or all persons may be excluded." On the West Coast, extending from the ocean 100 miles inland, the exclusion reached all persons of Japanese ancestry.

As Western Defense Commander, U.S. Army Lieutenant General John L. DeWitt took the lead against Japanese Americans, and he entered upon his task with no friendly views. "A Jap's a Jap. It makes no difference whether he is an American citizen or not," he publicly declared in a statement newspapers widely reported.[3] In testimony to a Congressional subcommittee, DeWitt described West Coast Japanese Americans as potential enemies. "We must worry about the Japanese all the time until he is wiped off the map," he declared.[4] DeWitt initiated a series of orders in March 1942. He imposed an 8:00 P.M. to 6:00 A.M. curfew for "all enemy aliens and all persons of Japanese ancestry."[5] He then sequestered such persons until May, when his Civilian Exclusion Order No. 346 directed all persons of Japanese ancestry, whether aliens or citizens, removed to detention camps officially dubbed "Relocation Centers."

Operated by the War Relocation Authority (WRA) created in FDR's March 18, 1942, Executive Order 9102, ten internment camps eventually opened in seven states. Arizona, Arkansas, and California each housed two camps. Colorado, Idaho, Utah, and Wyoming each had one. The removal and detention of nearly 120,000 persons of Japanese ancestry, more than two-thirds of whom were U.S. citizens, became the largest single forcible relocation in U.S. history.

Overwhelmingly, Japanese Americans obeyed military commands without much public complaint. Insisting on their loyalty, however, they challenged the lawfulness of their treatment up to the U.S. Supreme Court. In *Hirabayashi v. United States* (1943), a unanimous Court accepted the curfew, exclusion, and sequestration imposed on Japanese Americans as constitutional exercises of war powers. While the majority upheld internment, several justices displayed growing unease.

In December 1944, when the Court decided *Korematsu v. United States* and *Ex parte Endo*, Justice Frank Murphy in dissent denounced the internment as a "legalization of racism." Military necessity had mounted no similar en masse internment of German Americans and Italian Americans. Only after individual investigations did officials take them into custody. "Racial discrimination in any form and in any degree has no justifiable part whatever in our democratic way of life," he insisted.[6]

On the same day, Justice William O. Douglas, writing for a unanimous Court in *Ex parte Endo,* rejected any racial basis of internment. "Loyalty is a matter of the heart and mind, not of race, creed, or color," he ruled. "When the power to detain is derived from the power to protect the war effort against espionage and sabotage, detention which has no relationship to that objective is unauthorized," Douglas emphasized.[7]

The internment had already done much of its worst by December 1944. Stripped of their houses, furnishings, vehicles, and livelihoods, as well as their privacy and individuality, Japanese Americans suffered destitution and indignity herded under armed guard into "so-called Relocation Centers, a euphemism for concentration camps," as Justice Owen Roberts put it in his *Korematsu* dissent.[8] He there echoed Justice Murphy's reference in *Hirabayashi* to "a melancholy resemblance to the treatment accorded to members of the Jewish race in Germany."[9]

Yet Japanese Americans steadfastly persisted in their patriotism. Thousands volunteered as linguists for U.S. military intelligence in the Pacific and for heroic battlefield service in the U.S. Army's 100th Battalion, 442nd Infantry, one the most decorated units in the fighting in North Africa and Europe.

U.S. officials began in June 1944 to undo part of the internment mess. They did not return those officially called "evacuees" to their homes, however. Many Pacific Coast communities where prewar Japanese Americans concentrated resisted having them back. The WRA termination program that lasted through 1946 dispersed Japanese Americans. By the beginning of 1945, it had resettled about 30,000 in Colorado, Idaho, Illinois, Michigan, Minnesota, New York, Ohio, and Utah.

President Truman pushed the 1948 Japanese-American Evacuation Claims Act to partially redress internment outrages. In legislation championed by Japanese American Congressman Norman Mineta (Democrat, California), a former internee, the U.S. Government in 1988 formally apologized for the exclusion and internment program and offered reparations and redress.

THE BRACERO PROGRAM, 1942

Mexico and the United States agreed in August 1942 to begin the Bracero program. The diplomatic agreement suspended the two governments' regulations so as to allow Mexicans to enter the United States as temporary workers. The arrangement initially directed several hundred laborers to California's sugar beet harvest. It spread in response to U.S. employers' clamor over labor shortages World War II (1939–1945) created. Western agribusiness especially complained of having too few hands for the stoop labor needed to put fresh fruits, vegetables, and other staples on U.S. tables. The farm labor problem was national, however, not regional. And no less than farms, factories also were short-handed. Mexicans lent their *brazos,* the Spanish word for "arms," to help fill U.S. needs.

To advance the 1942 Mexican Labor Agreement, Congress in April 1943 authorized the Mexican Farm Labor Supply Program. It was part of a $26.1 million appropriation "for assisting in providing an adequate supply of workers for the production and harvesting of agricultural commodities essential to the prosecution of the war."[10] In February 1944, Congress added another $30 million. Working with the U.S. Department of Agriculture, the Department of State, and other public or private agencies and persons, the program facilitated labor contracts to import workers.

Officials presented the Bracero program as mutually beneficial. It aimed to furnish U.S. employers labor they craved and provide Mexican employees desirable work and wages. Bracero labor would help the U.S. economy run, and bracero earnings sent back home would help the Mexican economy stabilize. Limitations in the 1943 act suggested, however, that significant worries accompanied the touted benefits.

Many Americans held deeply entrenched hostility toward persons of Mexican heritage, often slandering them. Racial stereotypes projected them as unclean and unassimilable peons. Competition for jobs long fed anger against those crossing the Rio Bravo north for work. As Mexican laborers spread from the West and Southwest to the Northwest, the Midwest, and further east, hostility increased.

Mexican agricultural laborers topping sugar beets near Stockton, California, 1944. Courtesy of the Library of Congress, LC-USW3-026256-D.

Many U.S. employers showed little concern for whether their employees had U.S. work permits or other appropriate legal documents. Whether the Mexican workers were documented or undocumented, their increasing presence in America fed controversy. Claims swirled that they displaced U.S. workers and lowered wages.

Congress sought to ensure the braceros' temporary presence. The law granted them no continuing U.S. status or hope of legally staying north of the border. They were to work for a fixed time and return to Mexico. Their limited status offered few, if any, protections. Braceros worked in the United States, but outside the framework of U.S. labor law. No oversight existed for living conditions or terms of work. There was no minimum wage or maximum hours, such as the Fair Labor Standards Act of 1938 set for U.S. workers with eight-hour days and hourly rates of $.30 in 1939 and $.40 in 1945.

From one view, braceros became abused, virtual indentured servants. Routinely paid substandard wages, sometimes less than $.20 an hour or on a piecework basis, they often lived and worked in unsanitary, sickening conditions. They had no legal rights. They were fired at will and worked wholly subject to the whims of bosses. Many employers wanted them simply as cheap labor.

Braceros were only one source of cheap labor during the war. Agricultural employers imported workers from the Bahamas, Canada, and Jamaica, too. They contracted for U.S.-based German and Italian prisoners of war. The use of interned Japanese Americans and convict labor also persisted in some places. Armed guards thus patrolled some fields where braceros and other such workers found themselves.

Congress showed no interest in the braceros' plight. Agribusiness and binational concerns directed congressional action. Growers pushed for cheap labor, and Mexican officials bartered bodies to decrease agitation from lack of employment at home and to increase the inflow of cash and human capital. Congress limited federal officials to aiding in recruiting, placing, and transporting braceros. It specifically denied authority for any other supervision. There were to be no audits or workplace inspections. Indeed, little focus fell on braceros' problems. They sat segregated. They were officially in America, but not of America.

U.S. organized labor attacked the bracero program as corroding the position of U.S. workers, at least 2.6 million of whom officially sat unemployed at the bracero agreement's start in 1942. Importing foreigners into wholly employer-controlled workplaces distorted U.S. labor markets and undercut U.S. workers, union officials declared.

The end of World War II in 1945 removed the climate of emergency that furnished the bracero program's rationale. Fear of returning to prewar, depression unemployment moved Congress to readjust its labor policies to accommodate demobilized U.S. troops, among other things. So in August 1946, Congress began to phase out the bracero program. It later set an official end date of December 31, 1947. The official closing of the program was, however, not the end of the braceros.

U.S. Immigration and Naturalization Service (INS) practices permitted selected braceros to continue working the fields of selected employers. Lobbying for cheap labor, employers continued to arrange policy deviations or new policies to maintain a flow of men from Mexico. (And the braceros were exclusively male, which opened problems of social control. It was, nevertheless, in keeping with an overall policy discouraging permanent U.S. ties, such as family formation.) Employers sought alternatives also. One notable program called Operation Bootstrap (*Operación Manos a la Obra*), begun in 1948, shifted the source of imported labor from Mexico to Puerto Rico.

Lingering spillover reached beyond the important contributions of the 221,000 braceros who officially entered between 1942 and 1947. Popular American prejudices, heightened with the flow of braceros, drew no distinctions between imported Mexican laborers and Mexican Americans. Stereotyped profiles defaced complexities of culture, condition, and class. And that reached not only among Americans of Mexican heritage but Americans of Hispanic heritage, who became simply lumped together.

The longer on-again-off-again 22-year program (1942–1964) that at its height in its later stages imported 400,000 braceros annually further spotlighted northward migration as an explosive problem in U.S.-Mexican relations and in domestic relations for Mexican Americans. It showed the rhetoric of mutually beneficial bilateral international agreements fell far short of workers' everyday lived realities. Moreover, braceros' success encouraged hundreds of thousands of Mexicans and others from south of the border to bypass legal programs and enter the United States to work without permits. That proved no small problem.

THE INDIAN CLAIMS COMMISSION, 1946

Congress established a three-person Indian Claims Commission on August 16, 1946. Its mandate was to "hear and determine the . . . claims against the United States on behalf of any Indian tribe, band, or other identifiable group of American Indians residing within the territorial limits of the United States or Alaska."[11] The enabling legislation appeared to allow Indians something long denied them—an open, uniform tribunal with power to redress their grievances against the federal government.

Only briefly before had Indians had such an opportunity to contest in court the dispossession that marked their history with the U.S. government. Tribes had asserted legal rights to land, money, and other property in the Court of Claims Congress established in 1855 for those redressing injury at the hands of the government. Perceiving an unintended and undesired consequence, Congress moved in 1863 to exclude Indians from the Court of Claims' ordinary jurisdiction. Thereafter, if a tribe wanted to sue the federal government for treaty violations or for any other wrongs, it could do so only by a special act of Congress. And that proved less than likely. Only in 34 of 118 cases, less than one-third of the time (28.8%), did Congress act to allow Indian tribes to proceed on claims they presented between 1881 and 1950. In all, between 1863 and 1946, Congress allowed Indian claims to proceed only 65 times.[12]

The 1946 law ended tribal special pleadings. It provided a comprehensive, general process for Indian claims that the United States had failed at "fair and honorable dealings" with them.[13] Also, the new law seemed to promise a quicker and better likelihood of succeeding. Instead of cases dragging on for more than 10 years, like the Winnebago's case begun in 1928 only to be dismissed in 1942, the 1946 act aimed to finish all of the Indian claims in 10 years.[14] Such expectation proved wildly optimistic. It represented wishes overcoming realities.

What drove the legislation through Congress was a somewhat untoward desire to be rid of what some dubbed the "Indian Problem." Indeed, the law represented congressional sentiment then accelerating to end Indians' special relations with the government. It was part of a call for Congress to terminate protective and supervisory policies toward Indians. More than a call, creating the claims commission was part of a push to end federal Indian policy that critics alternatively described as wasteful, paternalistic, exploitative, or all of the above and worse.

The Claims Commission Act aimed to create a final settlement with Indians. It aimed to provide a process for "a full discharge of the United States of all claims and demands" and to "forever bar any further claim or demand against the United States" arising from past Indian grievances against the government.[15] In short, it aimed to wipe the slate clean. Removing all the spilled blood and other filth accumulated in Indian removal over generations since the nation's colonial roots was hardly possible. Congress hoped a good faith effort would advance reconciliation. It would at least settle questions in the eyes of the law. Whether the effort reached the blindfolded eyes of Justice was a different question.

Proponents of the process saw eliminating tribal claims as a step toward putting Indians' relations with the federal government on the same footing as that of all other Americans. It would end what the U.S. House Committee on Indian Affairs in a 1940 report termed "continued wardship of the Indians."[16] That was the vision of termination policy. Rhetoric promoted it as desegregation. It promised to integrate Indians fully into U.S. governance and society, according to advocates. Its starker reality promised to erase Indian identity. It pressed to end tribes as cultural, governmental, and social units. Its words about liberating Indians focused on recognizing only individuals and so making Indians indistinguishable from anybody else.

Indians saw termination policy clearly as another stratagem for the government to achieve what relentless white settlement had long sought—to terminate Indians. So they understandably eyed the Indian Claims Commission with suspicion. It held the allure of a kiss-off. For many Indians the invitation to settle their historical claims against whites was only tempting until examined. They saw their tribes as fully entitled to amends and compensation. Yet they saw also that the federal government was not offering reparations or recompense. It was seeking in a final, single money payment to liquidate its debts to Indians. The commission thus appeared as a hand-washing, final gesture.

Indians' history of sad experience with the federal government led them to be less than sanguine that the claims commission would settle their grievances once and for all. What they would get from the commission was no small question. U.S. law's emphasis on procedure and presentation had routinely confounded Indian claims earlier. What would be different now? Indians asked themselves.

The legislation offered some hope in directing the commission to operate by fairness rather than strict rules of legal pleadings. The commission's final determinations were to have the force of law. They would be equivalent to Court of Claims rulings. But the commission was not confined by court procedure. Legal culture nevertheless dictated process. The Department of Justice (DOJ) lawyers representing U.S. interests saw to that. They focused on winning cases, not on seeing justice done. Indeed, recognizing the commission's limited 10-year life, DOJ attorneys too often adopted a go-slow policy, sometimes delaying their answers for more than three years, in apparent hopes of killing Indian claims by having the law expire.

Congress's act to give Indians a place and time to air their accumulated grievances failed to work as designed. It was too small an effort to suit the vast bulk of claims. There was too much to cover. The ground reached back even before 1821 when Chief Justice John Marshall in the landmark case of *Johnson v. M'Intosh* denied Indians title to any land they occupied. Cultural divergence on concepts of value, title, and property degenerated much of the commission's proceedings.

U.S. insistence on a showing of "exclusive use and occupancy" defied traditional Indian understanding of their claims to land.[17] Besides, what would prove such occupancy? U.S. law preferred documents to oral testimony. But few Indians kept deeds or ledgers. Beyond all else remained the issue of value. What would set land prices where and when no sales or other market transactions created a standard for fair market value?

The Indian Claims Commission's problems proved many. It decided 102 claims before its 1956 deadline. It awarded $890 million in 78 claims and estimated liabilities of about $1.2 billion in other cases.[18] And it had yet to reach almost 800 cases already filed. Congress thus extended its life, eventually to 1978. But no extension really sufficed. What the nation owed Indians lay beyond settlement in any single commission.

VOICES OF THE DECADE

ADVOCATES OF INDIAN TERMINATION POLICY

American Indians stood in another "no man's land" as the 1940s opened. They faced renewed attacks from advocates pushing federal policy to terminate

Indians' special relations with the U.S. government. Such advocates contested the success of the 1934 Indian Reorganization Act, sometimes called the Wheeler-Howard Act, 48 Stat. 984 (June 18, 1934), that had announced a drastic shift in U.S. policy to promote Indian self-government and economic development. It moved to incorporate tribal government in market-based management of tribal resources. It reversed the federal policy of seeking to assimilate Indians by dissolving tribal lands into allotted small farm-holdings. It urged maintenance of Indian cultural identity and in many ways a fuller independence. Termination advocates criticized the IRA approach and all federal policy that recognized tribal sovereignty. They claimed such policies encouraged communalism and perpetuated dependency. They asserted that the correct federal policy was to terminate the federal government's so-called special relations with Indians. The critics called for the government to stop recognizing Indians as groups, to become blind to tribes, and to recognize only individuals. The U.S. House of Representatives Committee on Indian Affairs in 1940 reported the following view of the IRA's failings and how to correct them:

Arguments advanced against the Wheeler-Howard Act in general, can be summarized as follows:

1. Acceptance of the act changed the status of the Indians from that of involuntary wardship to voluntary wardship.

2. The act provides for continued wardship of the Indians and gives the Secretary of the Interior increased authority.

3. The act is contrary to the established policy of the Congress of the United States to eventually grant the full rights of citizenship to the Indians.

4. The act provides for only one form of government for the Indians, viz. a communal government, with all property, real and personal, held in common; and it compels the Indians to live in communities segregated from the rest of American citizens.

5. The act itself and the administration of the act violates the rights of citizenship, which the Indians have won through long years of efforts.

6. That the Indians prefer to be under the jurisdiction of the laws of the respective States where they reside.

Conclusion

Fundamentally, the so-called Wheeler-Howard Act attempts to set up a state or a nation within a nation which is contrary to the intents and purposes of the American Republic. No doubt but that the Indians should be helped and given every assistance possible but in no way should they be set up as a governing power within the United States of America. They shall be permitted to have a part in their own affairs as to government in the same way as any domestic organization exists within a State or Commonwealth but not to be independent or apart therefrom.

From *Wheeler-Howard Act-Exempt Certain Indians: Hearings on S. 2103 before the Committee on Indian Affairs of the House*, 76th Cong., 3rd Sess. (1940), 23–25.

PRESIDENT FRANKLIN D. ROOSEVELT

On June 25, 1941, President Franklin D. Roosevelt issued Executive Order 8802. He acted under pressure from the March on Washington Movement (MOWM) A. Phillip Randolph organized with other black leaders and allies. Threatening to have tens of thousands of blacks and their allies protesting at the national Capitol was too embarrassing a prospect for the president and his advisors and, also, for much of the nation. An order that federal defense jobs be filled on the basis of skill "regardless of race, creed, color, or national origin" seemed more than reasonable. To many it seemed simply right. The president, himself, framed the order as no new policy but only as an act to "reaffirm" basic American ideals. Nevertheless, the fact was that segregation shut out blacks and many others from wide ranges of jobs. The president's order opened important doors.

WHEREAS it is the policy of the United States to encourage full participation in the national defense program by all citizens of the United States, regardless of race, creed, color, or national origin, in the firm belief that the democratic way of life within the Nation can be defended successfully only with the help and support of all groups within its borders; and

WHEREAS there is evidence that available and needed workers have been barred from employment in industries engaged in defense production solely because of considerations of race, creed, color, or national origin, to the detriment of workers' morale and of national unity:

NOW, THEREFORE, by virtue of the authority vested in me by the Constitution and the statutes, and as a prerequisite to the successful conduct of our national defense production effort, I do hereby reaffirm the policy of the United States that there shall be no discrimination in the employment of workers in defense industries or government because of race, creed, color, or national origin, and I do hereby declare that it is the duty of employers and of labor organizations, in furtherance of said policy and of this order, to provide for the full and equitable participation of all workers in defense industries, without discrimination because of race, creed, color, or national origin;

And it is hereby ordered as follows:

1. All departments and agencies of the Government of the United States concerned with vocational and training programs for defense production shall take special measures appropriate to assure that such programs are administered without discrimination because of race, creed, color, or national origin;

2. All contracting agencies of the Government of the United States shall include in all defense contracts hereafter negotiated by them a provision obligating the contractor not to discriminate against any worker because of race, creed, color, or national origin;

3. There is established in the Office of Production Management a Committee on Fair Employment Practice, which shall consist of a chairman and four other members to be appointed by the President. The Chairman and members of the Committee shall serve as such without compensation but shall be entitled to actual and necessary transportation, subsistence and other expenses incidental to performance of their duties. The Committee shall receive and investigate complaints of discrimination in violation of the provisions of this order and shall take appropriate steps to redress grievances which it finds to be valid. The Committee shall also recommend to the several departments and agencies of the Government of the United States and to the President all measures which may be deemed by it necessary or proper to effectuate the provisions of this order.

From Exec. Order No. 8802, 6 Fed. Reg. 3109 (June 25, 1941).

MITUSHIKO H. SHIMIZU

Born in Japan in 1899, Mitushiko H. Shimizu immigrated to the United States in 1907 and worked his way up to being a successful businessman and community leader in Los Angeles, California. In the following excerpt from a 1978 interview for the California State University, Fullerton, Oral History Program Japanese American Project, he recalled his experience surrounding Japan's attack on Pearl Harbor on December 7, 1941, his arrest, and subsequent internment.

On the night of the day when the war started, FBI men came to my house in Los Angeles and told me they had something to ask me, and ordered me to go with them to the police station.

I said, "If you want to question me, do it right now." But they insisted that I should come with them.

So, I told my wife that I would not be able to come back that night. Then I went to the police station.

I found out they would not ask me anything, but put me into a jail. I was taken to the police station and then transferred to the Los Angeles City Jail.

All the Japanese leaders were taken there. . . .

I was a chairman of the Japanese Association at that time, and all the Japanese leaders of the Association had gathered before the war and made up the Emergency Service Committee.

The movement against the Japanese was strong at that time. So we, the committee, dealt with the hard situation and the relations between the United States and Japan. At movie theaters, they said that buying Japanese commodities was helping Japan to provide more ammunition. . . . When the Japanese walked on the streets, many young people spoke ill of us. . . . They said, "You are Japanese. We don't like Japs. . . ."

We stayed in the jail overnight, and when the morning came, we found out that they would not give us breakfast. . . . They gave us some food there twenty-four hours after we were confined. . . .

[T]he American authorities were frightened. They were afraid that Japan might attack the West Coast someday. So they blacked out San Pedro[, California]. I understand that they had to do that for protection, but it was inhumane not to give us food. We stayed there [at the Federal Penitentiary on Terminal Island] until just before Christmas, and then we were transferred to Bismarck, North Dakota [to the Fort Lincoln Internment Camp].

I think it was on December 20, 1941. We were taken there by train, in a freight car. The camp had already been built there. They [the barracks] looked like cottages. It was already in the middle of the cold winter. I felt very cold because I went there from a warm place. We walked in the snow when we went to the mess hall from the barracks. We had to cook for ourselves; they just gave us the food to cook. . . .

When it came to forced labor, the Japanese people hated to do that—especially people who had a college education or who had held a position like a branch president of a company. They were the sort of people who hadn't ever done such a thing and they hated it. Some of them made excuses saying they had flu or a stomach ache. The value of a human being shows under such circumstances.

From Mitushiko H. Shimizu, interview by Mariko Yamashita and Paul F. Clark, October 30, 1978, Los Angeles, California, Department of Justice Internment Camps—Internee Experience interview O. H. 1614, transcript, the Oral History Program, California State University, Fullerton, Fullerton, California, 92834-6846, and in collection Japanese American Relocation Digital Archive: Oral Histories at California Digital Library.

JUSTICE FRANK MURPHY, 1944

Japan's attack on the U.S. Navy Pacific Fleet headquarters and base at Pearl Harbor, Hawaii, struck panic across America. President Franklin D. Roosevelt responded to the emergency of war in part as presidents before him had. He sought first to reassure the public and to provide for domestic security by imposing restrictions on designated aliens. His Executive Order 9066 issued in February 1942, and confirmed by Congress in March, reached to unprecedented lengths, however. It allowed the interning of roughly 120,000 persons of Japanese ancestry, both aliens and citizens. The U.S. Supreme Court upheld the internment against challenges that the program amounted to what U.S. Ninth Circuit Court Judge William Denman of San Francisco described as imprisonment "buried in the euphemism 'evacuation,' without suggestion of its forced character."[19] Dissenting in the key decision in *Korematsu v. United States* (1944), Justice Frank Murphy in the following went further to denounce the Japanese American internment as racism.

This exclusion of "all persons of Japanese ancestry, both alien and non-alien," from the Pacific Coast area on a plea of military necessity in the absence of martial law ought not to be approved. Such exclusion goes over "the very brink of constitutional power" and falls into the ugly abyss of racism. . . .

The judicial test of whether the Government, on a plea of military necessity, can validly deprive an individual of any of his constitutional rights is whether the deprivation is reasonably related to a public danger that is so "immediate, imminent, and impending" as not to admit of delay and not to permit the intervention of ordinary constitutional processes to alleviate the danger. Civilian Exclusion Order No. 34, banishing from a prescribed area of the Pacific Coast "all persons of Japanese ancestry, both alien and non-alien," clearly does not meet that test.

Being an obvious racial discrimination, the order deprives all those within its scope of the equal protection of the laws as guaranteed by the Fifth Amendment. It further deprives these individuals of their constitutional rights to live and work where they will, to establish a home where they choose and to move about freely. In excommunicating them without benefit of hearings, this order also deprives them of all their constitutional rights to procedural due process. Yet no reasonable relation to an "immediate, imminent, and impending" public danger is evident to support this racial restriction which is one of the most sweeping and complete deprivations of constitutional rights in the history of this nation in the absence of martial law.

It must be conceded that the military and naval situation in the spring of 1942 was such as to generate a very real fear of invasion of the Pacific Coast, accompanied by fears of sabotage and espionage in that area. The military command was therefore justified in adopting all reasonable means necessary to combat these dangers. In adjudging the military action taken in light of the then apparent dangers, we must not erect too high or too meticulous standards; it is necessary only that the action have some reasonable relation to the removal of the dangers of invasion, sabotage and espionage. But the exclusion, either temporarily or permanently, of all persons with Japanese blood in their veins has no such reasonable relation. And that relation is lacking because the exclusion order necessarily must rely for its reasonableness upon the assumption that all persons of Japanese ancestry may have a dangerous tendency to commit sabotage and espionage and to aid our Japanese enemy in other ways. It is difficult to believe that reason, logic or experience could be marshaled in support of such an assumption. . . .

No adequate reason is given for the failure to treat these Japanese Americans on an individual basis by holding investigations and hearings to separate the loyal from the disloyal, as was done in the case of persons of German and Italian ancestry. It is asserted merely that the loyalties of this group "were unknown and time was of the essence." Yet nearly four months elapsed after Pearl Harbor before the first exclusion order was issued; nearly eight months went by until the last order was issued; and the last of these "subversive" persons was not actually removed until almost eleven months had elapsed. Leisure and deliberation seem to have been more of the essence than speed. And the fact that conditions were not such as to warrant a declaration of martial law adds strength to the belief that the factors of time and military necessity were not as urgent as they have been represented to be. . . .

I dissent, therefore, from this legalization of racism. Racial discrimination in any form and in any degree has no justifiable part whatever in our democratic way of life. It is unattractive in any setting but it is utterly revolting among a free people who have embraced the principles set forth in the Constitution of the United States. All residents of this nation are kin in some way by blood or culture to a foreign land. Yet they are primarily and necessarily a part of the new and distinct civilization of the United States. They must accordingly be treated at all times as the heirs of the American experiment and as entitled to all the rights and freedoms guaranteed by the Constitution.

From *Korematu v. United States*, 323 U.S. 214, 233–242 (1944) (J. Murphy, dissenting, citations omitted).

O. K. ARMSTRONG

The condition of American Indians collectively raised concerns throughout the United States at the end of World War II (1939–1945). The following article by O. K. Armstrong, a former college English teacher turned journalists and politician who would later serve as a U.S. Representative from Missouri (1951–1955), proved politically and popularly influential. An editorial staff member of the widely circulated magazine *Reader's Digest* in 1945, Armstrong captured a strong current of change about and among American Indians, although he himself was not an Indian. His underlying rationale promoted federal Indian termination policy.

Few know the shameful story of the present status of the Indians . . ..

In three important respects they have never been emancipated: They are restricted in property rights: without consent of their superintendent they cannot own land on the reservation, or sell it, or mortgage it, or lease it. They live under conditions of racial segregation. And they are subject to special limitations and exemptions *because they are Indians* . . ..

[T]he Indian problem is a national reproach . . ..

Why aren't the Indians free? The policy of segregation and special treatment is deeply rooted in the past. Early reservations were concentration camps, where troops kept the inmates subdued. By the middle of the 1870s, reservations had become centers of paternalistic control, where able-bodied Indians waited from week to week for the agents to distribute beef and clothing.

It became apparent that the reservation system was pauperizing these wards of the Government . . ..

Although all native Indians were declared citizens of the United States by act of Congress in 1924, the act made no provision for the details of their emancipation. . . . With their land held in trust by the Indian Office, Indians are in the anomalous position of being both citizens and wards of the Government. They cannot use funds owned by the tribe without consent of the Office, even for cooperative enterprises. Their money is not theirs until the superintendent doles it out for a specific purpose . . ..

Lands held by reservation Indians—56 million acres—are not subject to state, county or local taxes. Hence they cannot vote in Idaho, New Mexico and Washington, because of constitutional provisions forbidding suffrage to Indians not taxed. They cannot vote in Arizona because of a law denying the ballot to "persons under guardianship." North Carolina requires that voters be able to read and write to the satisfaction of the election registrar—and a Cherokee Indian holding an M.A. degree from the University of North Carolina was told by an election judge: "You couldn't read or write to my satisfaction if you stayed here all day." . . .

The latest government efforts to meet the Indian problem have been in the wrong direction . . ..

Despite government outlays, most reservation Indians live in poverty. Until war work came to their aid, not more than two percent of reservation families averaged more than a $500 income a year. Living conditions are often extremely bad. Disease is prevalent and infant mortality is high.

Two pressing tasks confront Congress and the Indian service:

The first is to provide legislation that will remove restrictions from—and thus emancipate—every Indian who is able to manage his affairs.

The second is to chart a new course for the Office of Indian Affairs, whereby its efforts, during the time it remains in existence, are directed toward assisting all Indians to be self-supporting . . ..

Frank Beaver, veteran leader of the Winnebago tribe, told me: "Give our boys and girls training as Americans, and not as Indians, and they'll set themselves free!"

From O. K. Armstrong, "Set the American Indians Free!" *Reader's Digest* (August 1945): 47–52.

JUDGE ALBERT LEE STEPHENS SR.

U.S. Ninth Circuit Court of Appeals Judge Albert Lee Stephens Sr. and his fellow judges upheld the complaint Gonzalo Mendez and other U.S. citizens raised in 1945 that their own and some 5,000 other elementary school-age children of Mexican or Latino descent were being segregated in California's Orange County Westminster School District public schools. The separate schooling was not officially race-based. In fact, the Westminster School District officially prohibited racial segregation. Yet it directed Spanish-speaking children to separate schools. And it was not alone. Other districts announced no formal policy, but they too segregated Spanish-speaking students by longstanding discriminatory custom, although California purported to maintain a unitary school system. Examining the pattern of public school practice in light of California's constitution and the U.S. Constitution's Fourteenth Amendment, Judge Stephens and his colleagues on the federal bench ordered an end to segregation of pupils of Mexican ancestry in the Westminster School District and other California elementary schools. Judge Stephens and the majority of his colleagues stopped short, however, of holding all racial or other segregation illegal in the California public school system.

> The segregation in this case is without legislative support and comes into fatal collision with the legislation of the state.
>
> The State of California has a state-wide free school system governed by general law. . . .
>
> Nowhere in any California law is there a suggestion that any segregation can be made of children within one of the great races. . . . [S]tate law permits of segregation only as . . . confined to Indians and certain named Asiatics. That the California law does not include the segregation of school children because of their Mexican blood, is definitely and affirmatively indicated . . . by the fact that legislative action has been taken by the State of California to admit to her schools, children citizens of a foreign country, living across the border. . . .
>
> It follows that the acts of [the school district] were and are entirely without authority of California law. . . . By enforcing the segregation of school children of Mexican descent against their will and contrary to the laws of California, [school officials] have violated the federal law as provided in the Fourteenth Amendment to the Federal Constitution by depriving them of liberty and property without due process of law and by denying to them the equal protection of the laws.
>
> From *Westminster School Dist. of Orange County v. Mendez*, 161 F.2d 774, 780–781 (9th Cir., 1947) (citations omitted).

RACE RELATIONS BY GROUP

AFRICAN AMERICANS

African Americans stepped unsteadily into the 1940s. Like most other Americans, they were reeling from the pain and suffering of the 1930s' economic collapse called the Great Depression. But few, if any, other groups collectively suffered the depths of privation blacks experienced as the nation's most numerous abused racial minority. When one-in-three other Americans had sat unemployed during the Depression, more than two-in-three black Americans stood jobless. And when blacks could find scarce jobs, they usually were relegated to the lowest-paying, most menial, and most insecure positions. Meager economic footing everywhere undermined African American life. Yet holding fast to faith in one day realizing long-delayed promises of American life, blacks in the 1940s renewed their energies in their persistent attacks against Jim Crow policies and practices.

Using the Depression ordeal as a catalyst, the nation's 12.9 million blacks in 1940 accelerated their determined demands to end the racial discrimination that isolated and segregated them from the full benefits of American life. Their energies, extended in the 1930s simply to surviving, shifted in the 1940s to gaining more of their rightful place as citizens, as workers, as human beings.

The hateful, race-based horrors of Nazism in Germany, with its doctrine of Aryan racial superiority and its ultimate crime against humanity in the outrage of the Holocaust, shifted the ideological context of racial thinking. Doctrines of innate racial inferiority or superiority fell into public disfavor. With them went much of the traditional intellectual justification for segregation.

A fresh accord arose for basic human rights. And in that context, enterprising and effective black leaders—such as labor organizer A. Philip Randolph and NAACP lawyers Charles Hamilton Houston, Thurgood Marshall, and Robert L. Carter, with Howard University law school dean William H. Hastie—pivoted the weight of blacks' numbers and position with interracial allies to increase public pressure to move U.S. law and society away from American apartheid.

Jobs were the priority in 1940. They were crucial for black progress everywhere. Union leader A. Philip Randolph saw that clearly. He saw also that, while jobs were opening up with increased defense industry demand from the 1939 outbreak of World War II in Europe, blacks remained closed out. In many places and for many positions, blacks were not being hired at all. Where they were being hired, the old pattern of being put in the most menial spots persisted.

Randolph determined to change job segregation so blacks received a fair shot to show what they could do and be rewarded for what they did on the same basis as anyone else. He saw the federal government's leading role in the economy, and he understood its leverage in the defense industry. So he worked with others, particularly NAACP Executive Director Walter White and National Youth Administrator Mary McLeod Bethune, on a plan to move federal policy and practice to eliminate racial discrimination in federal hiring and in hiring by employers doing business under federal contract. The plan announced in the early days of 1941 became known as the March on Washington Movement (MOWM).

The plan called for mass demonstrations to demand change or else. It aimed to rally at least 100,000 blacks in protest at the national capitol. It targeted President Franklin D. Roosevelt, particularly, and more generally the Congress and other federal policymakers. The simple idea was to threaten to embarrass the U.S. government by exposing to the nation and the world the dark realities of life for the 10 percent of Americans who were blacks. The prospect of civil disobedience loomed. It drew from the example of India's independence leader Mohandas Gandhi.

President Roosevelt saw the promised march as more than disagreeable. To head it off, FDR acceded to MOWM's demands. On June 25, 1941, he issued Executive Order 8802. It pledged nondiscrimination in federal hiring and training. Also, it banned racial discrimination in any defense industry receiving federal contracts and created the Fair Employment Practices Committee (FEPC) to investigate employment discrimination.

Black employment prospects brightened. The biggest fillip, however, was the nation's mobilization following Japan's attack on Pearl Harbor on December 7, 1941. Insatiable demand for labor changed not only blacks' position in the workforce but across the range of American life.

The face of the U.S. Armed Forces reflected the change. Before Pearl Harbor, the U.S. Army had only 4,450 black soldiers in six segregated units. The U.S. Marines barred blacks. The Navy employed blacks only as mess men. By the war's end in 1945, 1.1 million blacks served the nation under arms. The indignities of segregated service gave rise to a separate "Double V Campaign." The nation pursued victory in Europe and in the Pacific. In a push the black *Pittsburgh Courier* newspaper initiated on the front page of its issue of February 7, 1942, blacks fought for "Democracy: Victory at Home, Victory Abroad."

On the home front, mobilization and wartime industry further quickened the flow of blacks out of the rural South. It accelerated blacks' moving from farm to factory. That had been underway since the opening 1900s. In April 1940, 47 percent of employed black men nationwide worked on farms; four years later the figure was 28 percent. Southern cities, particularly war industry centers—such as Charleston, South Carolina, and Hampton, Virginia, with their shipbuilding—absorbed some of the flow. But northern and western industrial centers got most, about 1.75 million blacks between 1940 and 1950. This ongoing black urbanization would continue for generations.

Blacks' moving produced opportunities and collisions. Shifting racial employment and residential patterns deeply affected the size and shape of many U.S. cities. It affected the remainder of the twentieth century, not simply the remainder of the 1940s. More than a few white workers and residents resented what they viewed as black encroachment. White United Auto Workers (UAW) members went on strike in the midst of World War II to protest black hiring in Detroit, for example. The Motor City, along with Los Angeles, New York, and smaller cities, experienced race riots in 1943. Such turf wars were not new.

Whites preferred not to work with blacks who were not subordinate. They virtually refused to live in neighborhoods with blacks. Racially mixed neighborhoods entailed a social intimacy unacceptable to many whites. They were deeply invested in their neighborhoods, perhaps more emotionally than even financially. So much of American social life revolved around neighborhoods. Churches, schools, community association, and entertainment centered on neighborhoods.

For many persons neighborhoods stood as bastions of identity. They were preserves many whites protected by every means necessary.

Blacks were not going away, however. All over America outside the South
in the 1940s, blacks were coming to stay in greater numbers. And they were
coming with a determination not to be denied their equal rights. Black veterans
returning from battle overseas returned "fighting," much as NAACP publications
editor W.E.B. Du Bois described returning World War I veterans in 1918. They
had fought in the name of democracy abroad. They were determined to have democracy at home. Their fighting disposition joined the broadening black attack
against segregation.

Blacks insisted on having the "equal" part of the "separate but equal" bargain
the U.S. Supreme Court confirmed in its 1896 *Plessy v. Ferguson* segregation decision. The NAACP's Legal Defense and Educational Fund (LDF), organized in
1940, hammered hard to collapse the fiction that segregation was not unconstitutional discrimination. Thurgood Marshall and his fellow LDF attorneys repeatedly exposed the patent lies in separate but equal public practice, particularly in
public education. The 1948 LDF win in *Sipuel v. Board of Regents of the University
of Oklahoma* reinforced the U.S. Constitution's rule requiring a state to provide
the same educational opportunities to blacks as it provided to whites.

LDF work with two black married couples—J. D. Shelley and Ethel Lee Shelley
in Missouri and Orsel McGhee and Minnie S. McGhee in Michigan—also took
the battle against segregation home after World War II. The Shelleys purchased
a home in St. Louis, as did the McGhees in Detroit. White neighbors sued to
block each couple from living in the homes they bought. The suits argued that
the blacks' purchases violated deed provisions called restrictive covenants. The
McGhees' deed declared, for instance, that "This property shall not be used or
occupied by any person or persons except those of the Caucasian race."[20]

In *Corrigan v. Buckley*, the U.S. Supreme Court in 1926 had upheld the legality of such covenants as private contracts. It repeated that holding in its 1940
ruling in *Hansberry v. Lee*. Deciding *Shelley v. Kraemer* and its companion case
McGhee v. Sipes in May 1948, the nation's high court repeated that while no
law prohibited the *making* of restrictive covenants, the Fourteenth Amendment's
Equal Protection Clause prohibited any law *enforcing* such covenants.

Without legal backing, restrictive covenants became dead letters, and residential neighborhoods lost that element as segregated preserves. That opened urban
neighborhoods to black home buyers and renters, at least as a matter of law. The
reality of integrating neighborhoods, however, remained neither easy nor safe.
Yet the law, so long the adversary of African American aspirations, did seem to
be shifting. President Harry S Truman, himself, called on Congress in 1948 to
advance civil rights for all Americans.

So much changed during the 1940s for blacks, but stark realities of racial oppression remained. Indeed, a counter-assault loomed. Those committed to racial
segregation held firmly to resisting black and other nonwhite advances.

AMERICAN INDIANS

American Indians entered the 1940s in a welter. Opposing forces buffeted them all around. Being so beset was not new. They had long before become accustomed to the ebb and flow of appearing as a troublesome presence. The onslaught of European colonization and settlement had pulled and pushed them since the 1600s. They were early collapsed into what many white Americans called the "Indian problem."

The continuous popular and political question in America had long been what to do with Indians. The routine answer since colonial times was to get rid of them. That took various forms, but the end seldom wavered. Whether it was extermination, segregation, or assimilation, predominant white American policies and practices converged on somehow making American Indians go away or, at least, moving them from sight. The white-dominated, U.S. mainstream persistently marginalized Indians, even while announcing repeated programs to bring them into the mainstream. So Indians faced the chronic uncertainty stemming from questions about how joining the white mainstream would help or hurt Indians.

The 1940s challenged American Indians to negotiate the announced U.S. policy of President Franklin D. Roosevelt's New Deal. The Indian Reorganization Act of 1934 had championed Indian tribal self-governance, self-determination, and self-development. The question of the 1940s was what the new federal policy meant in fact. Its rhetoric touted freedom for Indians. It said it would reduce federal interference in Indian affairs. Indians had heard such claims too often before. Agents of the Great White Father in Washington had too frequently predicted the dawning of a new, better day. Indians worked to protect themselves from what they were not being told about federal policy, as they distinguished between what whites said and what whites did.

As with others throughout the United States, American Indians in 1940 were struggling with the Great Depression. The hardships were many for the 333,969 American Indians, Eskimos, and Aleuts the U.S. Census counted in 1940. Indians in the West dominated the four U.S. regions in number with 156,694. Then came the South with 94,139, the Midwest with 71,350, and the Northeast with 11,786. The former Indian Territory that in 1907 became Oklahoma led the states in Indian population with 63,125. Arizona followed with 55,076, New Mexico with 34,510, South Dakota with 23,347, North Carolina with 22,546, and California with 18,675.

Regardless of where they were, most Indians were not in a good position. Their unemployment rate was high. Their housing was substandard. Their health was chronically poor. High crude death rates ravaged their communities. Endemic and pandemic diseases sorely tested tribal health resources. Trachoma and tuberculosis, for example, plagued Indians. Cultural issues clashed in health beliefs about "white man's sicknesses." Lifestyle changes also warred against Indian health. Increasingly high-calorie and high-carbohydrate and fat-intake diets destroyed personal health on and off the reservation. Diabetes, heart disease, pneumonia, and syphilis were near epidemic in some Indian communities. Reservations appeared destitute,

Corporal Henry Bahe Jr., left, and Private First Class George H. Kirk, Navajo code talkers serving with a Marine Signal Unit, operate a portable radio set in a jungle clearing behind the front lines on the island of Bougainville in New Guinea (present-day Papua New Guinea), December, 1943. AP Photo/USMC via National Archives.

dispirited, and unhealthful places. Many were deserting them. Particularly the young were leaving the reservation and relocating from rural to urban living.

If the 1940s opened as what appeared a dark hour, it was not wholly so. Indians in growing numbers rose to the challenges of changing federal policy and Indians' prospects. They seized opportunities. Collectively and individually, they pursued economic development. They took new jobs and developed new skills. They reaffirmed their Indian identities, while also embracing more of conventional America, from English language to general education and advanced technology.

With other Americans, Indians rallied to the national defense when Japan's attack on Pearl Harbor in December 1941 drew the United States into World War II (1939–1945). Most noted were the Native Americans who served in the U.S. Armed Forces as "code talkers." The Navajo serving in the U.S. Marines' Pacific campaigns received special notice. The 2002 feature motion picture *Windtalkers* magnified their renown. It dramatized the World War II battlefield protection and service of Navajo Marines working their native language as an unbreakable radio cypher. Other tribes also served as code talkers. And the U.S. Army, as well as the Navy, used their services. Indeed, the code talkers were not an invention of World War II; they served also during World War I.

By the spring of 1945, enlisted American Indian men numbered 21,767 in the U.S. Army, 1,910 in the Navy, 121 in the Coast Guard, and 723 in the Marines. American Indian women served in various auxiliaries. Two American Indians received the Congressional Medal of Honor, the highest U.S. military decoration. At least 71 American Indians received the Air Medal, 51 the Silver Star, 47 the Bronze Star, and 34 the Distinguished Flying Cross. Further, to support the war effort tribes bought at least $17 million in war bonds.

World War II's most significant impact on American Indians did not develop on foreign battlefields, however. It developed from Indians' broader participation in U.S. society. The personnel shortages and other opportunities the war induced gave Indians, like other marginalized groups, work, training, travel, and other experiences they would otherwise probably not have had. "The war has indeed wrought an overnight change in the outlook, horizon, and even the habits of the Indian people—a change that might not have come for many years yet," the Dakota linguist Ella Deloria explained in her 1944 book *Speaking of Indians.*[21]

Accelerating change percolated among Indians. It produced fresh individual and collective efforts. The National Congress of American Indians (NCAI), organized in Denver, Colorado, in November 1944, showed shifting sentiments toward more concerted pan-Indian action. Intertribal confederacies reached far back in history. Indian leaders such as the Sauk and Fox Black Hawk (1767–1838) and the Shawnee Tecumseh (1768–1813) had urged tribes to organize for mutual benefits in opposing advancing white settlement. In 1912, the Society of American Indians organized to lead Indians beyond fraternal or religious association into a collective, nationwide, political reform movement. Its vision was something like that of the National Association for the Advancement of Colored People (NAACP) founded in 1909–1910 with a focus on African Americans.

Dissatisfaction with federal administration of Indian affairs united the NCAI's members. With delegates from about 50 tribes at its initial meeting in 1944, the group boasted representatives from 27 states. It expanded at its 1945 meeting in Browning, Montana, and at its 1946 meeting in Oklahoma City. It aimed at what one NCAI leader described as "a cross-section of the Indian population."[22]

The NCAI in many ways supplanted the American Indian Federation (AIF) founded in 1934. It shared basic AIF sentiments. It detested the dictates and notorious ineptitude of the Bureau of Indian Affairs (BIA). But neither were monotone or monolithic. Multifaceted in elements and outlook, the NCAI battled the threatening paradox of New Deal Indian policy. What Congress announced in 1934 as Indian emancipation was developing in the 1940s not so much as a beginning of a new federal-Indian relationship but as the ending of any special federal-Indian relationship.

Congress appeared in the 1940s bent on washing the federal government's hands of any distinct association with Indians. Its 1946 Indian Claims Commission Act illustrated the inclination. It aimed once and for all to settle all Indian claims against the federal government. It sought to set history at zero. It sought to nullify the federal policy U.S. Chief Justice John Marshall announced in 1831 in declaring that American Indians' relations to the United States resembled that of "a ward to his guardian."[23]

The NCAI and other Indians had no objections to no longer being relegated as wards. Nor did they object to receiving just dues for the long history of wrongs perpetrated against American Indians. They refused, however, to acquiesce to a policy bent on acting in the future as if nothing had happened in the past. The relationship they wanted to end was that of white domination, and they wanted to reach beyond simple pronouncements to the reality of Indian life.

The call they developed in the 1940s would resound in the 1950s and beyond. They wanted an end to being marginalized. They wanted an end to their cultural deprivation. They wanted an opening of American society to Indian identity with its cultural past and its present differences. They wanted recognition and acceptance of their differences. They wanted to determine their own order and stability. They wanted the American nation and its government to join in solving the real problems Indians faced.

In seeking solutions, American Indians in the 1940s found themselves again fighting uphill against the flow of the American majority. Their concern and commitment were hardly superficial. Nor were they temporary. Their grievances were complex, and so was their push for change. The issues of the 1940s would persist into the 1950s and beyond.

ASIAN AMERICANS

Americans from Asia and the Pacific Islands accounted for less than 1 percent of the U.S. population in 1940. U.S. immigration barriers deterred their growth. Beginning in 1882 with the Chinese, U.S. law excluded immigrants from Asia. By the 1920s, such exclusion included all Asians. That bar remained firm until 1943. It further prohibited Asians from becoming naturalized U.S. citizens. So lifting the exclusion of the Chinese in December 1943 as a gesture of friendship toward a war ally was more than a small act. The lifting was pointedly limited, however. It allowed a paltry entry quota of 100 immigrants per year from China. It was, nevertheless, a beginning; it was a seed, and it grew. During the latter twentieth century, it would expand to change the complexion and composition of the U.S. population.

In 1940, Hawaii was the center of the U.S. Asian American and Pacific Islander population. Just about three-in-four (73.3%) of the territory's 423,330 residents were Pacific Islanders and Asian Americans. Hawaii was, after all, a Pacific island chain. So it was hardly surprising that the bulk of its people were native Pacific Islanders. Nor was its large Asian American population so remarkable.

Before U.S. annexation in 1898, Hawaii welcomed Asian immigrants, particularly from China and Japan.

Outside of Hawaii, the Asian American population in 1940 was largely home-grown and isolated. Most (80.9%) of the mainland's 254,918 Asian Americans lived in the West. That essentially reflected California's leading position with 167,643 Asian American residents. The Golden State accounted for 65.8 percent of the mainland's total. Trailing California in Asian American population were New York (19,724), Washington (19,226), Oregon (6,794), and Illinois (4,969).

The U.S. racial climate segregated Asian Americans, as it did other nonwhites. This was despite Asian Americans' being relatively cosmopolitan—indeed, in some ways transnational—and open and eager to engage the ways of their U.S. homeland. While interacting daily with other Americans and being highly acculturated as native-born Americans, Asian Americans were not integrated into the U.S. mainstream. Persistent bias fixed on their racial appearance and cultural differences to hold them formally separate. So they tended to live and work in ethnic clusters, most notably symbolized in the Chinatowns of major U.S. cities such as San Francisco, New York, and Los Angeles.

Community remained strong for Asian Americans in the 1940s, fed by both a pull from within and a push from without. Their community ethos reflected contested identity as cultural values and social origins clashed with political realities of mainstream American rejection. Yet the various Asian American communities showed forward-looking flexibility and dynamism.

World War II (1939–1945) proved a watershed. It simultaneously increased and decreased racial discrimination against Asian Americans. Its varying effects also revealed the diversity of Asian Americans. Japan's being a detested U.S. enemy relegated Japanese Americans to what some saw as concentration camps. Issuing his Executive Order 9066 on February 19, 1942, President Franklin D. Roosevelt initiated what became the internment process. It reached about 120,000 Japanese Americans, confining them in 10 camps officially called "War Relocation Centers."

Located in seven states—Arizona (2), Arkansas (2), California (2), Colorado, Idaho, Utah, and Wyoming, the camps operated until June 30, 1946, when Executive Order 9102 officially decommissioned them. The U.S. Supreme Court, notably in its decisions in *Hirabayashi v. United States* (1943) and *Korematsu v. United States* (1944), upheld the internment process, but not without dissent. Justice Frank Murphy denounced the wartime Japanese American internment as "legalized racism."[24]

Other Asian Americans not distinguished from those of Japanese heritage suffered by association. Korean Americans, whose ancestral homeland Japan annexed in 1910, ironically became enemy aliens in the United States after Japan's December 7, 1941, attack on Pearl Harbor. In 1943 U.S. policy separated Koreans' identity from that of their ancient rivals. As enemies of Japan, Koreans became friends of America.

The shift in U.S. perspective showed also with other Asian Americans. Chinese Americans rose in status with China's prominence as an essential U.S. ally. The December 1943 repeal of the ban on Chinese immigration illustrated the turn in U.S.-Sino relations. The end of the war prodded racially reluctant America to accept so-called war brides from China. The July 1946 Chinese Alien Wives of American Citizens statutory provision allowed wives and children of U.S. citizens to apply for U.S. entry as non-quota immigrants.

The contentions of war, with racial overtones in the Pacific, accelerated American reconciliation in what was at one point the largest of its colonial holdings—the Philippines. Acquired in the 1898 in the War with Spain, the 115,831 square-mile Pacific archipelago, with its tens of millions of people, proved a thorny hold for U.S. administration. New Deal policy under President Franklin D. Roosevelt increased island self-governance, establishing the Commonwealth of the Philippines in 1935. Japan's occupation of the islands during World War II delayed U.S. promised independence until 1946. The U.S. connection with the Philippines landed a small but substantial Filipino population, particularly in California, Washington, and New York. At the end of the 1940s, there were about 62,000 Filipinos on the U.S. mainland.

The Cold War further shifted the position of Asian Americans as their ancestral homelands' positions shifted in relation to U.S. foreign policy. Post-World War II U.S. fixation on fighting communism for many Americans supplanted fear of a "race war." It moved them to reach out to, if not embrace, darker peoples as allies in a common struggle. Dictates of foreign policy came also to guide domestic policy. Peoples the Cold War displaced found homes in the United States. Such refugees from Asia trickled in from the generation-long Chinese Nationalist-Communist Civil War (1927–1950). The flow surged after October 1, 1949, when Chinese Communist leader Mao Zedong proclaimed the People's Republic of China.

Anticommunism hardly erased clumsy U.S. racial fantasies about Asian Americans. Even at the end of the 1940s, Asian Americans—predominantly Chinese and Japanese in ancestral heritage—remained unalterably alien in most American eyes. To start, the European-dominant U.S. perspective seldom acknowledged the separate, distinct identities of the diverse Asian American communities. They sat as a simplistic cluster. Popular images seldom distinguished Chinese Americans from Japanese Americans from Korean Americans, for example.

World War II forced a distinction. Telling friends from foes put the Chinese and Koreans on one side and the Japanese on another. Mass circulation U.S. magazines, such as *Life* and *Time*, featured instructions during the war on distinguishing Japanese from others. Yet superficial distinctions were not the real issue of group or individual identity for Asian Americans. They had developed populations of significant size on the U.S. mainland. They constructed their own communities with physical and psychological structures to mediate between American culture and their Asian heritage. Yet, for the most part, they had gained little entry into the U.S. mainstream. Race blocked their path.

HISPANIC AMERICANS/LATINOS

The 1940s was a dynamic and pivotal decade for Americans of Hispanic or Latin American ancestry. Their numbers in the United States grew explosively and focus sharpened on their confused public identities. Never defined as a racial group per se, although often treated as one, those in the multifaceted group called Hispanic or Latino could and did fit into any of the U.S. Census Bureau's racial or ethnic categories. Their national origins spread throughout the Americas, as well as into Europe and even the Pacific. They stood lumped as a political category, more than anything else. Indeed, politics shrouded their identities and their popular images.

As historically the single largest Hispanic/Latino community, Mexican Americans dominated the group's image. In spots around the nation, other Hispanics/Latinos established their identities separate from Mexican Americans. Yet they could not escape clumsy official U.S. categorization.

Sometimes identified as having "Spanish surnames" or being "Spanish-speaking" or of "Hispanic origin," persons grouped as "Hispanic" found themselves in shifting positions in U.S. census counts. The 1930 census, for the first and only time, counted Americans of "Mexican ancestry" separately and included them within the racial category "white." The 1940 census counted those "of Spanish mother tongue" and categorized them as white. The census viewed the category as including Mexican Americans and persons with origins from elsewhere in Central America or from South America. Persons from Cuba or Puerto Rico were also included in the category.

The sweeping categorization did not reach to all areas of the Spanish-speaking Caribbean. Nor was the reach of language identification consistent. Brazilians, for example, were included in the group. Although Latin American and Spanish-speaking in some cases, Brazilians' native tongue was Portuguese. So were their surnames. Most were not of "Hispanic origin," except in the U.S. census count. So there was much sorting to do to identify who was who within the clumsy official category. The situation became more ungainly over time as numbers pushed in or left out of the category grew, and that difficulty nowhere counted the official "discovery" of persons within the category who were not white but Indian or black or Pacific Islanders.

Reaching peoples from the Iberian Peninsula and the many nationalities of the Caribbean and Central and South America, Hispanic/Latino American demographic diversity pointed to a broad range of political and social problems across various communities. Within the diversity two themes competed. One demanded individuation. It fought the depersonalization of indiscriminate, omnibus grouping. The other embraced the political potential of a common identity in collective action. It did not reject the search for individual or communal identity. Rather, it focused on avenues to organize effectively for political clout to improve socioeconomic conditions. The Texas-based League of United Latin American Citizens (LULAC), founded in 1929, represented the broad political approach of a common cause Hispanic/Latino organization.

Zoot suit rioters leave jail to make a court appearance in Los Angeles, June 1943. Courtesy of the Library of Congress, LC-USZC4-4735.

The "Hispanic problem" at the opening of the 1940s arose most publicly from the tight U.S. labor market. Wartime mobilization stretched thin what people of the day called "manpower." That raised competing cries for and against importing labor. Agricultural employers in the West urged Congress to facilitate importing labor. They already had a long history of employing Mexicans and other Central Americans who crossed the U.S. southern border, often seasonally. Long depressed conditions and political unrest in Mexico disposed its government to embrace entreaties for a cross-border labor agreement.

In August 1942, Mexico and the United States began what became known as the Bracero program. Initially directing hundreds of Mexicans to stoop labor in California fields, the Bracero program expanded in April 1943. It spread from the West and Southwest to the Northwest, the Midwest, and further east. Braceros worked more than farms. They did factory work and, between 1943 and 1945, they formed a "box car" contingent of more than 100,000 workers on U.S. railroads.

Beyond those in the official program, other arms (*bracero* is the Spanish word for arm) crossed the border from Mexico. U.S. laws slotted braceros for only temporary work. Those who crossed the border officially and unofficially found more than temporary opportunities, however. Even at the lowest end of U.S. pay scales, workers from south of the border made far more than they could earn back home. The incentives of better money and higher standards of living moved many not simply to stay but to invite family and friends to unmatchable U.S. opportunities.

The influx became increasingly viewed as an incursion, and calls to stem it increasingly became cries to control the southern border and to control groups crossing the border. The numbers alone frightened many in the United States. Indeed, the 1940 census count itself startled many Americans. The official list-ing of 116,356,846 persons of "Hispanic origins" appeared incredible to many. It represented more than 88 percent of the U.S. population of 131,669,275. Such a count threw into question the much heralded Anglo-American legacy. It was clearly unacceptable to U.S. elites who moved in various ways to discount the census figures. The census would offer no official count or estimate of Hispanic or Latino Americans again until 1970, and debate would persist about whom such an identity included or excluded.

Separate counts of national origin sufficed to fix concerns in most places on persons of Mexican origin. A few states, such as New York, New Jersey, and Florida, hosted significant populations in which persons the census counted as "whites born in Cuba" or elsewhere in the Caribbean or in Central and South America out-numbered "whites born in Mexico." But the Mexican-born dominated states with the largest Hispanic/Latino populations. The top five in Mexican-born population in 1940 were Texas (159,266), California (134,312), Arizona (24,902), Illinois (10,065), and New Mexico (8,875). Four of those five—Arizona (5.0), Texas (2.5), California (1.9), and New Mexico (1.7)—were the only states where the census in-dicated the Mexican-born population exceeded 1 percent of the total population.

It was not so much those who were in place in 1940, but those who came there-after, that inflamed concerns in the United States. Yet popular opinion seldom paused to distinguish between generations-old Americans and recent arrivals. It appeared to take little notice of the more than 750,000 Hispanic/Latino Ameri-cans serving in the U.S. Armed Forces during World War II (1939–1945) and their relatively large share of military awards, such as the Congressional Medal of Honor. Rather, focus fell on the influx.

Diplomatically, the flow from Mexico eased U.S. relations, as the arrangement appeared mutually beneficial. Large U.S. agrarian interests delighted in the flow, as it provided them with cheap labor. U.S. labor interests balked, however, at the flow headed to bring almost 5 million Mexicans officially into the United States over 20 years. The number ballooned with the unofficial flow of those called "wetbacks" or *mojados*. Moreover, Mexico was not the only source of imported Spanish-speaking laborers. Puerto Rico, for example, also supplied laborers as an offshoot of its postwar Operation Bootstrap (*Operación Manos a la Obra*) initiated in the Industrial Incentives Act of 1947.

The labor flow heightened tensions. Booming opportunities of the war years changed attitudes among Hispanic/Latino Americans, as it did for many others. More self-assertive, self-confident activism pushed publicly for economic, politi-cal, and social improvements. That produced frictions. Los Angeles's so-called zoot suit riots in June 1943 displayed the explosive potential. A more insistent generation of Mexican Americans and others confronted segregation with their own self-identities and the cultural heritages from the lands of their ancestors and of their birth.

The long-brewing June 1943 riots focused on Mexican American youths called *Pachucos* for their flamboyant dress in oversized suits adapted from African American jazz culture. The fashion proclaimed defiance in the face of widespread discrimination and traditional subordination. Zoot suiters appeared "uppity" in many eyes. White U.S. Armed Forces servicemen, many from the segregated South, insisted on teaching the assertive zoot suiters lessons about minding their manners and keeping their social place.

The two groups clashed sporadically throughout May. On June 3, 1943, pitched battles erupted. U.S. sailors, soldiers, and marines—most teenagers themselves fresh from basic training and some from as far away as bases in San Diego—mounted "search and destroy" raids to clear downtown Los Angeles of Pachucos. Their 10-day long attacks spread into East Los Angeles. And from the barrio, they moved into the predominantly black section called Watts. At its height, the mayhem massed perhaps 5,000 white rioters. Military officials and California Governor Earl Warren scrambled to restore order in what First Lady Eleanor Roosevelt decried as a "race riot."[25]

Beyond the streets, LULAC and others moved from grassroots activism to attacking the institutional divides barring Hispanics from full participation in American life. They won significant legal results. In *Mendez v. Westminster School District* (1946) and its continuation on appeal, for example, federal courts in California outlawed public school segregation against "Spanish-speaking children."

In October 1948, California's Supreme Court struck further at segregation. Anticipating the U.S. Supreme Court by 19 years in examining the fundamental rights involved in marriage, the California court in *Perez v. Sharp* held that the state's anti-miscegenation statutes violated the U.S. Constitution's Equal Protection Clause. Andrea Perez thus prevailed not only in her wish to marry the person she chose, Sylvester Davis, regardless of racial classification. She also advanced the larger struggle against segregation.

Perez's win was another step toward correcting what President Harry S Truman identified as "the remaining imperfections in our practice of democracy." He declared in February 1948, "We know the way. We need only the will."[26] But he proved far more alone in his vision for a desegregated America than he wished.

The nation had opened in the 1940s to recognizing more Hispanics/Latinos. Hollywood was putting the likes of Ricardo Montalbán on screen actor as the Latin lover, but it was not all good. Bigotry barred Mexican American World War II veterans from even being buried with dignity and honor. The Hispanic/Latino image sat mired in the morass of both segregation and immigration.

EUROPEAN AMERICANS

For white Americans of European heritage, the 1940s opened as another world-shifting physical and psychic upheaval. The dislocations of the 1930s Great Depression had hardly ceased before many European Americans found their ancestral homelands engaged in the cataclysm of World War II (1939–1945). Old national and ethnic allegiances warred amid suspicions about loyalty and identity.

For many, the contested allegiances were not so old. The war that erupted in Europe in 1939 involved the land of their birth for one in every dozen Americans. The nation's 11.6 million foreign-born whites constituted more than 10 percent of the total population in 12 states in 1940. They were 21.2 percent of New York's 13.5 million population.[27] Even more were children of European immigrants. The war attacked not only their old world but their sense of personality and place. And they were not alone. World War II challenged how white Americans, whether new or old immigrants, whether native-born or recent arrivals, viewed themselves, their world, their America, and those with whom they inhabited the nation.

War production and mobilization transformed America as the 1940s opened. War-related activity moved millions. The Armed Forces alone mobilized more than 8 million men. The movement created new experiences, new perspectives, and new communities. It brought Americans into closer contact with many others they would not have so encountered. From the Armed Forces to factories to neighborhoods, European Americans found themselves faced with a diversity of other Americans insistent on enjoying equal rights with whites. From education to employment to housing to public facilities, whites from old-line families and from the most recent immigrants found themselves in a welter of race relations.

The war dented the cushions of racial segregation. Whites who perhaps never realized how their race made their lives more convenient found themselves increasingly confronted with uncomfortable realities of race. The German Nazi leader Adolf Hitler's race-based horrors pushed Americans to examine their own public culture and personal relations. But more than ideas of blood, nation, and race played in self and social reflections of personal identity and place. During the 1940s, many whites for the first time felt nonwhites' demands pressing on them, and many resisted. Some became recalcitrant. The South was the easy showcase for resistance to racial change, but resistance was no less sharp outside the South. The clash of race relations extended everywhere.

The 1943 race riots in Los Angeles, Detroit, and New York City more than illustrated increased racial friction nationwide. For many Americans in the 1940s, particularly those who were immigrants or the children of immigrants, their hard-won whiteness stood as symbol and substance of their achieved identity. It represented their progress and their place in the United States. They shared at least tacitly in idealized white supremacy. Its demands of social distance from darker peoples, especially blacks, shaped not only whites' self-images but the boundaries of their communities. It moved them to bristle at the presence of nonwhites in their workplaces, to say nothing of their neighborhoods. People of color posed a threat to such whites, even while for the most part they refused to think of themselves or of their attitudes as racist or even race-based.

European immigrant assimilation, with its scrambling up the social margins, often embraced racialized categories to set solidarity with white elites and to separate the strivers from nonwhite social subordinates. Even while espousing a multicultural vision of European ethnic diversity in America, most Americans constructed a white identity for themselves that politicized racialized norms as necessary standards. And that was no less true in the 1940s among the large foreign-born populations in New England and the Middle Atlantic states than among the small foreign-born populations in the southern states. For many white Americans, their definition of self and of nation, their image of being American, rested on an essential whiteness. And that was more than social image or memory. It represented an often unacknowledged whitewashing of American character and culture.

Explicit U.S. racism in the war against Japan contrasted with American abhorrence of racism in the war in Europe. African Americans' "Double V Campaign" for democracy abroad and at home might have clarified contradictions for many white Americans. Yet too few of them seemed aware of the gap between American rhetoric and racial reality. Many white Americans saw no connection, for example, between racial violence abroad and American apartheid. Many refused to acknowledge the self-serving white aesthetic that informed race-based public and private U.S. custom and culture.

Popular political imagination among whites tended to localize U.S. racist excess. A tendency existed also to transfer the causes of racial excess from white perpetrators to nonwhite victims. So, for example, in the view of many whites, Japanese Americans sat in concentration camps from 1942 to 1946 not because of official and popular American racism but because of Japanese Americans' inscrutable character, which included questionable allegiance. Similar apologetics sought to excuse white rioters attacking Los Angeles *Pachucos* for their zoot suits or blacks seeking jobs or housing in Detroit in 1943.

The war's end in 1945 signaled no return to normalcy. The nation had forever changed. Demobilization, the sharp decline in war-related demand and production, removal of price controls, and rising unemployment mixed with growing demands from the nation's racial minorities. The prewar racialized framework of U.S. life could no longer contain or fully support structural segregation against nonwhites' insistent challenges.

The seemingly perennial "Negro question" loomed largest for white Americans thinking about race relations in the postwar 1940s. It represented a dilemma, as Swedish economist Gunnar Myrdal famously explained in his multiyear Carnegie Foundation landmark study, *An American Dilemma: The Negro Problem and Modern Democracy,* published in 1944. Challenging the conservative American continuity of blaming blacks for their subordinate condition, Myrdal demonstrated the controlling white construction of black Americans' relative poverty, poor education, poor housing, and poor health. His work scandalized many white Americans, as it came in the context of unfolding Nazi racial atrocities in Europe.

President Harry S Truman courageously acknowledged the gaping contradiction between U.S. egalitarian rhetoric and the realities of race in America. He declared that "the preservation of civil rights guaranteed by the Constitution is essential to domestic tranquility, national security, the general welfare, and the continued existence of our free institutions."[28] And in December 1946, he established the President's Committee on Civil Rights to recommend reforms of federal law, policy, and practice to end segregation.

The commission's classic 1947 report, titled *To Secure These Rights*, emphasized the theme that "the American ideal still awaits complete realization."[29] It echoed President Truman's call to "make the Federal Government a friendly, vigilant defender of the rights and equalities of all Americans."[30] Also, it referenced the human rights and international contexts of postwar civil rights, noting the U.S. commitment to the 1945 United Nations Charter.[31]

In February 1948, President Truman urged Congress to enact a broad civil rights program to, in his words, "finally achieve the ideals for which this Nation was founded" and to end "discrimination as a result of [any person's] race, or religion, or color, or the land of his forefathers." Acting on his constitutional powers as commander-in-chief, in July 1948 the president ordered the desegregation of the U.S. Armed Forces.[32] While calling for institutional reforms, the president and his advisers recognized the need for both governmental and popular individual action to correct what *To Secure These Rights* termed "the imperfections of our social order, and the ignorance and moral weaknesses of some of our people."[33]

Desegregation met stiff resistance. Even before President Truman's postwar push, forces rose to resist what they viewed as the racial liberalization of President Franklin D. Roosevelt's New Deal. In Deep South states such as Alabama, Mississippi, and South Carolina, such resistance gave rise to Dixiecrats. Stalwarts such as governors J. Strom Thurmond in South Carolina and Fielding L. Wright of Mississippi split from the Democratic Party in 1948 to preach political and social conservatism that insisted on continued segregation.

Taking up the historic southern theme in their State's Rights Party, those popularly called "Dixiecrats" rejected the changing face of U.S. race relations. Although they spoke with southern accents, the Dixiecrats' message was not simply sectional. Their hierarchical vision of the United States rested on white supremacy. It reached nationally. It was not simply southern. The presidential ticket of Thurmond and Wright won 7 percent of the 1948 popular vote, winning majorities in Alabama, Louisiana, Mississippi, and South Carolina and garnering 39 electoral votes in all.

While the nation reelected President Truman, it did not entirely rally behind his call for racial readjustment. Many whites at least implicitly clung to their race as an important boundary in their lives. So although the 1940s had moved the nation away from prewar segregation, the decade closed with many white Americans not simply far from accepting nonwhites as equals but prepared to take flight or fight so as not to live near them or have much to do with them.

LAW AND GOVERNMENT

The 1940s was a decade of significant change in U.S. law and governmental policy related to race relations. The years featured breakthrough advances and also notable retreats. The drastic dislocations of World War II (1939–1945) unsettled much of the structure of the racial segregation that traditionally distanced whites from nonwhites throughout the nation. The Great Depression had already unsettled much. The unnerving economic collapse in the 1930s so fatigued many Americans as to allow President Franklin D. Roosevelt's New Deal to break down old barriers to the federal government's reaching and regulating individual Americans' everyday lives. Indeed, expectations grew for the national government to take increased responsibility for personal welfare and individual rights. Profound implications for U.S. race relations developed with contested visions of a more active federal role.

Congressional hearings on federal Indian policy in 1940 illustrated something of the persistent contradiction and ironies, not only in the decade but in the history of U.S. race relations. The House of Representatives Committee on Indian Affairs debated what critics considered advantages and disadvantages American Indians were reportedly reaping from their revived tribal independence under the 1934 New Deal Indian Reorganization Act (IRA). Critics contended during the hearings that rather than treating, or even recognizing, Indian tribes, the federal government should cease its so-called special relationship with Indians. It should stop recognizing Indians as separate or distinct from other Americans and treat them simply as individuals. IRA critics urged government to become blind to Indians' traditional identities.

The United States was the land of individuals, IRA critics insisted. So government should recognize only individuals, not groups. It had no proper business treating with Indian tribes. Fostering communal organization rather than advancing individual interests created and sustained group-think and dependence. It smacked of communism. It made Indians voluntary or involuntary wards of the government. U.S. Chief Justice John Marshall had declared Indians wards in 1831. The time had long passed to end that wardship, critics charged. They demanded an end to federal Indian policy that in their view did nothing more than "set up a state or nation within a nation which is contrary to the intents and purposes of the American Republic."[34]

The theme of terminating the federal-Indian special relationship was an old issue, and it would persist long after the decade. What it did in the 1940s was foster divergent government actions with the announced aim of making Indians independent or, at least, cutting them off from government supervision and support. A major measure in that direction was the Indian Claims Commission Act of 1946. It sought to provide a mandated legal forum to settle once and for all what, if anything, the federal government owed Indians. The notion of providing some formal, final monetary tally for historical depredations appeared realistic to some and ridiculous to others. It reflected money as the measure of damages in U.S. law. Moreover, the polar contrasts reflected distant perspectives on race relations in the nation.

The Indian Claims Commission's mechanisms and timeframes proved wholly inadequate to the task. Reviewing what tribes claimed as their due for centuries of depredations and dispossession at the hands of whites, in general, and the U.S.

government, in particular, was no little work. Nor was it necessarily suited for handling formalistic legal proofs. The register of differences contained subtleties beyond U.S. law. It was complex in ways U.S. law refused to recognize. And it ran longer than law usually allowed. Moreover, the register was bloody. It was filled with injury and insult. It contained the substance and significance of the past.

Settling the past was no simple matter, if it were possible at all. It resisted formulaic calculations. It was not a matter of numbers or balances. Nothing could wipe the slate clean and provide a fresh start, as if the past had not occurred. There was no way to declare history at an end. The fact was that the past was not past. In many Indians' perspectives, their historic injuries remained ongoing. Indeed, their injuries appeared never-ending. A genuine settlement of Indian grievances was a matter of repairing relations. It was a matter of fundamental changes. And that was unlikely to happen in a U.S. law court, even one with relaxed rules of procedure. A genuine settlement needed to reach the hearts and minds of the American population and affect their attitudes and behaviors.

In short, the Indian Claims Commission represented problematic elements in the government's approach. It represented insensitivities also in the general U.S. population. It reflected a perennial American tendency to hope for quick-fix solutions, and it reflected a tendency to focus on the future while trying to jettison the past.

A majority of Americans in the 1940s, and not then alone, seemed to prefer that problems with Indians, or with race relations in general, simply go away. They insisted on making the past *past*. To the degree they were interested in reconciling with minority groups such as Indians, the American majority appeared uninterested in anything that smacked of reparations. Many rejected any notion that anything wrong had in fact been done. Most simply resisted what they considered rehashing the past. They really did not care what had happened.

Many brandishing their immigrant descent claimed innocence for any historical injuries in America. They never harmed an Indian or held slaves or interacted with them or Asians or Hispanics or any other racial minorities. They claimed to have done no wrong and to have not benefited from any wrongdoing. So their being responsible for compensation for past injury was out of the question in their view.

Indians' historic and seemingly open-ended complaints, like those of other racial minorities, tended to rub many in the American majority the wrong way. The complaints contained fundamental indictments of the American way of life. They cast basic U.S. institutions as flawed. Such complaints generated fatigue and jaundice in the general population. They gave rise also to counter complaints about minorities such as Indians simply seeking special favors or pursuing special interests to the detriment of the general welfare. That view marked groups different from the white majority as undeserving to the degree of their difference. If Indians, or other minorities, wanted to be treated as equals in civil society, then they should work to become equals and simply be like everybody else. That, of course, meant being like the white majority. They should abandon their differences and melt into the mainstream, critics asserted.

As views of the Indian Claims Commission reflected, adjusting national and local race relations to accommodate demands from racial minorities in the existing official and popular U.S. climate in the 1940s required not so much setting new priorities as insisting on new patterns of popular and official behavior. Traditional rhetoric saturated U.S. society with a sense of freedom and equality. It instilled a notion of everyone in America achieving their position through personal talent and toil. It accepted equality of opportunity as fact rather than fiction. When minorities challenged the ideal as an illusion, they faced a daunting backlash. Yet they had few viable alternatives.

The nation's ambivalence to minorities' demands for equal rights showed further in response to the March on Washington Movement (MOWM) African American labor leader A. Philip Randolph spearheaded in January 1941. MOWM called for a massive demonstration at the national capital in July 1941 to protest employment segregation that excluded blacks from better jobs and relegated them to the lowest paid work, when they got any paid work at all. MOWM threatened to expose to the world the hypocrisy of America's claim of rewarding people according to the character of their personal contribution. It aimed to exhibit the lies of equality of opportunity in America.

To avoid the embarrassment of MOWM's demonstration, President Roosevelt negotiated a compromise to head off the planned July march. On June 25, 1941, he issued Executive Order 8802. It established the Fair Employment Practices Committee (FEPC) to monitor that there be no "discrimination because of race, creed, color, or national origin" in federal employment practices or in those of federal contractors. Yet typical of national antipathy since at least the framing of the U.S. Constitution in 1787, the president refused to concede that racial discrimination in fact existed. Nor did he declare any commitment to the principle of equal rights in employment. Rather, he blithely declared that it was "the policy of the United States to encourage full participation in the national defense program by all citizens of the United States, regardless of race, creed, color, or national origin."[35]

Opposition raged at the president's tepid endorsement of antidiscrimination. FEPC critics complained FDR had surrendered to a pressure group. Some complained the FEPC took an unconstitutional direction. It violated freedom of association, critics charged. The U.S. Constitution provided no authority for government to control private employment selection and retention, critics asserted. Moreover, with southern Democrats in the lead to defend segregation and states' rights, Congress balked at confirming the antidiscrimination principle. It resisted appropriations for the FEPC. With almost unprecedented parliamentary maneuvering, moreover, Congress bitterly refused during the 1940s to give the FEPC statutory standing.

Despite congressional and popular recalcitrance, FDR's establishing the FEPC initiated a role for government in combating job discrimination. Even hampered as it was, the FEPC contributed significantly to remarkable black economic progress in the 1940s. Primarily, it fostered black men's moving into manufacturing jobs. Between 1940 and 1950, the proportion of employed black men in manufacturing rose from 16.2 to 23.9 percent. Black men the U.S. Census classified as semiskilled workers nearly doubled from 12.6 to 21.4 percent. That proved crucial for African Americans far beyond the 1940s.[36]

The labor market was an area where government initiatives also boosted the position of Hispanics and Latinos and shifted their relations in the United States. The Bracero program with Mexico funneled temporary workers to U.S. sites in growing numbers beginning in 1942. The northward flow of labor fit into the wartime surges, changing U.S. demographics nationwide. It also built political pressures for and against social transformations and challenges to cultural continuity that accompanied the population shifts. Popular attitudes in many places hardly changed as swiftly as wartime demands escalated.

Nowhere during the 1940s did American racial prejudice surface with such ugly consequences as in U.S. governmental policies and practices that interned 120,000 Japanese Americans in the aftermath of Japan's attack on the U.S. Navy's Pacific Fleet Headquarters at Hawaii's Pearl Harbor in December 1941. Entering World War II, President Roosevelt immediately proclaimed nationals of Japan, Germany, and Italy in the United States to be "alien enemies." The proclamations limited their travel, restricted their property rights, and authorized their being detained into custody. Although U.S. agents arrested several thousand Germans and Italians, the scale of the roundup of Japanese Americans tagged as being of "foreign enemy ancestry" was unprecedented. Only U.S. removals of Indians from their homelands in the 1800s approached the scale of Japanese American internment that followed Executive Order 9066.

Issued in February 1942, the order authorized the U.S. military to exclude persons of Japanese descent, whether citizens or aliens, from designated "military areas" such as the U.S. Pacific Coast and much of the West. In April 1942, the Wartime Civilian Control Agency (WCCA) began evacuating Japanese Americans to 10 War Relocation Authority (WRA) centers. Located in Arkansas (2), Arizona (2), California (2), Colorado, Idaho, Utah, and Wyoming, these facilities operated as late as June 1946, essentially as concentration camps.

Protests challenging the constitutionality of the internment produced notable U.S. Supreme Court decisions in *United States v. Hirabayashi* (1943), *United States v. Korematsu* (1944), and *Ex parte Endo* (1944). In the first, Seattle-born, University of Washington sociology student Gordon Kiyoshi Hirabayashi challenged the military curfew and exclusion orders as unconstitutional discrimination that violated Fifth Amendment guarantees to due process. In an opinion Chief Justice Harlan Fiske Stone delivered in June 1943, a unanimous Court upheld the curfew and exclusion under the war powers. The Court held the government actions against Japanese Americans a warranted and reasonable response to "the danger of espionage and sabotage to our military resources [that] was imminent."[37]

On December 18, 1944, the Court similarly upheld the internment process against California-born Fred Toyosaburo Korematsu's challenge. "Compulsory exclusion of large groups of citizens from their homes, except under circumstances of direst emergency and peril, is inconsistent with our basic governmental institutions," Justice

Hugo Black conceded in writing for the six-to-three majority. "But when under conditions of modern warfare our shores are threatened by hostile forces, the power to protect must be commensurate with the threatened danger," he explained.[38] Justices Owen Roberts, Frank Murphy, and Robert H. Jackson strongly dissented. Justice Murphy condemned the Japanese American internment as a "legalization of racism."[39]

The *Korematsu* dissents signaled something of a shift. From broad deference and reluctance to second-guess military decisions in wartime, the Court moved to state limits on government's authority to roundup and hold persons indefinitely without judicial process. On the same day as the *Korematsu* decision, Justice William O. Douglas writing for a unanimous Court upheld 24-year-old former California state highway commission civil-service stenographer Mitsuye Endo's challenge to her confinement in the Tule Lake War Relocation Center in California.

Endo's habeas corpus petition declared her "a loyal and law-abiding citizen of the United States." It stated "that no charge has been made against her, that she is being unlawfully detained, and that she is confined in the Relocation Center under armed guard and held there against her will."[40] The Court ordered her unconditional release from detention. "A citizen who is concededly loyal presents no problem of espionage or sabotage," Justice Douglas explained. "Loyalty is a matter of the heart and mind, not of race, creed, or color. He who is loyal is by definition not a spy or a saboteur," he noted. "When the power to detain is derived from the power to protect the war effort against espionage and sabotage, detention which has no relationship to that objective is unauthorized."[41]

At President Truman's urging, Congress in July 1948 passed the Japanese-American Evacuation Claims Act. Without apology and considering "moot" the question of whether the internment was justified, the legislation accepted that "the principles of justice and responsible government require that there should be compensation" for losses interned Japanese Americans suffered.[42] Over 27 years, Congress appropriated $38 million to settle 23,000 claims for damages totaling $131 million. (In 1980, President Jimmy Carter would appoint a special commission to investigate the World War II Japanese Americans internment. The result was the Civil Liberties Act of 1988, which included an official apology and provisions to pay each surviving internee $20,000 as "redress." Also, based on government prosecutors' having deliberately suppressed evidence that Japanese Americans posed no security risk, San Francisco U.S. District Court Judge Marilyn Hall Patel vacated Korematsu's conviction in November 1983.)

Race relations was more than a domestic issue in the post-1945 United States. Nazi horrors, along with incessant agitation, heightened sensitivities everywhere to racial domination and subordination. International perspectives on U.S. civil rights and, indeed, on the U.S. position as a colonial power increasingly sharpened after 1945. Domestic race relations loomed ever more as an issue of international image and ideological consistency.

During his 1930s New Deal, President Roosevelt pushed forward U.S. decolonization, primarily in the Philippines. America seized the archipelago as a colony in its 1898 war with Spain. It secured its hold by brutal suppression of local independence in the Philippine-American War (1899–1913). The United States promised self-government in 1935 in declaring the Commonwealth of the Philippines. It completed the promise in recognizing Philippine independence on July 4, 1946.

Puerto Rico was another U.S. colonial possession that figured prominently in post-1945 race relations. Also acquired in the 1898 Treaty of Paris that ended the War with Spain, the Caribbean island developed a peculiar status under U.S. rule. The 1917 Jones-Shafroth Act granted Puerto Ricans U.S. citizenship. In 1948 Congress allowed Puerto Ricans to elect their own governor. Yet continuing tensions developed over the island's becoming independent. Significant migration after 1945, especially to New York City, made Puerto Ricans a notable group in U.S. race relations.

Puerto Ricans joined with African Americans and others in the United States to play out their grievances for a world audience. Even before World War II's end, the National Association for the Advancement of Colored People (NAACP) campaign to reform U.S. racial policies and practices on the basis of worldwide recognition of human rights. With the advent of the United Nations in 1945, the NAACP and others increased their push for international focus on U.S. racial injustice. The 1946 National Negro Congress (NNC) petitioned the UN to attend to inhumane conditions in the United States. The NNC saw its campaigned very much like that waged successfully to have the UN condemn South Africa's discrimination against its resident Asian Indians. The NAACP's 1947 UN petition "An Appeal to the World" pressed the theme, but without success.

As with President Truman's push for omnibus federal civil rights legislation, the press for a top-down solution from the United Nations or the world community failed for the moment. The more striking success in forcing U.S. governmental and legal change arose from local attacks against segregation. The 1946 Mexican American-led win in federal courts in *Mendez v. Westminster School District,* for example, outlawed public school segregation against "Spanish-speaking children" in California. Similarly, the 1948 victory in *Perez v. Sharp* struck down California's anti-miscegenation statutes as violations of the U.S. Constitution's Equal Protection Clause.

The Legal Defense and Educational Fund (LDF) that the NAACP founded in 1940 also chipped away at the constitutional support for segregation. Its 1948 win in *Sipuel v. Board of Regents of the University of Oklahoma* reinforced the U.S. Constitution's rule requiring a state to provide the same educational opportunities to blacks as it provided to whites. Also in 1948, the win in *Shelley v. Kraemer* struck a blow at residential segregation in holding the Fourteenth Amendment's Equal Protection Clause prohibited legal enforcement of covenants restricting nonwhites from buying or renting homes in certain areas.

So as the 1940s drew to a close, the legal segregation that served as the foundation of U.S. race relations was not what it had been. Time and tide were moving against it with increasing pressure.

MEDIA AND MASS COMMUNICATIONS

Mass communications flowed along two major media tracks in the United States in the 1940s, and each significantly shaped shifting race relations. Traditional print media, particularly newspapers and magazines, carried information and ideas of institutional elites. None enjoyed a truly mass audience. Even when they had national influence as the *Chicago Tribune* or *New York Times,* for example, single newspapers were for the most part local and seldom, if ever, had audited circulations above 1 million. Magazines reached tens of millions. Radio was, however, the mass medium of the 1940s. Its national programming helped increasingly to homogenize U.S. culture. That proved both good and bad for race relations.

As competing U.S. media were converging in the 1940s, with ownership becoming increasingly concentrated, race relations hardly appeared in the view of most American mass communications. To be sure, issues of race relations were not wholly absent. They were most notable, however, by their infrequent appearance. No major media producer made race an issue. All operated on the white standard. That meant a virtual blackout for nonwhites.

Relatively few perspectives were available. Four radio networks—the American Broadcasting Company (ABC), Columbia Broadcasting System (CBS), Mutual Broadcasting System (MBS), and National Broadcasting Company (NBC)— with a combined 1,136 affiliates—controlled more than half the nation's 2,183 AM radio stations operating in 1949. Print boasted wider ownership, but it too was becoming more and more concentrated. Hearst and Scripps-Howard were the two largest national newspaper chains. They competed also with regional clusters such as the McClatchy Company in California.

Whether broadcast or print, U.S. media in the 1940s appeared racing toward shared material and market-based attitudes that emphasized income and the propensity to consume over explicit race-based values. Their main interest rested in husbanding market revenue rather than offering a marketplace for ideas. That offered little prospect for doing other than promoting the racial status quo.

U.S. national radio broadcasting took big steps during the 1940s. Rural electrification during the 1930s and broadcasting and production advances put radio at the fingertips of most Americans. In part, military necessities for wartime applications and expected improvements in the developing medium advanced technology. Opening audiences to advertisers, as well as providing an outlet for information and propaganda, drove radio in the early 1940s to unprecedented national reach. Commentators often consider the 1940s a golden age of radio. The potential reach of the medium enticed commercial interests to scramble for audience share.

Programming was the crux. To what would audiences listen, when, and for how long? And who in the audience would listen? The radio business increasingly focused on matching program appeal to relevant listener characteristics. More and more in the 1940s, that focus shifted radio away from nonwhite offerings. In the 1930s, radio presented various black orchestras and singers. Such entertainment faded in the 1940s as daytime serial programs, dubbed "soap operas" because of the predominant advertisers, succeeded in edging out most else.

As the serials took increasing audience share, nonwhites fell from the radio dial. Nor did news and commentary programming that reached short-term and limited audiences give voice to nonwhites. Indeed, by the end of the 1940s, as one historian of the medium has explained, nonwhites had virtually disappeared as "the lily white dramas became the staple of radio."[43]

As soap operas became the most popular type of U.S. radio program, they altered the radio audience. In many ways they moved the audience away from reality, often under the guise of treating real life. Centered around personal relations, the serials usually featured courtship, marriage, and household drama. In exposing America's intimate life, however, the serials seldom introduced any realistic aspects of race relations.

The world of American radio was not colorless, of course: It was simply white. It was a world for the most part without community problems. It was certainly a world without racial problems, unless those arose in standard patterns that exhibited nonwhites—especially blacks—with weak or bad tendencies. The lowest common denominator approach affected attitudes so as to help distance most white Americans from the ugly realities of the nation's racial structure.

From its 1926 debut on Chicago radio station WGN as *Sam 'n' Henry*, to its 1928 appearance on the *Chicago Daily News* station WMAQ and the next year becoming a NBC 15-minutes-a-night, six-nights-a-week staple, *The Adventures of Amos 'n' Andy* became America's blackface radio voice of the 1940s. While offering near cartoon caricatures featuring rural black Southern migrants to the urban North (first Chicago's Southside then New York City's Harlem), the program provided snatches of black life few white Americans could otherwise imagine, let alone experience.

Old minstrel show and vaudeville routines carried the action with what was supposed to be black dialect. Yet standard English also surfaced. Exchanges on issues of the day, including race relations and politics, were thoughtful, if not provocative. No black-white confrontations ever occurred. Indeed, whites were a distant presence. It was almost as if blacks and whites did not inhabit the same America. On radio they were marginal to each others' lives.

Highly controversial but popular enough to become a 30-minute broadcast in 1943, *Amos 'n' Andy* demeaned and disparaged blacks in many perspectives. The NAACP bitterly opposed it. Yet the show offered several dignified black characters. Amos's wife Ruby, for example, radiated intelligence and a bearing worthy of respect. Black professionals also appeared at a time when most Americans had never heard of a black attorney or physician.

Not completely alone in providing black voices on U.S. radio, *Amos 'n' Andy* had a little, but less substantial, company in *Beulah* and the character Rochester on *The Jack Benny Program*. As black domestics in white households, the man-servant Rochester and the maid Beulah acted out scenes more familiar in white Americans' images of blacks. They, too, were caricatures and unflattering in many eyes, but there was also a difference between them.

Beulah developed from a 1939 introduction in the series *Hometown Inc.* She moved to *That's Life* in 1943. Then she went to work at the home of *Fibber McGee and Molly*, one of the most popular and longest-running network radio programs. She spun off in 1945 as a separate show. The well-meaning but servile and simpleminded meddler spoke in malapropisms and consorted with the shiftless, exemplified by her apparently good-for-nothing boyfriend Bill Jackson.

Beulah's minstrelsy was not only blackface but transgendered, as a white man, Marlin Hurt, portrayed the maid on radio until his death in 1946. Hattie McDaniels—the first black winner of an Academy of Motion Picture Arts and Sciences' Oscar Award, for best supporting actress for her portrayal of the character Mammy in the 1939 film *Gone with the Wind*—took over Beulah's character in 1947. She made a hit of the daily 15-minute CBS radio show.

In contrast to Beulah, black actor Eddie Anderson's Rochester Van Jones offered no simple stereotype. He was a key figure in the long-running *Jack Benny Program*. A cast original starting with the program in 1932, he remained throughout the radio series and also went to television. He proved integral to the show's appeal.

Rochester was not a fall man but a foil. Rather than being the butt of jokes in the comedic series, Rochester often in deadpan turned back jokes with snappy, sharp-tongued retorts. He stood as an equal personality with his employer Jack Benny. He was in the special sense the man's man, occupying a peculiar place in American broadcasting of the 1940s. The program's racial sensitivities showed further as its resort to race-based humor diminished as the horrors of the World War II Holocaust became more widely known in the 1940s.

Nonwhite presence on U.S. radio in the 1940s extended also to an occasional Asian, Hispanic, and Indian character. Like black domestics Beulah and Rochester, these others were also mostly in service. Two notable exceptions appeared.

The Potawatami sidekick Tonto on the popular and long-running *The Lone Ranger* serial, which premiered in 1933, provided perhaps the most sustained American Indian presence on U.S. network radio in the 1940s. Akin to Rochester, Tonto was very much his own man. Nevertheless he played a distant fiddle to the masked man riding "a fiery horse with the speed of light, [and] a cloud of dust" to the "cavalry charge" theme from the finale of Gioacchino Rossini's overture to his 1829 opera *William Tell*.

The Chinese American detective Charlie Chan aired first in 1932, and, by the serial's end on radio in 1948, he appeared on all four U.S. national networks under different eponymous show titles. Although portrayed by white actors in what might be called yellowface, akin to blackface minstrelsy, Charlie Chan was decidedly a representative Asian. Stereotyped as inscrutable and from time-to-time given to troublesome relations with other minorities, particularly his black domestics, Chan appeared as a virtually unparalleled character on U.S. airwaves: he was an intelligent nonwhite hero. He bested all comers. Always dignified, he ultimately won every battle of wits, usually against white villains, sometimes in semi-comic and sometimes in dramatic fashion. Still, this was no complex discourse on or about race relations. It portrayed thin identities.

As radio kept the nation turned on to program favorites, a few general-interest weekly magazines also had national reach. *Time*, created in 1923 as the first U.S. weekly news magazine, led the way. Its sister *Life* magazine, begun in 1936, and its competitor *Look*, begun in 1937, reached further with their mostly photographic and light-entertainment formats. They became keys to America's shared images and popular ideas, more than the multiplicity of daily newspapers, even as they dipped together into a common pool of pictures and stories wire services such as the Associated Press (AP) and United Press International (UPI) provided. The images were overwhelmingly white.

With smaller outreach than nationally circulated magazines or radio programming, most U.S. newspapers in the 1940s operated from an unchallenged position in reaching fragmented or somewhat insulated audiences. A single daily alone served more than 80 percent of U.S. cities that had a local daily newspaper. Even in cities with multiple newspapers, the publications more than likely came from a single source. More than 90 percent of U.S. newspaper communities in the 1940s had only a single publisher. To say the least, that concentration, along with localized focus, tended to close debate on more than race relations.

Regional and national newspaper chains reached multiple millions. Indeed, a few dozen publishers produced about half the newspapers circulated to the 40 million or so U.S. readers daily during the 1940s. But that was in combination. The readership did not represent the reach of any one newspaper alone. The trend was declining newspaper readership, anyway.

Whether owned locally or by chains such as Hearst or Scripps-Howard, the nation's newspaper dailies and weeklies focused on their immediate surroundings and reflected and molded prevailing biases and stereotypes in their predominant communities. They mirrored local culture. They thrived on local dynamics. Some were crusaders, but most rested on their immediate community's readers and advertisers. And they were under significant pressure to do so.

Cannibalistic competition and radio's widening reach focused newspapers sharply on dominating local markets. They were more in the business of selling than of shaping attitudes. Notable exceptions existed, such as Hodding Carter II's *Greenville Delta Democrat-Times* in Mississippi, but for the most part local papers tended to go with the flow on race relations. They often saw few options in light of their advertisers' powers.

With the major U.S. media and mass communication being English-language based, the foreign-language media supported by racial minorities had little impact nationally or even regionally. The Spanish-language press, reaching back to its start in Louisiana in 1808, contributed its voice to the national effort during World War II. Although regionally concentrated west of the Mississippi, it reflected a scattered but growing community with national aims and aspirations. Located mostly in New Mexico, Texas, California, and Arizona, it gained new outlets with shifting migration patterns prompted by the war. Tampa, Miami, and Chicago gained new Spanish-language papers during the 1940s. So did New York City, where the founding of *El Diario de Nueva York* in 1948 reflected the Puerto Rican migration. Yet these publications had limited, if any, reach outside their immediate communities.

The one minority press that had notable national impact was the black press. With admittedly a limited, occasional readership, the black press had stature beyond its circulation. Indeed, it operated in the 1940s as a remarkable exception to locally focused U.S. newspapers. From renowned leaders such as Robert S. Abbott's *Chicago Defender* or the *Pittsburgh Courier* with its boasted 5 million readers, to less noted publications such as *The Carolina Times* in Durham, North Carolina, the 230 black-owned papers published with a national agenda. During World War II, they invariably displayed their loyalty and patriotism. Yet they also campaigned to reform U.S. race relations to accord with the nation's egalitarian rhetoric.

The "Double V Campaign" was evident throughout the black press. The *Pittsburgh Courier* launched the theme in its February 14, 1942, issue. It drove for "Democracy: Victory at Home, Victory Abroad." News items early in the war detailed the discrimination prompting the black-led March on Washington Movement (MOWM)'s campaign against racial discrimination in employment. "This prohibiting of Negroes to work in defense industries merely because they are Negroes . . . to satisfy the desires of race hatred here in Durham and elsewhere in the South, under the pretense that it threatens 'white supremacy' and encourages 'social equality' is the most pernicious attitude ever concocted by mortal man," a *Carolina Times* editorial complained on August 22, 1942.[44]

An editorial in the September 26, 1942, *Carolina Times* further exemplified the black press's consistent connection of local circumstances with more transcendent perspective. "This war cannot be won with a 'hatred as usual' attitude," the editorial warned. Pointing up hypocritical race relations, the editorial lambasted local prejudices for blocking the national war effort. "Here in Durham are certain war-industry plants that are crying about their employees being taken by the manufacturing concerns in other cities," the paper noted. But, the editorial chided, "these same plants have indicated that they are not going to employ, if they can avoid it, competent Negroes, simply because some little short-sighted halfwit does not like to work beside Negroes."[45]

Persisting in the historic strategy of black protest echoing America's rhetorical claims to expose their hollowness and hypocrisy, the black press repeated U.S. propaganda on the meaning of World War II. It embraced the vilification of Naziism and retold the horrors to demonstrate the inhumanity of race-based systems. It linked the oppressed status of nonwhites worldwide to the vagaries of white supremacy on which the Nazis operated. It pilloried the German Third Reich as the leading edge of race-based segregation. It made America's treatment of its Negroes a test of adherence to the substance of the Four Freedoms President Roosevelt articulated in January 1941 as the aim of the nation and all civilized humanity. For many, those freedoms—freedom of speech and worship and freedom from want and fear—announced the Allied war purpose.

The black press campaigned like no other media sector with moral purpose for domestic reform to eliminate racism. And its campaign was not only domestic. It pressed worldwide human rights. It reached out to build liberal, progressive coalitions. It made racial justice a basis for world peace. Its global consciousness exhibited a focus on human rights not found elsewhere. Typically black papers during World War II devoted half or more of their editorial and news coverage to the war's implications for race relations.

The Pledge of Allegiance *The Chicago Defender* published in a special edition on September 26, 1942, gave full voice to the vision and verve the black press exhibited during the war. "The world will never be safe until every man, be he white or black, brown or yellow, wherever he may reside, shares the full measure of the blessings of civilization," the newspaper declared. "We pledge ourselves to fight segregation, discrimination, and all forms of racial bigotry and Hitlerism which impede our war effort, and give aid and comfort to the enemy," it stated.[46]

The black press, particularly *The Chicago Defender* and the four large regional black newspapers—the *Baltimore Afro-American*, the *New York Amsterdam News*, the Norfolk, Virginia, *Journal and Guide*, and the *Pittsburgh Courier*—accelerated their protest campaign after the war. They backed the NAACP and the National Urban League (NUL) challenges to segregation. Indeed, the papers advanced the attack on Jim Crow's legal foundation. They gave significant voice also to other nonwhites. *The Chicago Defender*, for example, furnished significant space to S. I. Hayakawa, the Canadian-born Japanese American psychologist and semanticist who was a sometimes Chicago resident in the 1940s. (He later became a California political figure, rising to U.S. senator.)

The black press's attention to civil rights laws and cases was second in frequency of coverage only to focus on the South as the citadel of antiblack segregation. The papers pushed for desegregation of public facilities and for black voting rights. That focus on democracy extended to Africa. The papers called for decolonization. They supported worldwide United Nation's human rights initiatives. That promised a worldwide revolution in race relations.

CULTURAL SCENE

The enormous dislocations, relocations, and developments of World War II (1939–1945) altered U.S. life and culture. War-related mobilization and manpower shortages changed where and how many Americans lived and worked. The war also changed with whom many Americans lived and worked. Previously isolated persons and places found themselves interacting more closely with others than ever before. Material shortages and rationing changed consumption patterns. Manners and tastes shifted, and not during the war alone. The America that emerged from the 1940s was not the America that entered the decade. Distinctive differences rippled through American culture, and shifting race relations flowed through many of the changes.

Both theaters of World War II profoundly acted on Americans' thinking about the concept of race and how their nation constructed and deployed it. Increasing information and images of Nazi atrocities in Europe and the costs to civilization of the brute rhetoric of racial superiority increased many Americans' reception of antiracist rhetoric. If the overwhelming American majority's willingness to recognize and respect nonwhites did not necessarily rise during or after the war, most Americans' sensitivity to unfavorable racial conditions and environments did increase.

The war in the Pacific heightened sensitivity with its reach into U.S. west coast communities. Interning Japanese Americans during the war moved many Americans to think more sharply about identity, loyalty, and being American. Many discussed essential qualifications for being an American. Race necessarily entered the discussion. So did the gross double standard white supremacy imposed in U.S. race relations. It was too stark not to perceive, although many white Americans accepted its benefits without attributing them to race.

Questioning the U.S. dropping atomic bombs on Japan at Hiroshima and Nagasaki in August 1945 fed the shifting discourse. As the 1940s stretched, race became increasingly challenged as a basis to justify legal, official, or popular treatment of persons or groups in the United States. Growing sensitivities on race were not mere war imports from abroad. Cultural trends brewing at home as the 1940s opened percolated in the flow of wartime change. Race was an edgy subject from the opening of the decade. If it were not a constant for media and mass communication, it was something of a constant in the text, subtext, and context of American popular and critical writing.

Richard Wright's 1940 premiere novel *Native Son* signaled the advancing position of race as an explicit issue for the U.S. cultural mainstream during the decade. The first black writer's work the powerful Book-of-the-Month Club ever selected for its mass readership, *Native Son* exposed American racism's life-destroying individual and institutional violence for the nation to ponder.

Set in Chicago's 1930s South Side ghetto to reflect black Americans' shifted locale from southern countrysides to northern cities, *Native Son* probed black character and identity, as well as the character and conditions of U.S. culture. Wright peeled away stereotypes to exhibit fundamental humanity and inhumanity in the tribulations of 20-year-old Bigger Thomas.

Standing as an American *bête noire*, Bigger personified the black brute whose murderous hands destroy fragile white womanhood. It was not quite so simple, of course. Accidents controlled Bigger's life and death. What he does and what others do to him were not without apparent cause, however. Wright unveiled systemic forces of racism that from birth make Bigger who and what he became.

Amid institutionalized inequality and injustice, Bigger faced limited choices in America's black-white divide. He made bad choices, Wright unapologetically conceded. But Bigger's were not the worst choices, Wright suggested. His immediate bestseller—with an initial hardcover print run of 250,000 copies—challenged America to consider its own choices of who and what it would be and what it would have African Americans be.

Wright became the black literary voice of the 1940s. The grandson of slaves, son of a sharecropper and schoolteacher, and onetime Communist Party member followed *Native Son* with the 39-page essay *How "Bigger" Was Born: The Story of Native Son.* To extend America's view of blacks, in 1941 he produced *12 Million Black Voices: A Folk History of the Negro in the United States.* Then in 1945, he offered the explicitly autobiographical novel *Black Boy* to depict the crushing racism of his native Mississippi and elsewhere in the South. It segued to blacks' dreams of a better life in the North. *Native Son* had exposed those illusions.

Richard Wright in his study in New York, 1944. Photograph by Gordon Parks. Courtesy of the Library of Congress, LC-USW3-030278-D.

America contained no haven from racism, Wright implied. In 1946 he made his feeling explicit, fleeing America to become an expatriate in France.

Wright insisted that changing scenery in America changed little, if any, of the substance of American racism. And that was true for more than blacks. U.S. culture's embedded stereotypes called for more than Wright's tragic Bigger Thomas to humanize nonwhites. And more than Wright were writing in the 1940s to provide readers with multidimensional nonwhite American characters.

Frank Waters's 1942 novel *The Man Who Killed the Deer* centered Indians' current conflicts with American culture. His young New Mexico Pueblo Indian protagonist Martiniano faces misjudgment for a killing, as did Bigger. Like Wright, Waters exposed the cultural conditioning and conflicts of his main character. Taken from his people for six years of forced boarding school education/indoctrination, Martiniano struggles with his identity. Returning to the Pueblos, he finds his self no longer fully Indian, not in his tribe's eyes nor, perhaps, in his own eyes. With his white man's ways he cannot simply be a Pueblo. And he clashes with more than tribal ways. He clashes also with white ways, for if he is no longer an Indian in Indian eyes, he remains an Indian in whites' eyes.

Martiniano confuses both Indians and whites. He is confused himself. Yet he is no simple, fallen soul awaiting external redemption. His killing a deer on traditional tribal lands the U.S. Forest Service then maintained focuses the symbolic and substantive conflict Martiniano personifies. As in *Native Son,* the unresolved systemic conflict in Martiniano's story exposes dislocations racist culture imposed on Americans, nonwhites and whites alike. Deftly, Waters has his character Rodolfo Byers, a white trader turned Indian-lover, mirror Martiniano's conflicts of culture and identity.

The Man Who Killed the Deer pointedly encapsulated episodic U.S. spasms to embrace or exterminate Indians. It told a larger story also. It related contradictions of U.S. culture in creating and confining nonwhites as a perennial American Other, torturing them with the decision to be or not to be. It spun the essentialist question of U.S. identity to inquire into human identity. What made Martiniano who he is? Was it cultural behavior, locale, phenotype, social recognition, or some combination?

Frank Waters's classic depicted the devastating tensions of the proverbial American melting pot. It exposed the physical conditions and emotional and psychological strains implicit in the U.S. bent toward assimilation and accepting standards of Anglo-European white supremacy used to torture those not Anglo-European whites.

Ella Deloria's 1944 *Speaking of Indians* supplied further factual basis about "This Man Called Indian," as she titled her study's introduction to Dakota tribal life.[47] A Yankton Sioux herself and a student of anthropologist Franz Boas's at Columbia University, Deloria sketched her people's development with a keen sense of their intricate kinship system and with a trained eye for social science significance. Her tribal portrait reached back to pre-Colombian times, discussing "A Scheme of Life That Worked" and moving through "The Reservation Picture" to "The Present Crisis."[48]

Deloria eloquently depicted how imposed white culture had disoriented the Dakota. She made the need to revive tribal responsibilities palpable. The mixed-blood Osage John Joseph Mathews, an Oxford University graduate, chipped in further on the theme of imposed white ways eroding traditional tribal harmonies in his 1945 *Talking to the Moon*. That built on his monumental 1932 history, *Wah'-Kon-Tah: The Osage and the White Man's Road*, detailing his tribe's plight since coming under U.S. control in 1878.

As one of the preeminent writers of his generation, Waters explored more than Indian-white race relations in treating the American Southwest. He probed aspects of Hispanics' struggles with imposed U.S. anglophile culture. His 1941 novel *People of the Valley* featured an isolated, old Spanish-speaking community high in northern New Mexico's Sangre de Cristo Mountains. The unspecified place lay close to paradise. "To three races and for generations, through all its many names, it has been known simply as the beautiful blue valley," wrote Waters in the opening.[49]

The story depicts an old and new America. The Spanish-speakers stand as old Americans. They form the long-settled community. The immigrants, the newcomers, are Anglos. The transition from old to new frames complex tensions. Progress looms. At least modern technology is coming in the form of a planned dam to control flooding to benefit the developing lowlands. "It is a great thing, perhaps, this dam," Waters has one of his Hispanic characters muse. "But who knows what to think? Who shall tell us?"[50]

The community's answer rises with old Maria del Valle. Skilled at survival on her own terms, she leads resistance to the dam. With fierce directness, she pushes for values of heritage, history, and humanity. She loses. The government will build the dam. Its institutional forms grind with their own undeviating vision. If the dominant U.S. society recognizes the values of the Others old Maria represents, it does not heed them.

In *People of the Valley*, *The Man Who Killed the Deer*, and his many other writings, Waters inquired into the place of minorities in America. He stimulated readers' awareness of cultural complexities minorities confronted. Without idealizing or romanticizing, he peeled layers of dominant America's incompatible beliefs about minorities. Rather than stereotypes, he portrayed complex personalities imprisoned in culture.

Hopeless, or at least unworkable, forms alienated Americans no matter their language or color in Waters's view. He offered no simple path to transcend alienation. He questioned without revealing solutions. Cultural genocide repeatedly failed. Indeed, in Waters's view, the attempt to erase cultural differences enhanced no one; rather, it diminished everyone. It lessened America. To be sure, minorities complicated American life. Collectively and individually, minorities perplexed the nation's cultural dichotomies. They also contributed to cultural values. They added alternatives to an overly rationalized, materialistic, power-hungry dominant society, Waters suggested.

The coming America Waters glimpsed in the 1940s appeared to have increasingly few, if any, places for minorities. The World War II Japanese American internment evidenced the reality of such racial exclusion. The "Jap" as enemy heightened American stereotypes of Asians. Yet it simultaneously sharpened distinctions among Asian Americans and opened many Americans' eyes to cultural differences.

Before the war, few popular efforts distinguished among peoples many Americans simply disparaged en masse as the "yellow peril." Chinese, Japanese, Koreans, and other "Orientals" usually fell together in a single ugly stereotype. World War II changed that. It offered an opportunity Asian Americans seized to promote a persistent theme of much of their writings, claiming their Americanness *and* their individuality. Indeed, the war prompted much-publicized identification to emphasize the *American* in Asian Americans. *Life*, and its sister magazine *Time*, featured repeated articles tutoring the American public on how to tell Japanese foes from Chinese friends.

Pardee Lowe's 1943 *Father and Glorious Descendent* illustrated the expanding U.S. reception World War II occasioned for refashioning Asian Americans' popular image in American culture. Relating his life from birth to Chinese immigrants in California, Lowe offered an assimilated voice of Asian American trials and tribulations in and around San Francisco. Mixing autobiography with a biography of his immigrant father, Lowe narrated the pain-filled cultural divides he continuously commends his father for negotiating.

Lowe consciously projected an image of successful melding of wisdom-filled heritage with hard lessons of New World experience from life in the United States to acquaint readers with their fellow Americans with Chinese roots. Boston-based publisher Little, Brown & Company touted Lowe's World War II U.S. Army service in promoting his work as that of "one of America's loyal minorities."[51]

Jade Snow Wong's 1945 novel, *Fifth Chinese Daughter*, also offered autobiography. Adding gender and more emphasis than Lowe on economic class, she related something of the assimilated success story China-born Lin Yutang also elaborated in his 1948 novel *Chinatown Family*. Both Wong and Lin, like Lowe, provided readers with powerful positive Chinese American characters. Indeed, they promoted in their own ways reverse stereotypes of Asian Americans, or at least Chinese Americans, as model minorities.

The featured Chinese Americans work hard, respect family, value education, exercise frugality, invest wisely, and succeed in business. They would also succeed in living the American dream were it not for the incubus of racism, Wong, Lin, and Low suggested. The import of their writing was not quite so simple, of course. Lin's teenage protagonist Tom Fong struggles, like Frank Waters's Martiniano, with his humanity and identity. His brothers wander from the straight path he straddles. And his own wondering is not simply about being Chinese or American but about finding and being himself. Wong pushed more realism in detailing cultural tensions. She challenged the limits of stereotypical gender confines. *The Fifth Chinese Daughter* transcended national cultures in confronting patriarchy and gender divides.

The more fully realized Asian American characters Wong, Lowe, and Lin presented to U.S. readers signaled further cultural shifts as issues of race became more

Jade Snow Wong. AP Photo/Ernest K. Bennett.

pressing during and after World War II. Race was not, however, an issue being raised only by minorities. It was percolating also in white Americans' minds. Southern white writer William Faulkner made clear race's centrality. He featured it from his early 1930s literary excavations of fictional Yoknapatawpha County, a *doppelgänger* of his native Lafayette County, Mississippi.

Faulkner's fragmentary thirteenth novel, *Go Down, Moses* (1942), drew its title from an antebellum Negro spiritual. It related American Negro slavery to ancient Jews' captivity in Egypt. The comparison reverberated in the 1940s in blacks' protest and in the plight of European Jews under the Nazis. Faulkner's tales reached back to slavery in tying together the McCaslin family's history. The story interrogated the values connecting humanity in sharing the earth's natural bounties and hardships. Like the McCaslin family, the South had no way to escape slavery and its history of race relations, Faulkner insisted. It could build on the past, as it chose, but it could neither ignore nor erase that past.

Faulkner's 1948 novel, *Intruder in the Dust,* carried forward from *Go Down, Moses* the characters of Lucas and Molly Beauchamp. It furthered the theme of the South's duty of truth and reconciliation in regard to blacks. It showed possibilities. It pointed to paths not without twists and turns. Offered as something of a crime mystery, the stream of consciousness narrative takes the black farmer Lucas to trial on false charges of murdering a white man named Vinson Gowrie.

Lucky to be in court rather than simply lynched, Lucas benefits from what might be called "a new New South." Old South racial prejudice did not prevail. It would have strung up Lucas, no questions asked. Being black and accused would have sufficed to pronounce him guilty and dead. Instead, Faulkner has legal process operate—to some degree. Institutions do not save Lucas, however, individuals do.

White lawyer Gavin Stephens defends Lucas. Prodded and assisted by his teenage nephew Chick Mallison, he cooperates in common cause with young and old blacks. Working together for justice regardless of race, the youth and some of their enlightened elders point to a more hopeful future, Faulkner suggests. If the complications of proving Lucas innocent do not add up to a first-class murder mystery, the process of exonerating him incisively explores race as a factor in U.S. law, justice, and culture. The 1949 MGM film of *Intruder in the Dust* further spread the story.

Faulkner's 1949 Nobel Prize for Literature gave further salience to race relations as a topic of serious public discussion among Americans. And in the realm of prizes, poet Gwendolyn Brooks moved toward becoming the first black to win a Pulitzer Prize. Her 1949 collection *Annie Allen* offered an insight-filled melody of a black girl's childhood and emerging womanhood. It brought readers to feel and see parts of black life and also boosted the public stature of black writers and their work.

Nonwhites were increasingly emerging then from virtual public invisibility into U.S. cultural mainstreams. Sports offered further entry grudgingly pried open in the 1940s. Segregation persisted, but clear cracks spread. Black champions had long stood tall in arenas of individual sports. Their prowess in the ring, for example, stretched back to the early days of prizefighting in the 1800s. Joseph Louis Barrow, known simply as Joe Louis or more popularly as "the Brown Bomber," dominated as heavyweight boxing champion from 1937 to 1949. The Sac and Fox Indian Jim Thorpe had won both the pentathlon and the decathlon at the 1912 Stockholm Olympics. He was widely recognized as one of the greatest athletes of all time.

Black track and field star Jesse Owens's triumphs at the 1936 Berlin Olympics were legendary. World War II canceled the Olympics of 1940 and 1944. At the 1948 summer Olympics in London, Harrison Dillard again demonstrated black sprinting prowess by winning the 100-meter dash. Don Barksdale became the first black to play for the U.S. Olympic basketball team. Alice Coachman became the first African American woman to win an Olympic gold medal, taking the high jump. Japanese American Harold Sakata won a silver medal in weightlifting.

While individual nonwhites could stand tall for America in the ring or on Olympic podiums in the 1940s, they were not welcomed in major team sports until late, particularly at the professional level. Those remained mostly all-white preserves.

Fledgling professional basketball and football teams had early allowed nonwhite players. Indeed, Jim Thorpe was president of the American Professional Football Association when it started in 1920. He played pro baseball for the New

Boxer Joe Louis with fight promoter Mike Jacobs, 1941.
Courtesy of the Library of Congress, LC-USZ62-135667.

York Giants, Cincinnati Reds, Chicago Cubs, and Boston Braves. But long before
the 1940s nonwhites had disappeared. Thorpe, for example, was relegated to all-
Indian basketball teams. Abe Saperstein's all-black Harlem Globetrotters, begun
in 1927, his Negro Midwest League, and the Negro Southern League further reflected basketball's segregation.

The "Great American Pastime," as Major League Baseball (MLB) styled itself,
epitomized the segregation of U.S. pro sports in the 1940s. Only whites played.
Prodigious black talent such as the Kansas City Monarchs' legendary hurler
Satchel Paige and Homestead Grays' homerun king Josh Gibson were relegated
to the "Negro Leagues." But postwar commercial and moral pressures increasingly
pushed talent, not color, onto the field of play.

Jackie Robinson's playing for the National League Brooklyn Dodgers on April 15, 1947, and Larry Doby's playing for the American League Cleveland
Indians on July 5, 1947, broke the MLB color line. In 1949 Cuban-born left
fielder Orestes "Minnie" Miñoso joined the Cleveland Indians. Outside the dia-
mond, nonwhites also caught the public eye. Los Angeles-born Richard "Pancho"
Gonzalez won the 1948 U.S. men's singles tennis championship at Forest Hills,

New York, and repeated in 1949. He also won the men's doubles championship at Wimbledon, England. Such triumphs on the fields of play became a broadening wedge for minorities in American culture.

In most popular cultural media, nonwhites remained stymied in the 1940s. Radio offered them only a small voice. Movies only edged them into the American popular eye. It was not that nonwhites had not appeared on the American screen. They had appeared, usually in unflattering roles. They performed at the margins in major studio productions. If they shared the spotlight, it was almost invariably for ugly purposes. Typical treatment showed early in American films such as director D. W. Griffith's notorious 1915 *Birth of a Nation*, which glorified Ku Klux Klan terrorists promoting white supremacy and denigrating blacks. The 1940s brought more positive and sympathetic nonwhite images to the American screen.

Spanish-language films, mostly made in Mexico, and so-called race movies by black producer-directors such as Oscar Micheaux and small white competitors had since the 1920s offered limited audiences some nonstandard, nonwhite fare such as all-black musicals and westerns. In the 1940s, movies featuring nonwhite heroes and more sympathetic nonwhite communities reached broader U.S. audiences.

The suave Robin Hood-like Latin bandit known as the Cisco Kid became big on the American screen in the 1940s. The Mexico-born one-time bullfighter Luis Antonio Damaso de Alonso, known in Hollywood as Gilbert Roland, played the character in a half-dozen 1946–1947 features. Mexican-born actor Ricardo Montalbán added to the Hispanic image with his portrayal of the Latin lover in a series of Metro-Goldwyn-Mayer (MGM) films. Beginning with *Fiesta* (1947), Montalbán played the lead in *The Kissing Bandit* (1948), *Neptune's Daughter* (1949), and *Border Incident* (1949).

The Chinese American hero Charlie Chan emerged on the big screen from his creator Earl Derr Biggers's six novels (1925–1932) and various radio serials. He began in the 1930s and carried on with two dozen films in the 1940s, starting with *Charlie Chan's Murder Cruise* (1940), starring Sidney Toler, and continuing to *The Sky Dragon* (1949), starring Ronald Winters. Chan's intelligence, honesty, and patriotism positively impressed broad American audiences. Similarly, 37-year-old Katharine Hepburn entranced American audiences as a young Chinese peasant turned guerrilla fighter, in the manner of Joan of Arc, in the 1944 film *Dragon Seed*. Adapted from Pulitzer Prize winner Pearl S. Buck's 1932 novel *Dragon Seed*, the film conveyed praise for a major U.S. wartime ally.

Propaganda needs also boosted blacks' screen image and the general cause of tolerance. The U.S. Office of War Information (OWI) early on urged major movie studios to show audiences a more racially integrated America. The casts of MGM's *Bataan* (1943), Twentieth-Century-Fox's *Crash Dive* (1943), and Columbia Picture's *Sahara* (1943) reflected multiracial U.S. war efforts. The real fighting was hardly integrated, of course, as the U.S. Armed Forces were solidly segregated. Yet nonwhites were everywhere making a war contribution. Just as in civilian life, they were almost everywhere present. Films such as Alfred Hitchcock's *Lifeboat*

(1943) and John Cromwell's *Since You Went Away* (1944) at least gestured toward acknowledging the nonwhite presence.

The OWI and other federal agencies offered footage and produced documentaries showing blacks in better light and generally urging more American tolerance. The "Double V Campaign" the *Pittsburgh Courier* newspaper initiated in 1942, and other black organs pressed, prodded government efforts. Screened in military outlets and civilian theaters, such government titles as *The Negro Soldier* (1944) featured blacks doing their patriotic duties under arms. Short films such as *Don't Be a Sucker* (1943), warning against racist propaganda, and *It Happened in Springfield* (1945), featuring a civics lessons to Massachusetts's public school pupils, pushed further against the injustice of intolerance in American life. The 11-minute 1945 film *The House I Live In* exemplified some of the best of the genre. It featured 30-year-old Frank Sinatra giving a gang of young white bullies lessons on tolerance. It won a Golden Globe and an honorary Academy Award "for tolerance short subject" in 1946.

Efforts to reach out on the one hand toward more tolerance in the national community underscored the fact that most Americans remained stuck in a culture of stereotypes. Their blinkered world was "Whites only." A trickle of change from Hollywood was a mere drop in the bucket. Indeed, most film flowing from the nation's celluloid capital and the center of its expanding culture industry continued to frame minorities in American life around central myths of dominant white culture, when it noticed them at all.

For the most part, minorities remained absent from the big screen throughout the 1940s. Director John Ford's *The Grapes of Wrath* (1940) won seven Academy Award nominations in adapting novelist John Steinbeck's gut-wrenching depiction of the Joad family eking out a living during the Great Depression. But those struggles on the screen, even with their heavy socioeconomic overlay, carried not a hint of color. Its struggle to survive "dust bowl" poverty was basically white.

With its seven Academy Award nominations in 1949, *All the King's Men* (1949) showed a similar lack of color. Adapting Robert Penn Warren's 1946 Pulitzer Prize-winning novel set in the rural deep South, mimicking Huey Pierce Long's rise and fall as Louisiana's populist Democratic governor (1928–32) and U.S. senator (1932–35), the film hardly glimpsed blacks, although more than one in three Louisianans (35.9%) in 1940 was black.

Other film classics of the decade, from Gothic mystery thrillers such as Alfred Hitchcock's *Rebecca* (1940) to the romantic melodrama *Casablanca* (1942), to Billy Wilder's film noir *Double Indemnity* (1944), similarly skipped any element of color. Whites filled the screen. Even in films such as *Casablanca*, set as it was in Africa with non-Europeans in the background, it was hard to tell who the non-Europeans were, as the actors portraying them were whites.

The popular sounds of the 1940s carried more color than the big screen. Latin music, with the Argentine tango, the mambo, the *paso doble,* samba, and rumba, were in high demand on America's dance floors. Vincent López, the Brooklyn, New York-born son of Portuguese immigrants, was one of most popular band leaders of the 1940s, building on radio fame beginning in the 1920s. Lopez's orchestra throughout the 1940s played in residence at the Grill Room at Manhattan's Hotel

Taft on 7th Avenue and 50th Street. The first song-hit of the teenage singer transformed into the star Judy Garland was the traditional Spanish language folk song *La Cucaracha*.

The 1940s were alive with fusion sounds. So-called Chicago blues, black jazz improvisations, swing, and other forms flowed in fresh musical directions. Bebop emerged in the mid-1940s to point uncharted directions. Moving away from dance music, pianists Thelonious Monk and Bud Powell, saxophonist Charlie "Yardbird" Parker, trumpeter John Birks "Dizzy" Gillespie, drummer Max Roach, vocalist Betty Carter, and others pioneered forms that re-centered musical innovation that would catch a worldwide postwar audience.

From older white big-band leaders like Woody Herman and Benny Goodman to the suave black Edward Kennedy "Duke" Ellington, the sounds of American music merged in fresh popular forms. Breaking through barriers of race, ethnicity, and class, the sounds of an increasingly commercialized mass-mediated music pulsed through post-1945 America. Narrow demographics no longer entirely determined who was listening to what. Music offered more and more desegregated sounds.

Duke Ellington directs his band from the piano at the Hurricane Cabaret in New York, 1943. Photo by Gordon Parks. Courtesy of the Library of Congress, LC-USW3-023947-C.

Increasingly after 1945, American popular music developed a pull and push of its own. It carried sounds of youth developing a culture of their own. The late 1940s sounded the early notes for a pervasive cultural influence that shaped consciousness and social context in the second half of the twentieth century. For a growing number of listeners, popular music increasingly conveyed a democratizing culture.

As music crossed over old lines of race in America, the nation itself was spreading farther apart in renewed cultural isolation. Growing suburbanization physically segregated the nation more than ever before. Postwar demobilization and population redistribution began to withdraw whites from metropolitan centers to which the war had drawn blacks and other minorities. Exercising mobility driven significantly by the automobile, large numbers of upwardly mobile white families detached themselves from urban tenements and row houses to live in homes not simply detached from others but separated from racial Others flocking to cities.

Suburbs projected a culture of homogenized gentility. Their distance established borders of social distinction. They offered cultural configurations for self-identity and association. So while the U.S. Supreme Court was holding residential restrictive covenants unenforceable in *Shelley v. Kraemer* (1948), whites were increasingly voting with their feet—or rather with their cars—to reconstruct self-contained, all-white communities. The suburbs allowed whites to live together, socialize together, school their children together, and minimize social contacts with racial minorities. The suburbs offered a sort of splendid isolation, at least from the perspective of many white Americans. From other perspectives, they perpetuated America's white/nonwhite divide. That remained the great cultural reality as the 1940s closed.

INFLUENTIAL THEORIES AND VIEWS ON RACE RELATIONS

In the United States and around the globe, World War II (1939–1945) changed much of the context of thinking about race and race relations. Revulsion at Nazi Germany's terror in Europe moved many to reconsider concepts of race and racial hierarchy and their symbols, substance, and significance. The war also destroyed European colonialism. Its demographic displacement surged migration worldwide. The effect raised questions about the meaning of race, particularly in cultural and national identity. Indeed, the onset, unfolding, and aftermath of the war elevated race as a topic in national and global discourse. The war created a context for broadly rearticulating human rights. That had momentous impact almost everywhere.

The shifting climate very much affected prevailing views and theories of race and race relations in the United States. It did not so much precipitate new thinking as it cleared the air to improve views of racial realities. It brought race and race relations home for the nation to face. The confrontation was not simply in the winds, as it were. It did not come naturally. It developed from insistent agitation and struggle from educational and intellectual elites and from persons in U.S. streets.

Moving most Americans' thinking on race and race relations was not easy. It surely was not quick. Levering American public support away from ideologies and institutions of white supremacy required getting some substantial part of the American public to acknowledge the nation's entrenched official and popular white standards that discriminated against and segregated nonwhites. It required putting America's race culture under intensifying scrutiny. It demanded widespread reconsideration of the validity of race as a basis for legal or social treatment. While it accelerated during the decade, the movement did not start in the 1940s. It built on struggles reaching back before the U.S. Declaration of Independence in 1776.

For many Americans in the 1940s, race and race relations were distant concepts. Many had never seen a nonwhite person. More had little, if any, contact with nonwhites. After all, 89.8 percent of the nation's population in 1940 was officially counted as "white." Outside the South, northern cities, and pockets in the Southwest and along the Pacific Coast, America's mostly homogenous white communities had few, if any, nonwhites. So for the overwhelming bulk of Americans, race was not something in their daily consciousness. It was not an everyday issue. Race relations loomed at most as a distant political topic.

Shifting American consciousness of race relations as a real problem about which the nation could and should do something was the great change in the 1940s. Beginning the decade, most Americans appeared to accept uncritically old notions of so-called scientific racism that dated back to the 1800s. They accepted race as a biological reality. They saw it as a matter of innumerable and immutable characteristics from physique to psychology and even moral disposition. They viewed people as naturally differing by groups. Many accepted, too, the idea of a natural hierarchy rising from race's supposed biological basis that made whites innately superior. Such thinking informed social views. It cemented the social structure of America's color caste.

Viewing the racial divide as the natural order of things with whites atop nonwhites had long settled much thinking in the United States. It disposed many whites to adopt a laissez-faire attitude. They took the existing order of things in their racial cast as unchangeable. They embraced racial stereotypes. They viewed nonwhites as naturally poor, unclean, uncultured, uneducated, and unqualified for any but menial labors. Perhaps they knew an exception, but they accepted racial difference as a general rule. They believed nonwhites, whatever their background, were unalterably as they were. Nothing was going to change how nonwhites lived and worked. They could do no better than they were doing. They could not help themselves, nor could they be helped to do better. There was no sense in interfering. Natural tendencies would prevail. So many white Americans believed.

Longstanding vilification lurked in the determinism scientific racism asserted. German leader Adolf Hitler and his Nazi adherents spewed such obscene notions in demonizing Jews and millions of others slaughtered as social deviants. They blamed their victims as if the victims inflicted death and desolation on themselves by being who they were. Versions of such thinking infected America. It surfaced in some explanations for interning Japanese Americans during World War II.

The dominant narratives of the emerging nation's history typically defamed nonwhites. Most varied little in viewing race in American social development. They ignored it. At most they made it background. They unfolded the Great American Experiment as virtually a whites-only enterprise. Nonwhites sometimes appeared at the margins but seldom for long. Occasionally they helped, but usually nonwhites were hindrances in the long run. When focus fell on them, it came for the most part in the run of modern progress. It justified dispossessing Indians and enslaving blacks. The dominant narratives typically described both as primitive and uncivilized. Dispossessing Hispanics came with a similar theme. The label tended, however, to identify religion or culture—rather than race—as the despised difference.

The dominance of the master narrative absent any color other than white remained clear throughout the 1940s. The decade's Pulitzer Prize winners for history exemplified the trend. Carl Sandburg's final of four volumes, *Abraham Lincoln: The War Years*, the 1940 winner for history, illustrated how invisibility arose without absolute exclusion. Sandburg necessarily admitted blacks to his narrative. They came, however, as objects not as actors; they formed no real part of his passionate story of people who touched Lincoln and whom he touched.

Marcus Lee Hansen's posthumous 1941 winner for history, *The Atlantic Migration, 1607–1860*, focused on explaining demographic flows that peopled the early United States and its colonial predecessors in British North America. It somehow missed millions of Africans forced across the ocean. Nor did it say anything substantial about Hispanics traversing the same waters to settle much that became the United States. Hansen's focusing on immigration from Europe, and more particularly from the British Isles and Germany, was understandable. He saw that an effective study needed limits. The difficulty with his work was its blinders. Offering its focus as exclusive perpetuated the virtual invisibility of nonwhites in the common American history.

Focusing often on themes cast in terms of progress, those who garnered the Pulitzer Prize for History in the 1940s tended to dismiss or, at best, marginalize the affect of race on U.S. history. Race formed little, if any, part of American development, expansion, or self-exploration in the works hailed to the public as distinguished U.S. history. Race had no face in the wartime capital depicted in *Reveille in Washington, 1860–1865*, Margaret Leech's 1942 winner for history, or in Esther Forbes's 1943 winner, *Paul Revere and the World He Lived In*. Arthur M. Schlesinger Jr.'s 1946 winner, *The Age of Jackson*, hardly paused over Indians and blacks. Extolling Jacksonian democracy as a reform tradition battling big business came without much of a nod to such "democracy" being confined to white males.

Similarly, Bernard De Voto's 1948 winner, *Across the Wide Missouri*, presented Indians only as background as it described the fur trading business and way of life in the Rocky Mountains from 1832 to 1838. Roy Franklin Nicols's 1949 winner, *The Disruption of American Democracy*, told how slavery splintered the Democratic Party from 1856 to 1861. It presented an argument among white men. Interestingly, the book's award came when Democrats were again splintering. They were arguing in the late 1940s over civil rights as southern Democrats insisted on maintaining "whites only" public privileges.

The significant exception among the Pulitzer Prizes for History in the 1940s was Merle Curti's 1944 winner, *The Growth of American Thought*. To be sure, it featured no focus on nonwhites. Yet in developing his social history of America's spreading democratic faith, the University of Wisconsin historian challenged racial typing and directed attention to individual character, regardless of race. Curti explained that "despite the stereotypes of the abolitionists and the southern apologist, the Negro did not conform to a single type." Treating enslaved blacks' capabilities, he described them as simply human.[52]

Referencing characters from Harriet Beecher Stowe's much-debated 1853 antislavery novel *Uncle Tom's Cabin*, Curti characterized slaves as "neither the saintly Uncle Tom nor the irresponsible, whimsical Topsy of Mrs. Stowe." Neither negative nor positive stereotypes applied, Curti insisted. The slave was not "necessarily endowed with all the elevated feelings and noble sentiments of the northern humanitarians. Nor was he merely the childish, docile, loyal, and at times rascally creature southern whites were prone to make him. He was probably all of these things, since individual and class differences were present in Negroes as in whites," Curti offered.[53]

The theory of common humanity regardless of race Curti suggested was hardly new in the 1940s. It was akin to the founding 1776 U.S. declaration that "all men are created equal." Most Americans accepted the rhetoric. Applying such theory proved another matter. Little helped most whites to see nonwhites simply in human terms or to move beyond stereotypes. Their schooling seldom helped. Segregated by law or in fact, few Americans in the 1940s attended schools with any significant racial mixture. Their textbooks almost never contained discussions or images other than those of whites or much of the world outside of Europe. Like the Pulitzer Prize winners for History, school textbooks covering the United States in the 1940s overtly and by omission fed unfavorable stereotypes.

Shifting from stereotypes was a struggle in the 1940s. Simply gaining minorities undeniable visibility as real people most influenced American views on race relations. Insisting on inclusion, nonwhites and Hispanics maneuvered to end the law and practice of segregation. They worked to expose public neglect of their humanity and individuality. They most often cast their insistence with the social ideals and values being contested in the war America officially framed as pitting democracy against totalitarianism. Blending historical protest with contemporary importance, minorities pressed to have the United States account for its racial dynamics, officially and in public opinion.

Protest pushed race relations to a marquee position in discourses on democracy in 1940s' America. Academics such as University of Texas educator and civil rights activists George I. Sánchez focused critical attention. His 1940 study, *Forgotten People: A Study of New Mexicans*, documented public and official neglect of Mexican American children's schooling in his native state. Becoming president of the League of United Latin American Citizens (LULAC) in 1941, Sánchez helped direct a civil rights agenda to expand public awareness of the U.S. culture of discrimination against Hispanics and other minorities.

The March on Washington Movement (MOWM) black labor leader A. Philip Randolph spearheaded in early 1941 to end job discrimination further illustrated minorities' insistence on no longer being segregated from the promises of American life. Such protests and violent clashes that hit the nation north, south, east, and west in 1943 made clear America's need to change its racial attitudes and behaviors. Fighting in the streets of Los Angeles, California; Mobile, Alabama; Beaumont, Texas; Columbia, Tennessee; Detroit, Michigan; and New York City's Harlem in the midst of World War II signaled the severity of America's racial problems. The race riots pointedly communicated, too, the need for solutions.

For Americans wondering about causes and consequences of U.S. race relations in the mid-1940s and thinking about what might be done, considerable enlightenment came from Swedish political economist Gunnar Myrdal. In 1938 the philanthropic Carnegie Corporation of New York commissioned him to direct a massive study of how America treated its most populous racial minority—blacks. The corporation funded the project as part of its mission to "promote the advancement and diffusion of knowledge and understanding." Founding U.S. steel magnate Andrew Carnegie framed the mission in his 1911 endowment. The corporation imported the Swede as a distinguished public policy scholar. Its board hoped that as "a stranger," Myrdal would be "someone who could approach this task with a fresh mind, uninfluenced by traditional attitudes or by earlier conclusions."[54]

With more than three dozen collaborators, Myrdal painstakingly detailed the hypocritical divide racism cleaved between America's ideals and its racial realities. His landmark signature two-volumes published in 1944 under the title *An American Dilemma: The Negro Problem and Modern Democracy* summarized an encyclopedic series of underlying social science studies. Myrdal cast U.S. treatment of minorities in general and blacks in particular as the critical test of America's contemporary national character.

The United States claimed to prize and protect the individual. It touted itself as an achievement society. It claimed to allow any and every person to rise or fall on personal merit. But entrenched American racism patently negated such promises. It denied equal opportunity, liberty, and justice for all. It revealed America as an intolerant and mean-spirited society, Myrdal noted.

The nation had choices, Myrdal posited with his dilemma framework. At opposing sides lay perhaps equally unpopular options for the white American majority. Whites could continue race relations as they were and acknowledge their hollow declarations of democracy. That was unappealing in terms of national self-definition and image. It was also particularly unappealing in the contested international arena of political ideologies and systems. In 1944 the hot war contest pitted democracy against fascist totalitarianism. It would shift soon to a cold war contest against communist totalitarianism.

The alternative for white Americans was to change race relations to embrace blacks and other minorities as full and equal participants sharing in the opportunities and outcomes of the American dream. That was unappealing because of deep prejudices and considerable advantages, both acknowledged and unacknowledged. White Americans collectively had a lot invested in being white, and most were unwilling to relinquish their dividends.

An American Dilemma exposed structural and systemic shackles U.S. society used to bind blacks interminably to the nation's bottom. African Americans' underclass position was no accident. Nor did it occur naturally. Dismissing the determinism of intellectually discredited theories bundled in scientific racism, Myrdal explained the social mechanics that fixed all Americans' socioeconomic positions by group according to their color, not their character or conduct. He described American race relations as a product of a vicious circle he called the "principle of cumulation," where "everything is cause to everything else."[55] He illustrated the fact from the voluminous findings of his project colleagues' underlying studies.

Myrdal's theoretical basis rested on worldwide anthropological fieldwork and other academic study of human behavior, particularly since the 1920s, detailing distributions of human traits. Anthropologists Bronislaw Malinowski, Franz Boas, his student Margaret Mead, and her student Ruth Benedict, for example, had dissected various societies and shown unmistakably that notions of race were cultural constructs. Race was no innate, natural, scientific, or unalterable reality. Race was human-made. It emerged from political processes. It flourished in America as a growth of European capitalism, colonialism, and white supremacy. U.S. race relations reflected those political processes. They reflected societal distributions of power. They set the broad boundaries of in-groups and out-groups, Myrdal explained.

America created its blacks' perceived character and their socioeconomic position, Myrdal noted. If white Americans wanted to understand "the Negro problem," they needed collectively only to probe their own beliefs and behaviors. Their attitudes and actions created and sustained the problems of race relations. To solve the problems they needed to change their attitudes and actions, Myrdal recommended. He urged affirmative action, pointing directly to the need for government intervention. He wrote that "the change of race relations is no longer determined by such 'natural' developments as migration but by a complex of intentional policies affecting not only migration but all other spheres of the problem."[56]

Myrdal's analysis profoundly influenced the immediate and ongoing debate about American apartheid. It became more than a book for the remainder of the

1940s. It became a classic. "*An American Dilemma,* in its comprehensiveness, in its originality, in its analysis, is the best thing that has been done on the Negro and is likely to be the best for a considerable time to come. To the social scientist and the 'intellectual' planners, publicists, and reformers, the book is a 'must,'" declared a prominent critic in October 1944.[57]

"Few serious studies of American society have been more widely read," historian Oscar Handlin, director of Harvard University Center for the Study of Liberty, noted in a 20-year retrospective. "Its analysis of the Negro problem in the United States has been a magnet to scholars and a catalyst to political groups. Its recommendations have helped shape the strategy of every organization interested in legislation and in judicial interpretations," Handlin wrote.[58]

An American Dilemma pulled back something like a veil. It made America's ignoring its too often publicly hidden problems with minorities further impossible. Myrdal's work did not go unchallenged, of course. Some questioned its empirical basis. Others criticized it as one-sided for postulating what white Americans needed to do without addressing what blacks or other minorities needed to do to improve race relations. "Not till more adequate proof is at hand will many people be convinced that the White domination is the only cause of the Negroes' troubles," carped one critic.[59] The book angered many.

Myrdal made the problem of America's color-caste something of a moral issue. He flatteringly described it as involving Americans' "high national and Christian precepts." At the outset of *An American Dilemma,* he declared that "The American Negro problem is a problem in the heart of the American. It is there that the interracial tension has its focus. It is there that the decisive struggle goes on."[60] His approach in many eyes cast attitudes as the ultimate key to U.S. race relations, and that had serious consequences as a call to public action.

Widespread interpretations distilled and diluted recommendations from *An American Dilemma* into simple attacks against prejudice. Myrdal's directions for changing behavior and public policies and practices lagged in many circles far behind discussions of changing Americans' hearts and minds. More than a few despaired at such a task as Herculean. They claimed it required superhuman will and virtue. Many dismissed the task as Sisyphean. Rolling back racial prejudice appeared to them even more impossible than King Sisyphus's succeeding in rolling uphill the boulder with which he was cursed in Greek mythology. Others simply refused to change. They dismissed Myrdal's proposed dilemma as no problem at all, insisting racial segregation was right and necessary. For some it was not merely an unalterable natural order of things, it was divinely ordained.

President Harry S Truman appeared to accept much of the vision of *An American Dilemma.* Declaring in December 1946 that "the preservation of civil rights guaranteed by the Constitution is essential to domestic tranquility, national security, the general welfare, and the continued existence of our free institutions," he moved forcefully to change U.S. race relations. Using his executive powers, he created a presidential committee on civil rights to recommend changes in U.S. law and other "more adequate and effective means and procedures" to make civil equality in America more than a theory.[61]

In his January 1948 State of the Union Message, President Truman further announced securing essential human rights as the first of five goals for postwar America to achieve. He followed up in February 1948 with a special message to Congress on civil rights. He recommended legislation to make the federal government an active and effective civil rights enforcer. Among his urgings, he exhorted Congress to outlaw lynching, to protect voting rights, to ensure fair employment practices, to prohibit discrimination and segregation in interstate transportation, and to redress the claims of interned Japanese Americans.

Truman's message and his moving by executive order in July 1948 to desegregate the U.S. Armed Forces clearly indicated his views and those of many hoping to move America past its old race relations problems. As evidenced in Congress's refusal to adopt the bulk of the president's civil rights proposals and by the split over civil rights in his own Democratic Party, Americans' views and theories on race relations were hardly in concert as the 1940s closed.

RESOURCE GUIDE

SUGGESTED READINGS

General and Cultural

Dixon, Wheeler Winston. *American Cinema of the 1940s: Themes and Variations.* New Brunswick, NJ: Rutgers University Press, 2005.

Erenberg, Lewis A., and Susan E. Hirsch. *The War in American Culture: Society and Consciousness during World War II.* New ed. Chicago: University of Chicago Press, 1996.

Gerdes, Louise I. *The 1940s: America's Decades.* San Diego, CA: Greenhaven Press, 2000.

Graebner, William. *The Age of Doubt: American Thought and Culture in the 1940s.* Boston: Twayne, 1998.

Lindop, Edmund. *America in the 1940s.* Brookfield, CT: Millbrook Press, 2008.

McMahon, Kevin J. *Reconsidering Roosevelt on Race: How the Presidency Paved the Road to Brown.* Chicago: University of Chicago Press, 2004.

Ward, Geoffrey C. *The War: An Intimate History, 1941–1945.* New York: Knopf, 2007. (The companion volume to the PBS TV series.)

Wills, Charles A. *America in the 1940s.* New York: Facts on File, 2005.

African Americans

Anderson, Carol Elaine. *Eyes Off the Prize: The United Nations and the African American Struggle for Human Rights, 1944–1955.* New York: Cambridge University Press, 2003.

Francis, Charles E. *The Tuskegee Airmen: The Men Who Changed a Nation*. Boston: Braden, 1993.

Garfinkel, Herbert. *When Negroes March: The March on Washington Movement in the Organizational Politics of FEPC*. Glencoe: Free Press, 1959.

Pfeffer, Paula F. *A. Philip Randolph, Pioneer of the Civil Rights Movement*. Baton Rouge: Louisiana State University Press, 1990.

Pitre, Merlene. *In the Struggle against Jim Crow: Lulu B. White and the NAACP, 1900–1957*. College Station, TX: Texas A&M University Press, 1999.

Reed, Merl E. *Seed Time for the Modern Civil Rights Movement: The President's Committee on Fair Employment Practice, 1941–1946*. Baton Rouge: Louisiana State University Press, 1991.

American Indians

Cowger, Thomas W. *The National Congress of American Indians: The Founding Years*. Lincoln: University of Nebraska Press, 1999.

Deloria, Vine Jr. *Frank Waters: Man and Mystic*. Athens: Swallow Press/Ohio University Press, 1993.

Durrett, Deanne. *Unsung Heroes of World War II: The Story of the Navajo Code Talkers*. New York: Facts on File, Library of American Indian History, 1998.

Hertzberg, Hazel. *The Search for an American Indian Identity: Modern Pan-Indian Movements*. Syracuse: Syracuse University Press, 1971.

Meadows, William C. *The Comanche Code Talkers of World War II*. Austin: University of Texas Press, 2002.

Taylor, Graham D. *The New Deal and American Indian Tribalism: The Administration of the Indian Reorganization Act, 1934–45*. Lincoln: University of Nebraska Press, 1980.

Asian Americans

Cheung, King-Kok, ed. *An Interethnic Companion to Asian American Literature*. New York: Cambridge University Press, 1997.

Daniels, Roger. *Concentration Camps USA: Japanese America and World War II*. New York: Holt, Reinhardt and Winston, 1972.

Gardner, Audrie, and Anne Loftis. *The Great Betrayal: The Evacuation of the Japanese-Americans during World War II*. New York: Macmillan, 1969.

Takaki, Ronald, Rebecca Stefoff, and Carol Takaki. *Democracy and Race: Asian Americans and World War II*. New York: Chelsea House, 1994.

Wu, Jean Yu-wen Shen, and Min Song, eds. *Asian American Studies: A Reader*. New Brunswick, NJ: Rutgers University Press, 2000.

Hispanics/Latinos

Foster, David William, ed. *Sourcebook of Hispanic Culture in the United States*. Chicago: American Library Association, 1982.

Guerin-Gonzales, Camille. *Mexican Workers and the American Dreams: Immigration, Repatriation, and California Farm Labor*. New Brunswick, NJ: Rutgers University Press, 1994.

Kaplowitz, Craig Allan. *LULAC, Mexican Americans, and National Policy*. College Station: Texas A&M University Press, 2005.

Mazon, Mauricio. *The Zoot-Suit Riots: The Psychology of Symbolic Annihilation*. Austin: University of Texas Press, 1984.

Rivas-Rodriguez, Maggie, ed. *Mexican Americans and World War II*. Austin: University of Texas Press, 2005.

Ryan, Bryan, ed. *Hispanic Writers: A Selection of Sketches from Contemporary Authors*. Detroit, MI: Gale Research, 1991.

FILMS/VIDEOS

The Black Press: Soldiers without Words. Produced and directed by Stanley Nelson. 86 min. California Newsreel, 1998. VHS/DVD.

The Code Talkers: A Secret Code of Honor. Directed by Brian DiMuccio. 23 minutes. Herzog Productions, 2003. (This documentary is featured on the 3-disc Collector's Edition DVD for *Windtalkers*.)

Hispanic-American Cultures in the U.S.A. Produced and directed by Tony Labriola. 60 min. Insight Media, 1993. VHS.

Stars and Stripes: Hollywood and World War II. 60 min. Marcia Ely Productions, 1991. TV documentary.

The War. Produced and directed by Ken Burns and Lynn Novick. ca. 430 min. Florentine Films and WETA-TV, 2007. DVD.

Windtalkers. Directed by John Woo. 134 minutes. Metro-Goldwyn-Mayer (MGM), 2002.

WEB SITES

African-Americans in Military History/World War II. www.au.af.mil/au/aul/bibs/afhist/afwwii.htm.

Asian/Pacific Americans in the US Army, "World War II." www.army.mil/asianpacificsoldiers/wars/ww2.html.

A Celebration of Women Writers, "Asian American Women Writers." http://digital.library.upenn.edu/women/_generate/ASIAN%20AMERICAN.html.

Department of the Navy, Naval Historical Center, "African-Americans and the U.S. Navy, World War II." www.history.navy.mil/photos/prs-tpic/af-amer/afa-wwii.htm.

Educational Broadcasting Corporation, "Harry S Truman supports civil rights (1947–1948)." http://www.pbs.org/wnet/jimcrow/stories_events_truman.html.

Exploring the Japanese American Internment through film and the Internet. http://www.asianamericanmedia.org/jainternment/.

The Hispanic Experience, "Hispanic Contributions to America's defense." www.houstonculture.org/hispanic/memorial.html.

Library of Congress, "African American Odyssey: The Depression, The New Deal, and World War II." http://memory.loc.gov/ammem/aaohtml/exhibit/aopart8.html.

Library of Congress, "Ansel Adams's Photographs of Japanese-American Internment at Manzanar." memory.loc.gov/ammem/collections/anseladams/.

The National World War II Museum, "World War II by the Numbers." www.ddaymuseum.org/education/education_numbers.html.

Presidential Task Force on Asian Americans / Northern Illinois University, "Landmarks in Asian American History." http://www3.niu.edu/ptaa/history.htm.

Smithsonian Education, "Letters from the Japanese American Internment" http://www.smithsonianeducation.org/educators/lesson_plans/japanese_internment/index.html.

Special Collections Department, J. Willard Marriott Library, University of Utah, and
Private Collections, "Japanese-Americans internment camps during World War II."
http://www.lib.utah.edu/spc/photo/9066/9066.htm.

NOTES

1. U.S. Bureau of the Census, *Statistical Abstract of the United States* (Washington,
DC: GPO, 1972), Series Y 904–916, Military Personnel on Active Duty: 1789 to 1970,
1141.

2. August Meier and Elliot Rudwick, *Black Detroit and the Rise of the UAW* (New York:
Oxford University Press, 1979), 171.

3. Gen. DeWitt's testimony before House Naval Affairs subcommittee, April 13,
1943, reported in "Japs in Coast Area Opposed: Gen. DeWitt Against Relaxation of Any
Evacuee Restrictions," *Los Angeles Times*, April 14, 1943, A1. See also editorial, "A Jap's
a Jap," *Washington Post*, April 15, 1943, 12.

4. "Japs in Coast Area Opposed," A1.

5. See "Japs Rush to Beat Army's Travel Ban," March 29, 1942, 1, 8, reporting on
Gen. DeWitt's orders issued in Civilian Exclusion Order No. 34 and public proclamations
of March 2, 24, and 27, 1942.

6. *Korematsu v. United States*, 323 U.S. 214, 242 (Murphy, J., dissenting).

7. *Ex Parte Endo*, 323 U.S. 283, 302.

8. *Korematsu*, 323 U.S. 214, 230 (Roberts, J., dissenting).

9. *Hirabayashi v. United States*, 320 U.S. 81, 110 (1943) (Murphy, J., dissenting).

10. The Farm Labor Act of 1943, 57 Stat. 70 (April 29, 1943).

11. "An Act to create an Indian Claims Commission, to provide for the powers, duties,
and functions," 60 Stat. 1049 (August 13, 1946).

12. Nancy Oestreich Lurie, "The Indian Claims Commission," *Annals of the American
Academy of Political and Social Science* 311 (May 1957): 56–70.

13. 60 Stat. 1049.

14. See "An Act Conferring jurisdiction upon the Court of Claims to hear, examine,
adjudicate, and enter judgment thereon in claims which the Winnebago Tribe of Indians
may have against the United States, and for other purposes," 45 Stat. 1027 (December 17,
1928).

15. 60 Stat. 1049.

16. Hearings on S. 2103 before the House Committee on Indian Affairs, 76th Cong.,
3rd Sess. (1940), 23.

17. 60 Stat. 1049.

18. Nancy Oestreich Lurie, "The Indian Claims Commission," *Annals of the American
Academy of Political and Social Science* 436 (March 1978): 97–110.

19. *Korematsu v. United States*, 140 F.2d 289, 291 (9th Cir. 1943) (Denman, Cir. J.,
concurring in the result, but dissenting from the grounds of the majority opinion).

20. *Shelley v. Kraemer*, 334 U.S. 1, 6 (1948).

21. Ella Deloria, *Speaking of Indians* (New York: Friendship Press, 1944; reprint, Lincoln:
University of Nebraska Press Bison Books, 1998), 94.

22. Peter Iverson, "Building toward Self-Determination: Plains and Southwestern Indians in the 1940s and 1950s," *Western Historical Quarterly* 16, no. 2 (April 1985): 166.

23. *Cherokee Nation v. Georgia*, 30 U.S. (5 Pet.) 1, 17 (1831).

24. *Korematsu v. United States*, 323 U.S. 214, 242 (Murphy, J., dissenting).

25. See Editorial, *Los Angeles Times*, June 18, 1943, 18.

26. Harry S Truman. "Special Message to the Congress on Civil Rights," February 2, 1948, *Public Papers of the Presidents of the United States: January 1 to December 31, 1948* (Washington, DC: GPO, 1964), no. 20.

27. Campbell J. Gibson and Emily Lennon, "Historical Census Statistics on the Foreign-Born Population of the United States: 1850–1990," Population Division Working Paper No. 29 (February 1999), Table 1: Nativity of the Population in Place of Birth.

28. Exec. Order No. 9808, 11 Fed. Reg. 14,153 (December 5, 1946).

29. *To Secure These Rights: Report of the President's Commission on Civil Rights* (Washington, DC: GPO, 1947), 3.

30. *To Secure These Rights*, 99.

31. *To Secure These Rights*, 110–111, quoting U.N. Charter arts. 55 and 56.

32. Exec. Order No. 9981, 13 Fed. Reg. 4,313 (July 26, 1948).

33. *To Secure These Rights*, 133.

34. *Wheeler-Howard Act-Exempt Certain Indians: Hearings on S. 2103 before the Committee on Indian Affairs of the House*, 76th Cong., 3rd Sess. (1940), 25.

35. Exec. Order No. 8802, 6 Fed. Reg. 3109 (June 25, 1941).

36. William J. Collins, "Race, Roosevelt and Wartime Production: Fair Employment in World War II Labor Markets," *American Economic Review* 91, no. 1 (March 2001): 272. White men in the semiskilled category barely moved from 19.0 to 20.2 percent at the same time.

37. *United States v. Hirabayashi*, 320 U.S. 81, 104 (1943).

38. *United States v. Korematsu* (1944) 323 U.S. 214, 219–220.

39. *United States v. Korematsu*, at 242 (Murphy, J., dissenting).

40. *In re Endo*, 323 U.S. 283, 294 (1944).

41. *In re Endo*, at 302.

42. Japanese-American Evacuation Claims Act, 62 Stat. 1231 (July 2, 1948).

43. Erik Barnouw, *A History of Broadcasting in the United States*, vol. 2, *The Golden Web, 1933–1953* (New York: Oxford University Press, 1968), 110.

44. As quoted in Lester M. Jones, "The Editorial Policy of Negro Newspapers of 1917–18 as compared with that of 1941–42," *Journal of Negro History* 29, no. 1 (January 1944): 29.

45. As quoted in Jones, "The Editorial Policy of Negro Newspapers," 24.

46. "Our Pledge of Allegiance," *The Chicago Defender*, special edition, September 26, 1942, 1.

47. Ella Deloria, *Speaking of Indians* (New York: Friendship Press, 1944), Introduction.

48. Deloria, *Speaking of Indians*. These are the titles of her three-part study.

49. Frank Waters, *The Man Who Killed the Deer* (Chicago: Swallow Press/Farrar, Rinehart, 1942), 3.

50. Waters, *The Man Who Killed the Deer*, 8.

51. Pardee Lowe, *Father and Glorious Descendent* (Boston: Little, Brown, 1943), book jacket.

52. Merle Curti, *The Growth of American Thought* (New York: Harper & Brothers, 1943), 432–433.

53. Curti, *The Growth of American Thought*, 432–433.

54. Gunnar Myrdal, *An American Dilemma*, 2 vols. (New York: Harper & Brothers, 1944), I:vi.

55. Myrdal, *An American Dilemma*, 78.

56. Myrdal, *An American Dilemma*, 201.

57. Howard W. Odum, "Problem and Methodology in *An American Dilemma*," *Social Forces* 23, no. 1 (October 1944): 95.

58. Oscar Handlin, "A Book that Changed American Life; A Revisit to a Classic Work on U.S.," *New York Times Book Review*, April 21, 1963, 1.

59. Kimball Young, "Review of *An American Dilemma: The Negro Problem and Modern Democracy* by Gunnar Myrdal; Richard Sterner; Arnold Rose," *American Sociological Review* 9, no. 3 (June 1944): 329.

60. Myrdal, *An American Dilemma*, xliii.

61. Exec. Order No. 9808, 11 Fed. Reg. 14153 (December 5, 1946), establishing the President's Committee on Civil Rights.

1950s

TIMELINE

1950

Cuban-born actor-musician Dezi Arnaz and his wife actress-comedian Lucille Ball form Desilu Productions and begin to create the Columbia Broadcasting System (CBS) television hit show *I Love Lucy* (1951–1957) and such other hit TV programs as *Our Miss Brooks* (1952–1956) and *The Untouchables* (1959–1963).

February 12   An Associated Press poll names Sac and Fox tribe member Jim Thorpe the best all-around American athlete of the first half of the twentieth century.

April 19   Congress authorizes rehabilitation of Navajo and Hopi Indian tribes.

May   The National Basketball Association (NBA)'s color barrier falls as the Washington Capitols sign blacks Earl Lloyd and Harold Hunter, the New York Knicks sign Nathaniel "Sweetwater" Clifton, and the Boston Celtics draft Chuck Cooper.

May 22   The President's Committee on Equality of Treatment and Opportunity in the Armed Forces, commonly called the Fahey Committee after its chairman Charles Fahey, issues its final report titled *Freedom to Serve*.

June 3   President Harry S Truman, in Executive Order 10129, creates the President's Commission on Migratory Labor to study social and economic conditions, especially those of workers of Mexican descent.

June 5	The U.S. Supreme Court in *Sweatt v. Painter* and *McLaurin v. Oklahoma State Regents* rules it illegal for state professional and graduate schools to deny blacks the same treatment as others based on race. *Henderson v. United States* rules so-called separate but equal racial discrimination in interstate commerce illegal.
June 16	The Displaced Persons Act of 1950 opens U.S. immigration further to refugees.
June 25	The Korean War (1950–1953) begins.
July 3	Congress provides for Puerto Rico's self-government, laying the basis for its becoming the *Estado Libre Asociado de Puerto Rico,* literally the "Free Associated State" but translated as the Commonwealth of Puerto Rico.
August 1	Congress authorizes civil government for the Pacific island territory of Guam.
	The film *Broken Arrow* premieres in theaters as a new type of Hollywood western, as it reflects Indian humanity in its focus on Apache chief Cochise; a successful TV series of the same title will pick up the theme (1956–1958).
August 28	Althea Gibson becomes the first black player in the U.S. Open Tennis Championship at Forest Hills, New York (she becomes the first black winner in 1957 and repeats as champion in 1958).
September 1	Gwendolyn Brooks receives the Pulitzer Prize for Poetry for her 1949 collection *Annie Allen,* becoming the first black to win a Pulitzer.
November 1	Two Puerto Rican nationalists attempt to assassinate President Harry S Truman across from the White House in Washington, D.C.
December 16	Ralph Bunche receives the Nobel Peace Prize for his Mideast mediation as principal secretary of the U.N. Palestine Commission, becoming the first black to win a Nobel Prize.

1951

March 29	Puerto Rican-born actor José Ferrer wins the Academy Award for Best Actor for his portrayal of the title character in the film *Cyrano de Bergerac* (1950).
June 28	*Amos 'n' Andy* becomes the first all-black cast U.S. television series (on air until June 11, 1953).

July 10	Venezuelan-born shortstop Alfonso "Chico" Carrasquel of the Chicago White Sox becomes the first Hispanic American player in Major League Baseball (MLB)'s All-Star game.
July 12	Congress extends the Bracero temporary worker program with Mexico.
September 4	Television for the first time broadcasts coast-to-coast in the United States, airing a speech by President Harry S Truman.
November 1	John H. Johnson launches *Jet* magazine in his growing black publishing empire.
December 3	President Truman establishes the Committee on Government Contract Compliance to enforce antidiscrimination provisions in federal contracts.

1952

March 10	Cuban military strongman and former president Fulgencio Batista again seizes power and suspends constitutional process in Cuba, sparking opposition led by Fidel Castro and Cuban flight to the United States.
March 18	Rosa Minoka Hill, the second American Indian woman to become a physician, dies in Oneida, Wisconsin.
March 19	Mexican-born actor Anthony Quinn wins an Academy Award for his supporting role in *Viva Zapata!* (1952).
April 17	California's Supreme Court in *Fujii Sei v. California* declares the state's 1913 Alien Land Law unconstitutional.
June 27	The Immigration and Nationality Act of 1952 (McCarran-Walter Act) removes U.S. immigration exclusions of Asians and grants them the right to become naturalized U.S. citizens.
July–August	Japanese Americans Tommy Kono (weightlifting), Ford Konno (swimming), and Yoshinobu Oyakawa (swimming) win gold medals at the Olympic Games in Helsinki, firsts for Asian Americans; Evelyn Kawamoto (swimming) becomes the first Asian American woman to win an Olympic medal (bronze).
July 3	Congress approves Puerto Rico's home rule constitution.

1953

January 13	Don Barksdale becomes the first black to play in the National Basketball Association's All-Star game.

March 31	Oklahoma's Otoe-Missouria Indians become the first tribe to get a land settlement ($1.5 million after offsets) in the Indian Claims Commission process.
June 8	The U.S. Supreme Court in *District of Columbia v. John R. Thompson Co., Inc.*, rules racial discrimination illegal in public accommodations in the District of Columbia.
June 16–23	Blacks conduct a successful eight-day bus boycott in Baton Rouge, Louisiana, to protest segregated seating on city buses.
July 27	The Korean War (1950–1953) ends.
August 1	House Concurrent Resolution no. 108 establishes Congress's termination policy, aiming "to end [Indians'] status as wards of the United States."
August 7	Congress enacts the Refugee Relief Act to admit persons escaping war or persecution and for the first time admits Asians as refugees.
August 15	Congress in Public Law 280 advances termination policy, transferring federal law enforcement authority over specified Indian tribes to states.

1954

	D'Arcy McNickle publishes novel *Runner in the Sun: A Story of Indian Maize*, treating an unnamed Southwest cliff-dwelling tribe's prehistoric struggles.
	Juan José Arreola wins the National Institute for Fine Arts Drama Festival first prize for his play *La hora de todos* (Everyone's Hour).
March 1	Three Puerto Rican nationalists fire about 30 shots from a visitors gallery in the Capitol and wound five members of the U.S. House of Representatives on the 37th anniversary of Congress's 1917 law declaring Puerto Ricans U.S. citizens or, in some eyes, permanent colonials.
May 3	The U.S. Supreme Court in *Hernandez v. Texas* outlaws racialized discrimination against Mexican Americans or others of Hispanic descent.
May 17	The U.S. Supreme Court in *Brown v. Board of Education of Topeka* outlaws separate-race public schools.
June 17	The U.S. Immigration and Naturalization Service (INS) launches "Operation Wetback," a dragnet to roundup undocumented persons, mostly identified as Mexicans.

September	Mexican-born Cleveland Indian second baseman Roberto "Beto" Avila becomes the first Hispanic American to win a MLB batting championship (.341).

1955

January 7	Contralto Marian Anderson becomes the first black soloist to perform at New York City's Metropolitan Opera.
May 31	The U.S. Supreme Court in *Brown v. Board of Education II* directs public school desegregation to proceed under the general supervision of federal district courts "with all deliberate speed."
June 7	Lumbee Indians of North Carolina win federal recognition but with stipulations barring their receiving federal funds or services.
July 1	As part of Congress's termination policy, the federal government transfers Indian healthcare from the Bureau of Indian Affairs (BIA) to the U.S. Public Health Service, which opens a Division of Indian Health.
August 28–31	Black 14-year-old Chicagoan Emmett Louis Till is kidnapped and lynched in Money, Mississippi.
November 7	The U.S. Supreme Court in *Mayor and Council of Baltimore City v. Dawson* and *Holmes v. City of Atlanta* outlaws racial segregation in public parks, playgrounds, and golf courses.
November 14	The U.S. Supreme Court in *Naim v. Naim* leaves standing Virginia's anti-miscegenation statutes, declaring itself unable to reach any constitutional issue.
December 1–5	Montgomery Bus Boycott begins as blacks in Alabama's capital protest racial segregation on city buses, following Rosa Parks's arrest on December 1, in what becomes a 381-day campaign that elevates local minister Rev. Martin Luther King Jr. to national prominence.

1956

	The U.S. Immigration and Naturalization Service (INS) reports entry of more than 350,000 aliens to the United States, the highest number since 1924.
February 1	A dynamite bomb explodes at the Montgomery, Alabama home of E. D. Nixon, a leader of the bus boycott and former president of the state chapter of the National Association for the Advancement of Colored People (NAACP).

February 3	Autherine Lucy becomes the first black student enrolled at the University of Alabama, but white mobs prevent her attending classes and the university expels her in violation of a federal court order (February 29–March 1).
March 11	Dozens of Southern members of Congress issue what is called *The Southern Manifesto*, denouncing U.S. Supreme Court desegregation decisions and federal interference in racial matters asserted to be issues of states' rights.
March 22	Rev. Martin Luther King Jr. convicted of illegally boycotting Montgomery City Bus Lines and fined $500 plus $500 in court costs, converted to a jail sentence of 386 days.
May 26	Rev. C. K. Steele leads a black boycott of city-run buses in Tallahassee, Florida (runs until December 23, 1956).
June 5	In *Browder v. Gayle*, a class action arising from the Montgomery Bus Boycott, a U.S. District Court in Alabama rules segregation illegal on intrastate public transportation carriers, vindicating boycotters.
July 30	Congress provides for job training centers under the Indian Vocational Training Act to help alleviate Indian unemployment and advance their relocation from reservations to cities as part of Congress's termination policy.
September	Venezuelan-born shortstop Luis Aparicio of the Baltimore Orioles becomes the first Hispanic American named MLB Rookie of the Year.
November 6	California's Imperial Valley congressional district elects India-born Dalip Singh Saund as the first Asian American member of Congress.
	In a general ballot referendum the Japanese American Citizens League initiated, California voters repeal the state's 1913 statute that prohibited Asian immigrants from owning real estate.
November 13	The U.S. Supreme Court in *Gayle v. Browder* affirms the lower court decision outlawing segregation in intrastate transportation.

1957

Septima Clark, Bernice Robinson, and Esau Jenkins begin opening Citizenship Schools in the South to teach blacks literacy sufficient to pass state voting tests.

January	Rev. Martin Luther King Jr. and others begin organizing what becomes the Southern Christian Leadership Conference (SCLC).
March 27	Mexican-born actor Anthony Quinn wins an Academy Award for his supporting role in *Lust for Life* (1956).
September 9	Congress passes the first Civil Rights Act since Reconstruction, emphasizing protection of voter rights and creating the U.S. Civil Rights Commission.
September 24	President Dwight D. Eisenhower orders U.S. 101st Airborne troops to quell rioting over school desegregation in Little Rock, Arkansas, so as to protect the first black students to attend the city's Central High School.

1958

January 3	The U.S. Civil Rights Commission swears in six members and begins work.
January 18	Three hundred armed Lumbee Indians rout Ku Klux Klan (KKK) rally and cross-burning in Robeson County, North Carolina.
June 29	KKK dynamites Rev. Fred L. Shuttlesworth's Bethel Baptist Church in Birmingham, Alabama.
June 30	The U.S. Supreme Court in *NAACP v. Alabama ex rel. Patterson* upholds against state harassment the privacy and integrity of the NAACP in promoting its "beliefs and ideas."
August 18	The Rancheria Act advances Congress's termination policy by ending federal trust responsibility for tribes on 41 California reservations.
September	Publisher Harper & Row releases Martin Luther King Jr.'s book *Stride toward Freedom: The Montgomery Story.*
September 28	A black woman stabs the Rev. Martin Luther King Jr. near his heart outside the National Broadcasting Company (NBC) studios in New York City.
September 29	The U.S. Supreme Court in *Cooper v. Aaron* unanimously and emphatically reaffirms that state-supported segregated schools are unconstitutional.

1959

January 1	Fidel Castro-led revolution seizes power in Cuba, triggering U.S. influx of Cuban refugees.

January 3	Alaska becomes the 49th state with its significant population of Native groups such as the Aleuts, Inupiaq, and Yupik Eskimos.
January 12	The U.S. Supreme Court in *Williams v. Lee* upholds tribal sovereignty and jurisdiction over Indians and non-Indians on reservations.
	Berry Gordy Jr. founds Tamla Records, the future Motown, in Detroit, Michigan.
January 21	Atlanta, Georgia, officially desegregates public buses but governor requests voluntary segregation.
March 18	Congress votes to admit Hawaii, with its majority nonwhite population, as the 50th state of the Union (admission occurs on August 21).
May 20	Congress restores citizenship to Japanese Americans who renounced allegiance on being interned during World War II (1939–1945).
July 21	African American Elijah Jerry "Pumpsie" Green breaks the color barrier on the Boston Red Sox, the last MLB team to integrate.
August 21	Voters in Hawaii elect Hiram Fong as the first U.S. Senator of Asian American and Chinese American descent. They also elect Daniel Ken Inouye as the first Japanese American to the U.S. House of Representatives.
September 14–19	William Wright becomes the first black to win a United States Golf Association (USGA) title, emerging victorious at the U.S. Amateur Public Links Tournament.
September 22	Congress authorizes additional admission of 57,000 aliens.

OVERVIEW

The 1950s was a decade when the American public more and more noticed rumblings of the volcano of U.S. race relations. Later decades got more attention for erupting. Much of their venting arose, however, from 1950s' thrusts that cracked the segregated status quo. Just as the activities of the decade built on momentum from the 1940s, later decades built on compelling forces formed in the 1950s.

An American Revolution was underway. And it was being televised. Increasingly transcending local and sectional communities, TV made national media events of items that might have been only local or otherwise had limited circulation. A prime example was 14-year-old black Chicagoan Emmett Louis Till's August 1955 lynching in the tiny river delta town of Money, Mississippi.

With the glare of television lights, few Americans could any longer view segregation as merely a sectional difficulty to be left to local resolution. Nor could they see it simply as an isolated black/white issue. The 1954 U.S. Supreme Court decision in *Hernandez v. Texas*, treating racialized discrimination against Mexican Americans, upheld the view that segregation was an issue for all Americans, not merely blacks. Moving in their own ways during the decade, America's racialized minorities everywhere pushed across the board for recognition and rights.

Blacks pushed at the forefront of intensifying protests against entrenched racial structures that excluded them and other nonwhites from the American Dream. Numbering 15 million and constituting almost exactly 10 percent of the U.S. population in 1950, blacks stood as primary targets for white supremacy and its imposed racial segregation. The U.S. Census had stopped counting "Hispanics" for the time. The category appeared too expansive and too threatening to entrenched views of America's having an Anglo character. Official counts of American Indians and Asian Americans put each at about one-third million. All stood at some distance from one another. Yet they all stood similarly situated as American outcasts.

Segregation's structural impediments routinely retarded nonwhites' progress. If anything, their economic position improved at a snail's pace. Generally, they remained stuck at the lower rungs of occupational ladders. The 1950s' booming business cycle advanced some. Expanding government employment also opened significant opportunities. Growing demand for non-unionized labor offered other opportunities. Still, most unionized jobs remained closed as white-only shops. The rapidly enlarging service sector further opened many workplaces to nonwhites. Usually they gained only clerical jobs, at best. Yet they got a foot in the door. The opening did not quiet them; it quickened their efforts.

Substantial shifts in racial stratification on the job were yet to come in the 1950s, particularly among men. Among women, nonwhites converged more quickly with whites. That largely reflected stultifying gender discrimination. Women generally sat at the low end of job ladders. So nonwhite women on the climb usually had less far to go to reach their white sisters. Nonwhite men had much further to go. White men far outdistanced everyone else. They stood atop America's sex- and race-based structures. They generally enjoyed the quintessential quality of life ascribed to the American Dream. They were understandably jealous of their dominating position. Few would yield it except grudgingly.

Breaking down segregation offered a first step for nonwhites to reach previously exclusive white preserves. That assault was the focus of 1950s' race relations. It was no sudden surge. It flowed in a long struggle, but it grew more effective during the decade. It drew strength from post-World War II concerns that escalated the force of human rights. And television bolstered it mightily.

TV focused an unblinking, worldwide eye on U.S. racism. It put the American ulcer on display. The image was nowhere flattering. It appeared sickeningly in international circles. Segregation's antidemocratic character colored world perceptions and painted America a hypocrite. Such ridicule stung especially in the context of America's cold war against the communist Union of Soviet Socialist Republics (USSR). Yet the battle was not so distant; it raged at home. It pitted determined nonwhite elements for change against determined white conservative elements.

Television reflected a national schizophrenia on race relations in the 1950s. The ugly realities and ridicule aired on the news side contrasted with much on the money-driven entertainment side. There with its cautious, corporate sponsors, TV showed primarily a homogenous, social serenity filled with dazzling technologies and glistening household appliances. It projected as typical a virtual, lily-white, all-American world.

Nonwhites made few sustained appearances on television outside of news and special programming in the 1950s. Nevertheless, their appearances were significant. Especially on the entertainment side, straitlaced white America progressively met nonwhites. Singing and dancing, running and jumping, batting, catching, and shooting, blacks particularly grew as prime players in professional sports that TV began to embrace during the decade. Enlarging Jackie Robinson and Larry Doby's 1947 breakthrough in Major League Baseball (MLB), scores of nonwhite athletes became household names in the 1950s. Baseball's Roberto Clemente and Willie Mays, basketball's Bill Russell, boxing's Sugar Ray Robinson, and football's Jim Brown dominated play, although their sports remained predominantly white. And they were not alone.

Indians and Hispanics joined the televised fields of play. In 1952, Creek Indian Allie P. Reynolds pitching for the MLB New York Yankees led the American League in strikeouts and in earned-run average. Recognition came also for those who had excelled in earlier decades. In 1953, for instance, pitcher Charles Albert "Chief" Bender, son of a Chippewa mother and German Canadian father, became the first American Indian admitted into the Baseball Hall of Fame in Cooperstown, New York. More remarkably, a 1950 Associated Press poll named Sac and Fox tribe member Jim Thorpe the best all-around athlete of the first half of the twentieth century.

The sounds of America also took a colorful, radical shift during the decade. Rock 'n' roll's riotous notes became the music of the 1950s with its rising king, Elvis Presley. Television boosted his star, and race relations resonated in his performances. Presley mixed sounds from hillbilly "Mississippi Slim" (stage name of Carvel Lee Ausborn) and black Memphis blues and soul. Indeed, some critics claimed Elvis sang black music in white face with a country-folk voice. He personified the fact of a racially changing America.

Radio broadcast Elvis's sound along with the black music crossover that by the end of the 1950s began to integrate American popular music. Motown propelled the legacy. Berry Gordy Jr. founded the label in 1959 as Tamla Records in

Michigan's "Motor City," Detroit—then the world's automotive industry design and manufacturing capital. The segregation that dominated America was crumbling under popular pressure. The soundtrack of the nation's future turned the table on white supremacy.

Nonwhites refused in the 1950s to be silenced any longer or relegated as a national underclass. Their insistence changed the shape of U.S. race relations. The face of America became more colorful during the decade. Asian Americans for the first time became members of Congress. California's 29th congressional district elected the Democrat Dalip Singh Saund, a Sikh from India's Punjab region, to the U.S. House of Representatives in November 1956. With Hawaii's becoming the 50th state in August 1959, the Chinese American Republican Hiram Fong entered the U.S. Senate. Yet Asians remained largely unwelcome as immigrants to U.S. shores as a much heralded view of the day proclaimed Americans should look alike, speak the same language, sound alike, and as much as possible descend from the same ethnic stock. Such sentiments also spurred the U.S. "Operation Wetback" dragnet that swept perhaps a million Hispanics in the Southwest across the border to Mexico.

Dalip Singh Saund, c. 1958. Courtesy of the Library of Congress, cph 3c0384.

The First Americans, too, found themselves again fighting for their collective lives against the recurrent American thinking represented in the termination policy Congress settled in 1953. Notions that American Indians should just go away were hardly new. Termination pushed, however, for Indians' final surrender. It planned to close reservations. It aimed to end tribes' being federally recognized entities. It hoped to erase Indians' identity as a feature of public policy. Termination advocates pushed a frame of reference to extinguish the so-called Indian problem by dispersing Indians from reservation segregation to official elimination.

Nonwhites belied Americans' general appearance as a people of plenty in the 1950s. Vast material gaps yawned along old race lines, and only meager, slow-developing gains edged toward bridging the divide. Nonwhites demanded better. Particularly blacks in the South rose in grassroots movements with a singular purpose. Spreading with insistent pressure, they pushed along primary paths to progress. They pressed to secure their place in public discourse and the political process. They demanded to vote and to have their votes count. They got fresh guarantees in the Civil Rights Act of 1957. More than written assurances were needed, however.

Blacks led a parade of nonwhites insisting on equal access to public accommodations. Forcing the point, they took to the streets. They boycotted segregated buses in 1953 in Baton Rouge, Louisiana, in 1955–1956 famously in Montgomery, Alabama, and in 1956 also in Tallahassee, Florida. And unrelentingly they insisted on improving education for their children. That accounted for the fierce legal battles over public schools. The cases in the U.S. Supreme Court's landmark 1954 decision in *Brown v. Board of Education* highlighted the struggle. More than anything else, the school desegregation cases signaled the 1950s as a breakout decade in U.S. race relations.

KEY EVENTS

INDIAN TERMINATION POLICY, 1953

On August 1, 1953, drastic change stabbed American Indians. Congress struck the blow with House Concurrent Resolution 108. It hit the cord of U.S.-Indian relations that stretched back to the era of the nation's 1776 Declaration of Independence. It shredded centuries of treaties. In a stroke, it thrust Indians and the nation into a policy called "Termination."

The policy's sharp point was deceptively simple. It declared Indians should be recognized and treated only as individuals, like any other U.S. citizens. That was easy to grasp. Indeed, it appeared easy to embrace. It seemed to announce an end to discrimination. It resonated with the American ideal of all persons being equal before the law.

The resolution's apparent commitment to democratic equality flourished in its opening lines. "It is the policy of Congress, as rapidly as possible, to make the Indians within the territorial limits of the United States subject to the same laws and entitled to the same privileges and responsibilities as are applicable to other citizens," the resolution declared. It continued by proclaiming a desire "to end [Indians'] status as wards of the United States, and to grant them all the rights and prerogatives pertaining to American citizenship." It directed all U.S. Indians to "assume their full responsibilities as American citizens."[1]

"With the general objective, there can be no quarrel," the *Washington Post* noted.[2] Voicing its opinion as one of the U.S. capital's leading daily newspapers, the editorial further explained, however, that the congressional resolution advanced more than a "general objective." It committed the nation to ending tribal authority and jurisdiction. It would cease federal recognition of tribes. It would eliminate Indian reservations. As a later *Washington Post* editorial put it, termination directed the United States to "get out of the Indian business."[3]

The resolution's wording suggested it was freeing Indians. Actually, it was more like getting rid of Indians. It was giving Indians nothing. Rather, it was taking what Indians had. It pronounced Indians to be "freed from Federal supervision and control and from all disabilities and limitations specially applicable to Indians." Behind the words lay the harsh directive that "all of the offices of the Bureau of Indian Affairs whose primary purpose was to serve any Indian tribe or individual Indian freed from Federal supervision should be abolished."[4] Congress was cutting off Indians from federal funding and customary services. It was moving to rid itself and the nation of a perceived burden.

Termination promised to end tribal autonomy, community, culture, and collective welfare. Its attack was not new. Resolution 108 simply reestablished an old objective: to wipe out tribes under the guise of democratic assimilation. Congress began unveiling its means two weeks after passing the resolution. It effectively stripped tribes of their sovereign jurisdiction. It put them under state authority. What became known as Public Law 280 transferred from tribes to the states, where they were, criminal and civil jurisdiction on Indian reservations. This statute of August 15, 1953, applied immediately only in California, Minnesota, Nebraska, Oregon, and Wisconsin. But subsequent acts quickly expanded application nationwide.

Termination proponents carried the day initially by speed, if not by stealth. Its sponsors and supporters pushed Public Law 280 to passage with little notice. Proponents displayed a decided bent not to pause for debate or public comment. They refused to ask what Indians thought, as if Indian collective self-determination were anathema. Such attitudes and actions engendered swift and sustained protest.

The *Washington Post* ridiculed 280's passage. "Among the bills that slipped through in the last hours of the congressional session that ended last week was a little-known measure which seeks to wash out Federal responsibility for law enforcement on Indian reservations," an editorial derided. "The President would do well to veto this abdication of Federal responsibility and to urge a more thoughtful approach to the problem at the next session of Congress," the *Post* urged.[5]

Indians organized against the outrage. Rosebud Sioux Tribe president Robert Burnette would fiercely fight Public Law 280 in South Dakota, for example. But non-Indians also sounded the alarm. The New York City-based Association on American Indian Affairs bitterly denounced termination. So did the New York City-based Institute of Ethnic Affairs. Its president John Collier, commissioner of Indian affairs from 1933 to 1945, lambasted Congress's "almost desperate haste" to enact termination. The process had, he noted, "stifled the voice of the Indian peoples and of the public at large."[6]

Termination's apparent backroom process violated democratic principles of open government, many critics complained. Opponents such as Collier, focusing on Indians' welfare however, attacked termination's outrageous consequences. It imposed "white-man law as a substitute for the voluntary but intimately controlling code of conduct, exemplified in the Indian law-and-order systems developed through ages."[7] It promised disaster, Collier predicted. And he was not alone. The *Washington Post* labeled termination "Trouble for the Indians." The policy promised to destroy with no hope of rebuilding.[8]

Rather than veto termination, President Dwight D. Eisenhower signed it into law. He endorsed its aim. Yet he, too, chided Congress on its process. All he did, however, was simply to urge Congress to amend the termination process so as to provide "full consultation in order to ascertain the wishes and desires of the Indians."[9] That produced nothing. It skirted the central issue of outcome.

Termination promised to destroy traditional Indian tribal life. That was the fundamental problem. It was not simply a matter of process. Results mattered. Termination proponents agreed, but from a contrary perspective. They were impatient for results to divest the federal government of relations with Indians. They spared no time for detail. They seemed prepared to do little more than turn a blind eye to Indians. They wanted, after all, to make Indians disappear as recognizable Indians. They acted as if declaring an end to Indians' federal status would end the nation's "Indian problem." It clearly was not going, however, to end Indians' problems.

Simply turning a blind eye was no real solution. "It would be one thing if this policy were carefully worked out as a long-range proposition to be applied only to those advanced tribes that were unmistakably ready for it," the *New York Times* explained with clear sympathies on both sides of the issue. "It is another one that permits the federal government to shed its responsibility and to throw even the most pitiable and wretched tribes on the tender mercies of the surrounding civilization for which they are so clearly unfitted," it concluded.[10]

All objections failed. Termination became the law of the land, and that had dire consequences for Indians and the nation for the remainder of the 1950s and beyond.

BROWN V. BOARD OF EDUCATION, 1954

The United States entered a bracing era of race relations on Thursday, May 17, 1954. The U.S. Supreme Court that day collapsed a central pillar of racial segregation. In an opinion by Chief Justice Earl Warren, the Court unanimously pronounced that "in the field of public education the doctrine of 'separate but equal' has no place. Separate educational facilities are inherently unequal."[11]

The ruling peeled away part of the imprimatur the Court itself bestowed on segregation more than a half-century earlier. In its infamous 1896 decision in *Plessy v. Ferguson*, the Court sanctioned states' legally requiring railway companies carrying passengers to provide "equal but separate accommodations for the white, and colored races."[12] That authority allowed apartheid to legally overrun American life. It became the signature of the South. It was far more than regional, however.

The five public school cases the Court decided on May 17, 1954, evidenced segregation's reach. The cases arose in the District of Columbia, Delaware, Kansas, South Carolina, and Virginia. *Brown v. Board of Education of Topeka, Kansas*, the parties to the lead case from the four states, which the Court consolidated to hear together, became the historic caption for the decisions. The D.C. case—*Bolling v. Sharpe*, heard separately, became all but lost in the splash of *Brown* and its state companions.

All the cases treated public schools. They raised a single question: Did the U.S. Constitution allow "segregation of children in public schools solely on the basis of race, even though the physical facilities and other 'tangible' factors may be equal"?[13] The answer in U.S. law had traditionally been "yes." That arose in part from the *Plessy* doctrine's being extended to public education.

Commentators usually cited *Cumming v. Richmond County Board of Education* for separate but equal school precedent. But the Court decided the otherwise obscure 1899 case from Georgia on the basis of the state's discretion in funding and managing its public schools. The Court's unanimous ruling in an opinion by Justice John Marshall Harlan—famous for his prescient, vigorous dissent in *Plessy*—carefully skirted the separate but equal question.

Black parents and taxpayers had argued vehemently in *Cumming* for the Court to rule on the Fourteenth Amendment equal protection issue. They had sought an injunction to restrain the county board of education from temporarily closing the colored high school for announced fiscal reasons while keeping open the white high school.

The Court had no evidence the board acted in bad faith or abused its discretion, Justice Harlan emphasized. So the Court lacked evidence to say the board acted on account of race. It could not rule "the case [one] of a clear and unmistakable disregard of rights secured by the supreme law of the land," he explained.[14]

Supporters of public school segregation liked to repeat part of Justice Harlan's *Cumming* opinion. In their eyes it settled the constitutional issue. Harlan's words were:

the education of the people in schools maintained by state taxation is a matter
belonging to the respective States, and any interference on the part of Federal
authority with the management of such schools cannot be justified except in
the case of a clear and unmistakable disregard of rights secured by the supreme
law of the land.[15]

Proponents perennially used those words to insist on public school segregation as
a matter of states' rights.

Segregation supporters liked also to point out that the legal doctrine for separate public schools originated in the North, not in the South. Part of the reason
was that before the Civil War the South lacked general public school systems.
Nevertheless, the 1850 case of *Roberts v. City of Boston* was the leading school
segregation precedent. Famed Massachusetts Chief Justice Lemuel Shaw had
there affirmed a local school board committee's discretion to maintain separate
schools for black and white children.

"In the absence of special legislation on this subject, the law has vested the
power in the committee to regulate the system of distribution and classification;
and when this power is reasonably exercised, without being abused or perverted
by colorable pretences, the decision of the committee must be deemed conclu-
sive," Shaw ruled. "The committee, apparently upon great deliberation, have
come to the conclusion, that the good of both classes of schools will be best
promoted, by maintaining the separate primary schools for colored and for white
children, and we can perceive no ground to doubt, that this is the honest result
of their experience and judgment," Shaw opined.[16]

The Massachusetts legislature responded to outcries against Shaw's decision. In
1855 it enacted what the chief justice had described as "special legislation on this
subject." It outlawed racial segregation in the state's public schools. Elsewhere
much of the North persisted with public school segregation. It spread west, too.

When the Supreme Court decided *Brown* in 1954, only 15 of the 48 states
positively forbade school segregation. Four states—Arizona, Kansas, New Mexico, and Wyoming—allowed segregation as a local or limited option. Eleven
states provided no law on the subject. All 15 states that maintained slavery in
1860, plus Oklahoma, West Virginia, and the District of Columbia, mandated
segregation.

Many whites accepted all-white schools as a fact of American life. Segregation
existed whether or not law mandated it. The fact was not confined to the 21
states and the District of Columbia with their legal directives. The neighborhood
public school system guaranteed highly segregated schools. In most U.S. locales,
whites and nonwhites lived apart. That was particularly true for blacks. America
was a land of racially separate urban neighborhoods and rural landscapes. The
homogeneity extended further, because residence segregated not only races but
classes. As long as students went to schools nearest where they lived, they would
most often go to schools overwhelmingly, if not exclusively, white or nonwhite.

In deciding *Brown*, the Court confronted more than law. It faced facts of
American life and history. The justices understood the stakes, and they did

not rush to judgment. They twice heard arguments in the state cases—once in December 1952 and again in December 1953. In the end, they decided to squarely confront whether racially separate schools could be equal.

The Court focused on whether segregated public schools "deprive the children of the minority group of equal educational opportunities?"[17]

"We believe that it does," the justices unanimously answered.[18]

The Court ruled "that such segregation is a denial of the equal protection of the laws."[19] The justices understood at least something of the "problems of considerable complexity" that attended their decision.[20] Outlawing the old system proved immeasurably easier than negotiating a new system in which whites and nonwhites would learn side-by-side in the nation's public schools.

OPERATION WETBACK

More than any other single event in the 1950s, the "Operation Wetback" dragnet campaign sharply displayed mounting concerns in many circles about immigration changing U.S. character, complexion, and culture. The coordinated Immigration and Naturalization Service (INS) action launched on June 17, 1954, responded to outcries, particularly in California and the Southwest, about the United States being overrun with illegal aliens. The concerns reached far into race relations.

The dragnet focused on persons who illegally crossed the U.S. border from Mexico. The derogatory label "wetback"—or in Spanish *mojado* (meaning simply "wet")—arose from the image of illegals swimming or wading across the Rio Grande border flowing from El Paso, Texas, to the Gulf of Mexico. All such crossers were not Mexicans. Yet almost all of Hispanic heritage crossing from the south were commonly classified as Mexicans.

Observers did not always distinguish Mexicans from Mexican Americans. Indeed, more than a few Americans recognized no difference. Their real worry was the growing Latino presence. They seemed more concerned with who descended from south of the border than with who legally was or was not American. In their view who was an American was not a matter of law. It was a matter of blood. It was a matter of race and culture. They embraced a roundup slated to grab anyone "Mexican-looking."

The operation had a military feel. The sense of a battle campaign in part reflected the stamp of new INS Commissioner Lt. General Joseph M. Swing. President Dwight D. Eisenhower appointed his retired 1915 West Point classmate to head the INS in April 1954 for the very purpose of turning what he viewed as the dangerous tide of alien invasion.

While posturing for his presidential nomination in advance of the 1952 election, Eisenhower had worried publicly about the nation's being undermined by un-American activities and aliens. In a reported exchange with Democrat U.S. Senator J. William Fulbright of Arkansas, Eisenhower underscored a March 1951 *New York Times* report of a "rise in illegal border-crossing by Mexican 'wetbacks' to a current rate of more than 1,000,000 cases a year."[21]

Operation Wetback announced a target of 1.2 million deportations. The Eisenhower administration cast those to be deported as a subversive menace. From the president on down, officials described the near 2,000 mile border from Texas west to the Pacific Ocean as if it were something of a soft underbelly where a vulnerable America was being massively attacked. They talked of aliens thwarting U.S. law, distorting the national and local economies, and corrupting social welfare and cultural values. Expelling wetbacks and taking control of the border became primary steps toward national security, administration spokesmen insinuated.

While hailed as thwarting subversion and halting an alien influx, Operation Wetback was very much caught up in a national debate over the character and quantity of U.S. immigrants. Many who pushed the action insisted it had nothing to do with immigration policy or even with immigrants. They vehemently denied it was about race or culture. They declared the sweep was simply about apprehending criminals. Wetbacks broke U.S. law. They entered the United States illegally. They needed to be caught and deported. It was that simple. Those who focused on wetbacks as criminals wanted to hear nothing other than the need, indeed, the public duty, to uphold U.S. law.

The actual roundup came as no surprise. The president and Attorney General Herbert Brownell Jr., under whose jurisdiction the INS fell, had talked up the action for weeks. In fact, the operation appeared as much a public relations campaign as a campaign on the ground. It appeared aimed to threaten more than to seize those given eight-days' actual notice of its kickoff.

On the first full day of action, the 700-strong INS task force made its presence clearly felt. From roadblocks to raids on workplaces suspected of hiring wetbacks, the INS effort drew great fanfare. It concentrated in southern California, west Texas, and Arizona. Agents packed detainees into special trains and buses for hauling back to Mexico. In Texas, the INS hired two ships, the ironically named *Emancipation* and the *Mercurio*, to ferry detainees the 500 or so miles to Veracruz, Mexico. Snatched from their homes and jobs and in some cases separated from family, those nabbed were herded south in conditions one reporter described as "human misery" and "the biggest human cargo ever to cross the Mexican-American boundary in a single deportation shipment."[22]

The first day's take was about 2,000—about the same as the daily average before the sweep. The numbers nabbed remained relatively small. After six weeks, Attorney General Brownell could report only 150,000 apprehensions.[23] Much more effective was what newspapers reported as "the concerted voluntary exodus of 'wetbacks' southward since the special drive was announced."[24] The INS estimated 500,000 to 700,000 illegals fled to Mexico "voluntarily" to escape detention and deportation. INS district supervisor Herman Landon pronounced the action "a success from our point of view."[25]

Most deportees were understandably devastated. Their lives were upended. Rather than despair, many were defiant. "These uncounted thousands drawn to the golden land of the North by a combination of economic mishaps and pinches in Mexico were agreed, almost to a man, in their comments here today. They're coming back to the Golden Land. The best way they can," a *Los Angeles Times* reporter noted in Nogales, Mexico, as INS agents surrendered detainees to Mexican officials on the roundup's second day.[26]

The operation touched nothing of the core problem. Ample work was to be had in America at wages and under conditions only illegals or other migrants were willing to accept. Big money was to be made. Employers pocketed significant profits from paying such workers low wages. For the workers, even the lowest U.S. wages were more than they could make south of the border, where many sent most of what they earned. Most looked for the day when either they would have enough to return south and live comfortably or to bring their families north for a materially better life.

Operation Wetback in the end appeared a repeat of U.S. moves that beginning in 1929 deported or "voluntarily repatriated" to Mexico perhaps as many as 2 million persons of Mexican ancestry. Approximately 1.2 million were native-born U.S. citizens.[27] Many cheered the expulsions as America reeled under Great Depression unemployment. Early in what some commentators euphemistically called "The Mexican Repatriation," the lead news story in the *Los Angeles Times* of April 24, 1931, trumpeted "Horde Departs for Native Soil."[28] So rather than a conclusion, Operation Wetback appeared to some as another chapter in a sorry saga.

ASIAN AMERICAN DALIP SINGH SAUND ELECTED TO CONGRESS, 1956

The Tuesday after the first Monday in November of every even year has ordinarily marked a special event in the United States. Congress has set it as general election day. In November 1956 that Tuesday was the sixth, and it marked an even more special day for the nation and its race relations. That day voters in California's 29th congressional district elected Dalip Singh Saund to the U.S. House of Representatives. The 57-year-old Sikh from India's Punjab region became the first Asian American in Congress.

Saund's election symbolized more than personal achievement. Indeed, different people took his win as evidence for several different things. The U.S. State Department, for instance, hoisted Saund as a shining star. In the midst of the so-called Cold War between the United States and the Union of Soviet Socialist Republics (USSR), Saund became prime propaganda material. He reportedly demonstrated that the American system gave every individual a chance. That contrasted with the closed possibilities of the USSR's communist totalitarianism. Saund, himself, exulted that his victory "just demonstrates that American democracy is real."[29]

Saund was touted, too, as showing that fame and fortune did not determine everything in American life. He defeated celebrity aviator Jacqueline Cochran Odlum. Wife of a multimillionaire Republican, candidate Odlum enjoyed the support of her wealthy Palm Springs friends and neighbors. She reportedly outspent Saund more than three-to-one in campaigning. But he pressed the flesh. Touring his sprawling 110,880 square mile district in his own car, he communicated more of a personal touch than money could provide. He shook enough hands and chatted with enough voters to win what commentators reported as "one of the most dramatic contests in the annals of California politics."[30]

More than representing any populism, Saund's election highlighted clashing perspectives on the place of race in U.S. politics and society. To some his win showed race was no bar to political and social achievement—at least in some places in America. It stood in stark contrast to the dark segregationist drama unfolding in the U.S. South in the mid-1950s. Race there clearly barred blacks, and nonwhites generally, from broad political participation. So Saund's triumph at the polls elevated split national images. In one, race dominated. In the other, race appeared inconsequential in some views.

The spotlight on Saund further illuminated the diversifying American character. It signaled the entry of a fresh set of players in American public life. Outside of Hawaii, Asian Americans and Pacific Islanders had been mostly invisible politically. World War II had shifted some attention to them. Nodding to wartime allies and refugees, Congress partly lifted the bar that excluded most Asians from immigrating. In 1946 it also rescinded prohibitions on some Asians becoming U.S. citizens. That was how Saund became naturalized. Until 1946 federal law blocked him and his fellow Asian Indian immigrants from becoming U.S. citizens. He had campaigned hard to overturn the law, and he had won there, too. He and other Asian Americans organized to make their voices heard. They showed that further in 1946 when Chinese immigrant Wing F. Ong became the first Asian American elected to state office, as he won a seat in the Arizona House of Representatives.

Unlike blacks and Hispanics, Asian Americans had relatively small numbers nationally and locally. They lacked the bulk to dominate any election. Their voting strength seldom, if ever, promised any electoral edge. Moreover, although often lumped together in official categories, the nation's 321,033 Asian Americans in 1950 represented anything but a monolithic group. They scattered among several dozen nationalities and ethnicities. They represented different and diverse, if not new, models for American minority group relations.

Saund stood then on the cusp of hopes for a brighter future and a bleak racial past. He represented something of an American rags-to-riches success story. His life also illustrated race-imposed highs and lows in segregated America. His becoming a member of Congress reflected the steep climb Asians in America negotiated to gain civil rights and U.S. citizenship.

Saund's personal trek began when he immigrated for graduate study at the University of California, Berkeley, in the 1919–1920 academic year. He earned a master's degree in 1922 and a doctorate in 1924, both in mathematics. He moved from the San Francisco Bay Area to the Imperial Valley in southeastern California and, despite the state's alien land laws, succeeded as an agricultural entrepreneur selling lettuce, other farm products, and fertilizer.

California's alien land laws, first adopted in 1913 as bars against Japanese immigrants, came by 1923 to bar immigrants from India, also. They could own no California real estate. They could not even lease land or related property for agricultural purposes longer than three years. The restrictions aimed to keep Asians and others not "eligible to citizenship under the laws of the United States," as the legislation phrased it, from competing as farm owners or being more than agricultural wage-workers or sharecroppers.[31] State records showed Punjabis lost control of at least 32,300 acres in the Imperial Valley and 56,052 acres elsewhere in California as a result of its 1923 act.[32]

California's alien land law was not itself the low point. The state's May 1923 act reflected results from federal action. It followed a February 1923 U.S. Supreme Court ruling. That was the low point. It was where Saund and his fellow Punjabis found themselves labeled legally nonwhites. That was key to their rights in segregated America.

U.S. courts conceded persons from India were technically Caucasian. The human grouping traced its lineage to Europe through western Asia to parts of India, after all. Yet, a unanimous Court in an opinion by conservative Justice George Sutherland—himself an English-born immigrant—ruled in the case of the Punjabi Sikh Bhagat Singh Thind, a World War I veteran, that he and similar Asian Indians were not "white persons" within the meaning of U.S. law.[33]

So Saund had come a long way to win election to Congress in 1956. He had battled his way to simple legal recognition, civil rights, and U.S. citizenship.

VOICES OF THE DECADE

CONGRESSMAN PAT MCCARRAN

Four-term Nevada U.S. Senator Patrick Anthony "Pat" McCarran (1876–1954) was a prominent figure in the early 1950s. Notable for shaping U.S. immigration policy, he reflected an early cold war sense that America was under siege. A staunch conservative, maverick Democrat, and law-and-order advocate, he was a one-time county district attorney and state judge. He opposed President Franklin D. Roosevelt's New Deal of the 1930s as socialism and feared the communist menace and other elements he considered "un-American" would subvert the nation. Immigration and internal security went hand-in-hand in his view. He pushed to squelch what he saw as human seepage and subversion flowing from the wrong kind of immigrants. The following excerpt from a speech he delivered in the Senate in March 1953 against increasing the flow of immigrants to the United States reveals something of his narrow views of America and who should inhabit it.

I believe that this nation is the last hope of Western civilization and if this oasis of the world shall be overrun, perverted, contaminated or destroyed, then the last flickering light of humanity will be extinguished.

I take no issue with those who would praise the contributions which have been made to our society by people of many races, of varied creeds and colors. America is indeed a joining together of many streams which go to form a mighty river which we call the American way. However, we have in the United States today hard-core, indigestible blocs which have not become integrated into the American way of life, but which, on the contrary are its deadly enemies.

Today, as never before, untold millions are storming our gates for admission and those gates are cracking under the strain. The solution of the problems of Europe and Asia will not come through a transplanting of those problems en masse to the United States. . . .

I do not intend to become prophetic, but if the enemies of this legislation succeed in riddling it to pieces, or in amending it beyond recognition, they will have contributed more to promote this nation's downfall than any other group since we achieved our independence as a nation.

From 99 Cong. Rec. 1518 (March 2, 1953) (statement of Sen. McCarran).

CARLOS CADENA AND GUS GARCÍA

Attorneys Carlos C. Cadena (1918–2001) and Gustavo "Gus" C. García (1915–1964) joined their voices in advancing a definitive statement of Mexican Americans' relegation in U.S. law. They argued the landmark 1954 case of *Hernandez v. Texas.* It was the U.S. Supreme Court's first ruling on racialized discrimination against persons of Mexican ancestry and, more generally, of Hispanic heritage. The case arose in 1950 when Texas convicted Mexican American migrant cotton-picker Pete Hernández of murdering José Espinoza. An all-Anglo white jury in Jackson County rendered the verdict. Excluding persons of Mexican descent from juries was part of Texas's segregating them in a "two classes" system, where as "whites" by law they were denied all equal protection, even that extended to blacks. Working as legal counsel with the League of United Latin American Citizens (LULAC) and the American G.I. Forum, Cadena and García attacked Texas's black-or-white, "two classes" theory. Systematically excluding persons of Mexican descent from juries violated Fourteenth Amendment Equal Protection, Cadena and García argued. In an opinion by Chief Justice Earl Warren, the unanimous U.S. Supreme Court agreed. Cadena and García's voice heralded a later day in 1971 when U.S. law would recognize Hispanics as an identifiable racialized group.

In demanding the right to participate fully in the government of their state by serving on juries, persons of Mexican descent are not demanding . . . recognition "as a special class" which is entitled "special privileges. . . ." Petitioner [Hernández] merely demands a right which is accorded to all: the right to a trial by a fair and impartial jury from which persons of his national origin are not arbitrarily and systematically excluded. . . .

[T]he evidence in this case establishes beyond any doubt that the jury commissioners of Jackson County, Texas, have for at least 25 years, consciously and deliberately excluded persons of Mexican descent from jury service. To attribute the complete absence of persons of petitioner's national origin from Jackson County juries to coincidence strains all credulity. Such uniformity of result betrays the existence of a master plan. If my name appears on 14% of the lots from which repeated drawings are made over a period of 25 years, and my name is never drawn a single time, I would be more than justified in suspecting that the person doing the drawing was cheating. . . .

The invalidity of the "two classes" theory becomes apparent when it is examined in the light of the minority status of persons of Mexican descent in Texas. They occupy an inferior social and economic position. . . .

While the Texas court elaborates on its "two classes" theory [distinguishing only whites and blacks], in Jackson County, and in other areas in Texas, persons of Mexican descent are treated as a third class—a notch above the Negroes, perhaps, but several notches below the rest of the population. They are segregated in schools, they are denied service in public places, they are discouraged from using non-Negro restrooms. They are excluded from juries, and a Texas court upholds their exclusion by a paternal reminder that they are members of the dominant white race. As members of the dominant class, they are chided by the Texas court for seeking "special privileges." They are told that they are assured of a fair trial at the hands of persons who do not want to go to school with them, who did not want to give them service in public places, who did not want to sit on juries with them, and who would prefer not to share rest room facilities with them, not even at the Jackson County Courthouse. . . .

All of the talk about "two classes"; all of the verbal pointing with alarm at a "special class" which seeks "special privileges" cannot obscure one very simple fact which stands out in bold relief: the Texas law points in one direction for persons of Mexican descent, like petitioner, and in another for Negroes. Under such circumstances, can it be said that the State of Texas has accorded to petitioner the protection of equal laws? Distinctions negate equality, and "distinctions between citizens solely because of their ancestry are by their very nature odious to a free people whose institutions are founded upon the doctrine of equality."

From Brief for Petitioner, *Hernandez v. Texas*, 347 U.S. 475 (1954), vii, 4–5, 27–28. (citations omitted.)

U.S. CHIEF JUSTICE EARL WARREN

Earl Warren (1891–1974) became the 14th Chief Justice of the United States in October 1953. The former governor of California was the 1948 Republican vice presidential candidate and a rival to Dwight D. Eisenhower for the 1952 Republican presidential nomination. Some considered Warren's 1953 appointment as chief justice a political payoff. Whatever the case, he found himself as chief justice spotlighted in an intensifying national drama of individual rights and race relations. Perhaps more reviled than revered, his leadership nevertheless unified the Court on public-school desegregation. His opinions in *Brown v. Board of Education* (1954) and its 1955 continuation called Brown II articulated fresh constitutional visions for the nation. The direction and reasoning offered in Warren's opinions for a unanimous Court in Brown I and II shifted the character and course of U.S. race relations. He viewed school desegregation as furthering the public interest and urged good faith compliance. He understood the momentous change the Court had decreed. He called for no miracles, only for "a prompt and reasonable start" with progress at "all deliberate speed."

[I]

The plaintiffs contend that segregated public schools are not "equal" and cannot be made "equal," and that hence they are deprived of the equal protection of the laws. . . .

In approaching this problem, we cannot turn the clock back to 1868 when the [Fourteenth] Amendment was adopted, or even to 1896 when *Plessy v. Ferguson* was written. We must consider public education in the light of its full development and its present place in American life throughout the Nation. Only in this way can it be determined if segregation in public schools deprives these plaintiffs of the equal protection of the laws.

Today, education is perhaps the most important function of state and local governments. . . . In these days, it is doubtful that any child may reasonably be expected to succeed in life if he is denied the opportunity of an education. Such an opportunity, where the state has undertaken to provide it, is a right which must be made available to all on equal terms.

We come then to the question presented: Does segregation of children in public schools solely on the basis of race, even though the physical facilities and other "tangible" factors may be equal, deprive the children of the minority group of equal educational opportunities? We believe that it does. . . .

To separate them from others of similar age and qualifications solely because of their race generates a feeling of inferiority as to their status in the community that may affect their hearts and minds in a way unlikely ever to be undone. . . .

We conclude that in the field of public education the doctrine of "separate but equal" has no place. Separate educational facilities are inherently unequal. Therefore, we hold that the plaintiffs and others similarly situated for whom the actions have been brought are, by reason of the segregation complained of, deprived of the equal protection of the laws guaranteed by the Fourteenth Amendment.

[II]

All provisions of federal, state, or local law requiring or permitting such discrimination must yield to this principle. . . .

[T]he courts will require . . . a prompt and reasonable start toward full compliance with our May 17, 1954, ruling. Once such a start has been made, the courts may find that additional time is necessary to carry out the ruling in an effective manner. . . . To that end, the courts may consider problems related to administration, arising from the physical condition of the school plant, the school transportation system, personnel, revision of school districts and attendance areas into compact units to achieve a system of determining admission to the public schools on a nonracial basis, and revision of local laws and regulations which may be necessary in solving the foregoing problems. . . .

[T]he cases are remanded to the District Courts to take such proceedings and enter such orders and decrees consistent with this opinion as are necessary and proper to admit to public schools on a racially nondiscriminatory basis with all deliberate speed the parties to these cases.

From *Brown v. Board of Education* 347 U.S. 483, 487, 492–493, 494, 495 (1954); and *Brown v. Board of Education* [*Brown II*], 349 U.S. 294, 298, 299, 300–301 (1955). (citations omitted.)

U.S. SENATOR WALTER GEORGE

Georgia Democrat U.S. Senator Walter F. George (1878–1957) on March 12, 1956, presented to Congress a statement dubbed "The Southern Manifesto." Its formal title was "Declaration of Constitutional Principles." George and 18 other senators endorsed it. So did 81 members of the U.S. House of Representatives. They repudiated the "segregation cases," as many then called *Brown v. Board of Education* (1954) and its 1955 continuation. Dubbing the Supreme Court's decisions "unwarranted" and "a clear abuse of judicial power," the endorsers articulated a southern states' rights view. Resistance was their watchword. Violence was in the offing, they said, although they pointedly counseled those whom they called "our people" to "scrupulously refrain from disorder and lawless acts." They insisted the U.S. Constitution and long custom and tradition supported their view that racial segregation was lawful, morally right, and wholly within states' rights to protect the public welfare of their people. The manifesto offered one of the fullest shorthand defenses of southern segregation.

Declaration of Constitutional Principles

The unwarranted decision of the Supreme Court in the public school cases is now bearing the fruit always produced when men substitute naked power for established law. . . .

We regard the decisions of the Supreme Court in the school cases as a clear abuse of judicial power. It climaxes a trend in the Federal Judiciary undertaking to legislate, in derogation of the authority of Congress, and to encroach upon the reserved rights of the States and the people.

The original Constitution does not mention education. Neither does the 14th Amendment nor any other amendment. The debates preceding the submission of the 14th Amendment clearly show that there was no intent that it should affect the system of education maintained by the States.

The very Congress which proposed the amendment subsequently provided for segregated schools in the District of Columbia.

When the amendment was adopted in 1868, there were 37 States of the Union. . . . Every one of the 26 States that had any substantial racial differences among its people, either approved the operation of segregated schools already in existence or subsequently established such schools by action of the same law-making body which considered the 14th Amendment. . . .

Though there has been no constitutional amendment or act of Congress changing this established legal principle almost a century old, the Supreme Court of the United States, with no legal basis for such action, undertook to exercise their naked judicial power and substituted their personal political and social ideas for the established law of the land.

This unwarranted exercise of power by the Court, contrary to the Constitution, is creating chaos and confusion in the States principally affected. It is destroying the amicable relations between the white and Negro races that have been created through 90 years of patient effort by the good people of both races. It has planted hatred and suspicion where there has been heretofore friendship and understanding. . . .

We pledge ourselves to use all lawful means to bring about a reversal of this decision which is contrary to the Constitution and to prevent the use of force in its implementation.

In this trying period, as we all seek to right this wrong, we appeal to our people not to be provoked by the agitators and troublemakers invading our States and to scrupulously refrain from disorder and lawless acts.

From 102 Cong. Rec. 4459–4460, 4515–4516 (March 12, 1956).

PRESIDENT DWIGHT D. EISENHOWER

Texas-born Dwight David Eisenhower (1890–1969), U.S. president from 1953 to 1961, sympathized with segregation. He was no fan of the Supreme Court's public-school desegregation decision in *Brown v. Board of Education* (1954). He preferred deliberation to speedy implementation and wholly disfavored any federal effort to compel desegregation. As a constitutional conservative, he held to limited federal government and broad state discretion. He wrote in his diary in July 1953 that he believed "improvement in race relations is one of those things that will be healthy and sound only if it starts locally. I do not believe that prejudices, even palpably unjustified prejudices, will succumb to compulsion."[34] Circumstances nevertheless moved Eisenhower to dispatch U.S. Army troops and to federalize the Arkansas National Guard to support desegregation in Little Rock in September 1957. He acted to vindicate the rule of law. The following excerpt offers Eisenhower's justification of his actions. It describes the contention of the day and what was publicly at stake.

WHEREAS on September 23, 1957, I issued Proclamation No. 3204 reading in part as follows:

"WHEREAS certain persons in the state of Arkansas, individually and in unlawful assemblages, combinations, and conspiracies, have wilfully obstructed the enforcement of orders of the United States District Court for the Eastern District of Arkansas with respect to matters relating to enrollment and attendance at public schools, particularly at Central High School, located in Little Rock School District, Little Rock, Arkansas; and

"WHEREAS such wilful obstruction of justice hinders the execution of the laws of that State and of the United States, and makes it impracticable to enforce such laws by the ordinary course of judicial proceedings; and

"WHEREAS such obstruction of justice constitutes a denial of the equal protection of the laws secured by the Constitution of the United States and impedes the course of justice under those laws:

"NOW, THEREFORE, I, DWIGHT D. EISENHOWER, President of the United States, under and by virtue of the authority vested in me by the Constitution and Statutes of the United States, . . . do command all persons engaged in such obstruction of justice to cease and desist therefrom, and to disperse forthwith"; and

WHEREAS the command contained in that Proclamation has not been obeyed and wilful obstruction of enforcement of said court orders still exists and threatens to continue:

NOW, THEREFORE, by virtue of the authority vested in me . . .

I hereby authorize and direct the Secretary of Defense to order into the active military service of the United States as he may deem appropriate to carry out the purposes of this Order, any or all of the units of the National Guard of the United States and of the Air National Guard of the United States within the State of Arkansas to serve in the active military service of the United States for an indefinite period and until relieved by appropriate orders.

The Secretary of Defense is authorized and directed to take all appropriate steps to enforce any orders of the United States District Court for the Eastern District of Arkansas for the removal of obstruction of justice in the State of Arkansas with respect to matters relating to enrollment and attendance at public schools in the Little Rock School District, Little Rock, Arkansas.

From Exec. Order No. 10,730, 3 C.F.R. 89 (September 24, 1957) (Desegregation of Central High School, providing assistance for the removal of an obstruction of justice within the state of Arkansas). See also *Public Papers of the Presidents of the United States: Dwight D. Eisenhower, 1954* (Washington, DC: GPO, 1960), 293.

RACE RELATIONS BY GROUP

AFRICAN AMERICANS

Blacks entered the 1950s with accelerating momentum. Their battle against racial segregation appeared quickening. Their stony road seemed tilting toward their long deferred dream of functional, not merely nominal, legal equality as U.S. citizens. They had long been Americans in name. They longed to enjoy with all others fulfilled opportunities of the renowned American Dream. They had long labored. In the decade of the 1950s, they intensified their demands to have the fruits rightfully theirs.

Blacks of all classes, rich and poor, schooled and unschooled, manual laborers and professionals, seemed to seize the time collectively in the 1950s. Their movement captured the nation's and the world's attention. They pushed hard along legal avenues. Largely through the National Association for the Advancement of Colored People (NAACP) and its Legal Defense Fund (LDF), blacks' press for their rights reached the nation's highest courts.

More and more, however, blacks took to the highways, byways, and streets. They pressed their cases directly in the court of public opinion. They pushed, in the words of the U.S. Declaration of Independence, to "let Facts be submitted to a candid world." Protesting en masse, they demonstrated undeniable terrors and troubles of American apartheid.

Blacks demanded change. Standing almost exactly as 1-in-10 Americans, they were the nation's single largest racial minority in 1950. The census counted them as 15,042,286 persons. Marching in the forefront then, they carried a broad banner. With other racialized groups, they asked for no favors. They urged no special treatment. They pressed simply to be treated equally under the law. They wanted to vote. They wanted their voices listened to, like others, on public issues. They wanted jobs. They wanted the same pay as others who did the same work. They wanted to be allowed to work where they shopped and to shop where they worked. They wanted to get the same service others received for the money they paid.

When they bought a ticket or paid a fare, blacks wanted the same opportunity for service and a seat. They wanted to live where they could afford, not where they were confined. They wanted their children to have access to the same quality public schooling seemingly reserved for white children. They wanted full access to public facilities built and maintained with their taxes, and often with their labor. In short, blacks demanded discrimination's stultifying load off their backs.

Their drive did not suddenly start in the 1950s. It stretched back before the nation's beginning. It ran with slavery's tearful centuries. It developed in unrelenting discrimination. Its direction was not new. It repeated timeworn petitions for basic rights. They had been heard from time to time, but seldom heeded. Yet blacks persisted. Their patience was legendary. In the post-World War II era, impatience increasingly characterized their mood. The running sores of segregation seemed finally festering beyond bearing in the 1950s.

Blacks' strengthening push in the 1950s carried over from the 1940s. They continued their World War II "Double V Campaign" for democracy's victory abroad and at home. President Harry S Truman lent a hand. He pushed Congress on civil rights. When it balked, he forged ahead. For example, as commander-in-chief he ordered the U.S. Armed Forces to desegregate. They complained but slowly began to comply in the 1950s. Over time the military would create broad avenues for black mobility.

The U.S. Supreme Court, too, responded to blacks' push against segregation. Under Chief Justice Earl Warren's direction it shouldered a significant load in the work to eliminate race-based public policies and practices. Even before Warren joined it in October 1953, the Court had begun hefting the burden. In June 1950 it issued back-to-back decisions limiting states' rights to exclude blacks from public educational opportunities at the postgraduate level.

In May 1954 the Court ruled on basic primary and secondary public schools. It directly confronted segregation's controlling legal doctrine. Described as "separate but equal," the theory sanctioned in the Court's 1896 *Plessy v. Ferguson* decision allowed states to use separate schools for whites and nonwhites. Chief Justice Warren's opinion for a unanimous Court sweepingly declared, "We conclude that in the field of public education the doctrine of 'separate but equal' has no place. Separate educational facilities are inherently unequal."[35]

Simple pronouncements were not going to suffice. Shifting from segregated schools, indeed shifting from segregation itself, promised diehard battles. The frontlines lay in the South. The citadel of antebellum slavery refused to retreat from its culture and legalized structure of segregation. Encounters flared almost everywhere. Everything seemed a racial issue. As the school segregation cases indicated, public services became the central contested arena.

Even before the *Brown* decision, the 1953 Baton Rouge Bus Boycott illustrated the intransigence. White bus drivers in Louisiana's capital flatly refused to abide by a February 1953 compromise opening seating on city buses. A new ordinance approached, but did not fully allow, first-come first-served seating. It directed whites to take seats starting in the front and blacks to start in the back. As the bus filled, whoever had a seat got to keep it. Blacks would not have to yield to whites. But bus drivers rejected the rule. Insisting on traditional supremacy, white drivers ordered blacks to give up seats to whites. Tired of being left standing, blacks boycotted.

As 70 percent of the Baton Rouge Bus Company's fares, black riders made their absence felt. They edged the company toward bankruptcy. Their pressure ultimately ended white supremacy on the city's buses in June 1953. Their bold steps opened fresh directions. As one boycotter noted, "we could see a change coming, and this was the beginning of it."[36]

The more heralded 381-day Montgomery Bus Boycott in Alabama's capital from December 1955 to December 1956 elevated to national prominence Mrs. Rosa Parks and the young Reverend Martin Luther King Jr. They pushed

Left to right: Rosa Parks, Eleanor Roosevelt, and Autherine Lucy, before a civil rights rally at Madison Square Garden in New York City, 1956. Courtesy of the Library of Congress, cph 3c11444.

forward in the direction the Reverend T. J. Jemison of Baton Rouge's Mount Carmel Baptist Church, the black-organized United Defense League, and the rank-and-file, real heroes of the 1953 Baton Rouge boycott pointed.

Black boycotts of city buses stretched back to the struggle for equal access to transportation that produced the 1896 *Plessy* decision. Blacks lost there. In the 1950s, they won. The Supreme Court outlawed segregation on municipal buses and other intrastate public transportation in *Gayle v. Browder* (1956), a case arising from the Montgomery Bus Boycott. To start the decade, the Court had outlawed discrimination in interstate transportation in *Henderson v. United States* (1950). Throughout the decade, the Court repeatedly chipped away at the base and extensions of de jure segregation.

To vindicate their rights to equal access, blacks put life and limb on the line. Frighteningly for black parents, to desegregate schools they sometimes had to put their children in jeopardy. The desegregation crisis in Little Rock, Arkansas, in September 1957, illustrated the danger. Governor Orval Faubus and other officials' obstruction forced President Dwight D. Eisenhower to order U.S. 101st Airborne troops to protect the first black students to attend Central High School.

African American student Elizabeth Eckford endures
epithets outside Central High School in Little Rock,
Arkansas, 1957. National Guardsman in upper left
of photo. Courtesy of the Library of Congress, cph
3c26826.

Public schools became a primary battleground. The Supreme Court's 1955
direction for schools to desegregate "with all deliberate speed" gave rise to
massive white resistance. Blacks refused to be turned around, however. They
persisted to vindicate their rights. Even the U.S. Congress grudgingly came
around. In September 1957, it enacted the first federal civil rights legislation
since the 1870s. But, again, as blacks well knew, gaining legal backing was only
another step, not the end of their stony road.

AMERICAN INDIANS

The 1950s saw the full force of the so-called termination policy long pushed
against American Indians in many circles. It advanced a desire to wash America's hands of Indians. The 1946 Indian Claims Commission Act had already
signaled the direction. Termination sought to finish the course. It aimed to end
Indians' federal status. It rode high on a wave of intolerance for things considered

un-American. That included cultural diversity. Conservative calls to curb federal spending also carried it forward. Western congressmen, such as Senators Richard Neuberger (Democrat, Oregon) and Arthur Watkins (Republican, Utah), pushed termination to advance their constituents' interests in grabbing Indian-held resources, especially minerals and water. They succeeded. Congress enacted and implemented termination in August 1953 with two measures, House Concurrent Resolution 108 and Public Law 280.

Termination positioned Indians to be recognized only as individuals, like any other U.S. citizens. It moved to cease federal recognition of tribes. It supplanted tribal authority and jurisdiction. It moved to do away with America's approximately 250 Indian reservations. The lands and people in what U.S. law quaintly called "Indian country" would fall under state jurisdiction where they were. In rough summary, termination directed the United States to "get out of the Indian business."[37]

Indians across the United States entered the 1950s then having to fight again for their tribal lives. It was an old battle. The bloody ground stretched back at least a generation before the U.S. Civil War (1861–1865). The early action came to a head in the 1830s. States asserting unilateral authority over Indian tribes within their borders provoked a constitutional crisis. President Andrew Jackson acknowledged the problem in December 1829, in his first State of the Union address. He pointed specifically to Georgia and Alabama. "These states, claiming to be the only sovereigns within their territories [had] extended their laws over the Indians," he noted.[38]

Jackson sided with the states. His clear sympathies lay with Georgia. The future Peach State had taken the lead in asserting states' rights against Indians. It pressed its authority particularly against the largest and most prosperous tribe within its borders—the Cherokee. Pointing to their treaty relations with the United States, the Cherokee Nation and other Indians refused to yield to state authority. As independent sovereigns, Indian tribes claimed immunity from state interference. Moreover, the tribes invoked repeated assurances of federal protection of their sovereignty.

The early 1830s' confrontation produced two of the Supreme Court's foundational rulings on U.S. law controlling Indians. Among the issues *Cherokee Nation v. Georgia* (1831) and *Worcester v. Georgia* (1832) settled as constitutional doctrine was that states had no authority on Indian lands. Both Georgia and President Jackson spurned the ruling. Neither the Cherokee nor any other Indians found any immediate solace, for although the Court's ruling may have settled legal theory, it did little to control actual practice.

Raw relations between states and tribes appeared destined to fester. President Jackson predicted as much. He warned in 1829 that Indian tribes could not exist as separate sovereigns within states. That would only create persistent problems between tribes, the states, and the federal government, he suggested. If Indians remained within states, then they must at some point "submit to the laws of those States," Jackson insisted.[39]

The president's general prescription for future Indian tribal peace and security lay essentially in tribes' going away or ceasing to be tribes. The future for Indians in his view lay in their ceasing to be identifiable as Indians. "Submitting to the laws of the States, and receiving, like other citizens, protection in their persons and property, they will ere long become merged in the mass of our population," Jackson proposed.[40] That was the path to the future he insisted in the 1830s. Congress and President Dwight D. Eisenhower agreed in the 1950s. They endorsed Jackson's old prescription as the path of Indians' present and future.

Old rhetoric resounded in termination policy. It clearly echoed Jackson's assimilationist call for Indians to be "merged into the mass of our population." Yet it appeared to many more like annihilation. It pushed entry into the great American melting pot not so much to make Indians harmoniously one with America but to reduce them to invisibility.

If termination had its way, there would be no identifiable Indians left from the 343,410 the U.S. Census counted in 1950. Federal trusteeship with tribes would end. Indeed, no officially recognized tribes would exist. Before the decade ended, Congress in fact terminated 61 of the approximately 500 federally recognized tribes and bands. It started with the Klamath of Oregon and Menominee of Wisconsin. It later reached 109 tribes and bands before reversing course.

Termination policy promised to end all official Indian government. So Indian reservations would close. The 61 tribes terminated in six states in the 1950s illustrated the process. They were removed from their lands. Many were sent to cities. As part of the larger process, the federal Bureau of Indian Affairs (BIA) set up 12 relocation centers between 1952 and 1957, but these served perhaps only one-in-four of the 100,000 Indians who relocated in the decade before 1957. The effort reflected the pro-termination rhetoric of "freeing" Indians from federal dependency.

Being released from restrictions and being abandoned were hardly the same. BIA services to help Indians make the transition from open plains tepees to urban skyscrapers might have appeared comic if the outcomes were not so tragic. As bad as reservations were, U.S. cities proved even more disastrous for many Indians. Urban Indians usually became more destitute and disillusioned than their reservation brethren. They tended to become jobless, homeless, and sick. Dumped with inadequate support, the dispersed tribal members were left to sink or swim. That was the sort of assimilation termination produced.

The policy proved another rejection of Indians. Under the guise of liberating Indians, termination "implied the ultimate destruction of tribal cultures and native life-styles, as withdrawal of federal services was intended to desegregate Indian communities and to integrate Indians with the rest of society," in the words of an Indian analyst.[41] The policy was hardly realistic. It neglected Indians' pressing needs for economic development. It gave short shrift to their general welfare, public education, and their physical and psychic health.

Termination ignored the confines of American apartheid. A cemetery in Sioux City, Iowa, showed how deeply the discrimination cut in the 1950s. It refused to bury U.S. Army Sergeant John Rice, killed in action in the Korean War (1950–1953), because he was an Indian. Perhaps more tellingly, although recognized as

U.S. citizens in 1924, Indians stood in many states deprived of basic civil rights. Voting discrimination remained rampant in the 1950s, for instance. At least six states proffered constitutional arguments to disfranchise Indians. Utah, for example, denied Indians the vote claiming they were not state residents. It did not relent until 1957, when it became the last state to formally enfranchise Indians.

Terminationists took no account of Indian self-determination. They dictated policy. That outraged Indians. They uniformly denounced the process, which long lingered as a bitter memory. In complicated tribal politics, most—but, notably, not all—also opposed the policy itself. None craved federal dependency. Dispute arose primarily on how to maintain tribal integrity. Private enterprise rather than public largess appealed to tribes with decent development prospects. No one size fit all. Yet termination pushed Indians collectively to step up their efforts at independent self-determination. It pointed the way to a coming surge dubbed "Red Power."

ASIAN AMERICANS

Asian Americans took major steps forward in the 1950s. Accelerating post-World War II developments pushed their growth. Numbering 321,033 in 1950, they began an unprecedented increase as part of the U.S. population. During the decade they moved toward doubling. Over the next 30 years they would increase more than 10-fold.

Natural increase from American-born generations contributed significantly to the growth. Perhaps even more significantly, new immigrants from Asia and the Pacific Islands began flowing into America on a rising tide. Relaxed U.S. immigration restrictions, particularly openings for refugees, fed the flow in the 1950s. The extensions of U.S. empire broadened the stream. So did America's acting as something of a global policeman amid cold war strife. Unrest in East Asia also directed immigrants to America. Displaced persons from China, Korea, India, Indochina, and other unsettled Asian places sought U.S. shores in small but growing numbers.

Demographics made telling impact. Public perceptions, nevertheless, continued to clumsily frame race relations for Asian Americans in the 1950s. Despite growing diversity, a Chinese face persisted as the popular image of all Asian Americans. While the oldest and largest group among Asian Americans, Chinese Americans were hardly alone or typical. Moreover, popular perceptions seldom recognized wide cultural, ethnic, and language differences among Asian Americans. Class differences were almost wholly ignored.

Popular images of Asian Americans reflected something of a cannot-tell-them-apart, if-you-have-seen-one-you-have-seen-them-all perspective. Also, popular perceptions of Asian Americans only rarely distinguished between recent immigrants and long-settled or U.S.-born Americans. That mistake plagued Hispanic Americans, too. It heightened immigration as a cause of anxiety among Asian Americans, as it did among Hispanic Americans. Backlash against recent arrivals or immigrants in general hit long-term Asian Americans who happened to share regional connections, physical features, or ethnic heritage with the more immediate targets of popular ire.

Yet increasingly in the 1950s, two contradictory glimpses of Asian Americans flitted in the U.S. popular views. One had an international perspective. It lent to distinguishing among Asian Americans. As unrest shifted the spotlight, individual nationalities came into sharper focus in the United States. For example, the end of the British Raj in the Asian subcontinent had elevated attention to Asian Americans from India in the 1940s. Turmoil following the creation of the Republic of India and the partitioning of Pakistan and eventually of Bangladesh sustained focus in the 1950s.

Mao Zedong's declaration of the Communist People's Republic of China in October 1949 sharpened focus on Chinese Americans. So did its continuing struggles with the Republic of China. Tensions over the island of Taiwan and its associated territories made China almost everyday news during the 1950s. The Korean War (1950–1953) added to the focus on China. Also, it sharpened focus on Korean Americans. U.S. international involvements in Asia throughout the remainder of the twentieth century would increase U.S. popular information about Asian Americans, while also increasing their numbers in the United States.

The second flitting glimpse reflected more domestic perspectives. Despite clear images of diversity, popular U.S. perceptions in the 1950s frequently held out Asian Americans as a monolithic model racial minority. They stood separated as a special case. Attention often emphasized their economic and other marks of achievement. They commonly appeared in the image of astute, frugal, hardworking entrepreneurs. They appeared as uniformly prosperous, never as poor. Attention frequently contrasted them with other racialized minorities. If they could succeed, why not others, such as blacks noted for their relatively low comparative economic progress? Asian Americans became touted in some views as showing U.S. racial barriers were not insurmountable, if they existed at all.

Yet the common view cast Asian Americans as perpetual strangers, not as true Americans. Common misconceptions stereotyped their appearance, customs, and speech as un-American. It imputed to them unassimilable heritages. It crowded them into clannish urban enclaves that sheltered dark subcultures. It imputed to them strong crime elements. Indeed, popular perceptions often vilified Asian Americans as gangster-ish exploiters of their own people and other Americans.

Rarely did popular images show Asian Americans' general Americanness. They ignored similarities, for example, between Asian immigrants and European immigrants. Their ethnic enclaves seldom appeared comparable. Yet, in fact, immigrant experiences, whether from Asia or Europe, shared much. Discrimination persisting to the point of persecution made Asian Americans' experience different as racial minorities. Yet their activities, aspirations, and organization often followed a common American pattern.

As the single largest group among Asian Americans, Chinese Americans continued their group protest leadership in the 1950s. Historically, they had been first to organize. The Chinese Equal Rights League that Wong Chin Foo founded led the way. It arose to combat virulent exclusionism in California in the 1870s. Groups such as the Chinese American Citizens Alliance and the Chinese Hand Laundry Association of New York followed in that tradition in the 1950s. They pushed general and specific agenda.

Japanese Americans had similar organizations. The Japanese American Citizens League, founded in 1929, was in the 1950s probably the largest Asian American civil rights organization. Various other national and ethnic groups among Asian Americans also maintained their separate organizations. They struggled in common cause for civil rights, but in the 1950s they had not yet joined together under a significant umbrella Asian American advocacy organization.

In the political arena, Asian Americans emerged as national players in the 1950s. In November 1956, Dalip Singh Saund—a 57-year-old Sikh from India's Punjab—became the first Asian American elected to the U.S. Congress. Winning California's 29th congressional district seat, Saund drew attention to Asian Americans as a political presence with both domestic and international bearing. Asian Americans could function at home and abroad as symbols of U.S. ideals, Saund suggested. "It just demonstrates that American democracy is real," he said of his election. And making foreign linkages, he said further, "I honestly hope that I shall contribute to removing misunderstanding between the people of the United States and India."[42]

The single greatest political boost for Asian Americans came in a stroke at the end of the decade. In August 1959, Hawaii became the 50th state. Its overwhelmingly Asian American/Pacific Islander population almost assured the group of national attention and impact. The island chain immediately provided the first Asian American U.S. senator. The then 52-year-old Chinese American Hiram L. Fong joined Rep. Saund in Congress. So did Daniel Ken Inouye, as the first Japanese American in the U.S. House of Representatives.

Many touted both Fong and Inouye as American success stories. Both were World War II U.S. Army veterans. Indeed, Inouye won the Congressional Medal of Honor for extraordinary bravery in battle, where he lost his right arm. Both became lawyers. Inouye graduated from George Washington University Law School in Washington, D.C. Fong graduated from Harvard Law School. Both shared a hardworking, populist ethos. "I am a product of the American public school system, a product of the American way of life," Fong exulted. "I hope the American people will see my life as symbolic of the opportunity offered only in a democratic society such as ours," he added.[43]

"Being the only non-Caucasian senator, and coming from a state which lives the principle of democracy, it is natural to assume that I will fight against anything that interferes with civil rights," Fong pledged.[44] He there acknowledged more than his unique position as a Chinese American. He gave voice to the common cause of all Asian Americans and other racialized minorities. Senator Fong signaled Asian Americans' growing political presence and also the expanding significance of U.S. attention to its race relations as a matter of domestic and international necessity. Becoming a U.S. senator himself, Inouye would long persist in the extraordinary service that won him the highest U.S. military decoration.

HISPANIC AMERICANS/LATINOS

The 1950s proved a pivotal decade for Hispanic Americans. They moved beyond local and regional attention. Increasingly visible outside California and the Southwest, Hispanics became a national focus. Indeed, in many Americans' eyes Hispanics became a national problem. They joined the "Indian problem" and the "Negro problem." Their growing numbers threatened Americans who hugged homogenized images of America and its people. Often popular stereotypes cast Hispanics as different in religion, language, culture, and class. They stood in many popular views as un-American, and in many places they were largely unwelcome.

Yet the decade yielded significant distinctions. Perhaps primary was the emerging disparate identities of the many peoples lumped as "Hispanic." The single stone face with chiseled Mexican features fell away in significant part in the 1950s. Puerto Ricans and Cubans particularly drew attention that marked them apart among Spanish-speaking peoples.

Entertainers and sports figures helped give a face to differences. Cuban-born actor-musician Desi Arnaz became a U.S. household personality. His work with his wife actress-comedian Lucille Ball made their television show *I Love Lucy* a smash. Puerto Rican-born actor José Ferrer distinguished himself in movies. Baseball players added to the mix. Venezuelan-born shortstops Alfonso "Chico" Carrasquel of the Chicago White Sox and Luis Aparicio of the Baltimore Orioles became stars in Major League Baseball. So did Puerto Rican outfielder Roberto Clemente of the Pittsburgh Pirates. (He would in 1973 become the first Hispanic American elected to baseball's Hall of Fame in Cooperstown, New York.)

Public attention could no longer fix simply on Mexico as the source of Hispanic Americans. By 1950 Puerto Ricans had become a significant presence in New York City. The direct airline connection from San Juan, the Caribbean island's capital and main city, accounted for their immediate location. Shortly, they would make New York City second only to San Juan in Puerto Rican population. They spread to the remainder of the Northeast. New Jersey, Massachusetts, Pennsylvania, and Connecticut developed significant Puerto Rican populations. So in time did Washington, D.C., Chicago, Los Angeles, and major Florida cities such as Miami and Tampa.

Florida would become more Cuban territory. That began in the late 1950s. Unrest with Cuban strongman Fulgencio Bautista, and then with insurgent Fidel Castro, pushed Cuban refugees to their nearest U.S. landfall. The opening waves of those fleeing the Caribbean's largest island came with significant assets. Politics pushed them, not poverty as with Puerto Ricans.

Those from the island Puerto Ricans fondly called *Borikén* in the aboriginal native tongue, or *Borinquen* in the Spanish, were certainly not without politics. They had issues aplenty. Many viewed unhappily what they saw as U.S. colonial

Desi Arnaz behind the camera, 1958. Courtesy of the
Library of Congress, cph 3c16050.

domination. Two Puerto Rican nationalists demonstrated their displeasure on
November 1, 1950. With guns blazing, they stormed the temporary presidential
residence at Blair House, across Pennsylvania Avenue from the White House
then undergoing long-term renovations.

The attackers killed one Secret Service guard and wounded two others. In
turn one of them was killed. "We came here with the express purpose of shooting
the President," the surviving assailant reportedly confessed.[45] President Harry S
Truman witnessed a bit of the action from a second-floor bedroom window. The
Secret Service said he was never in danger.

Tried for the killing of the White House guard, the 37-year-old surviving Puerto
Rican assailant stood unrepentant. "I did it for a just cause, for the liberty and
independence of my people," he declared in a District of Columbia courtroom on
being sentenced in April 1951 to die in the electric chair.[46]

Many shook their heads at the Puerto Ricans' clamor for independence. Congress had granted the island self-government in July 1950, after all. And Puerto
Ricans had U.S. citizenship since 1917. So what was their grievance? Could they
really be pushing to separate from the United States when hundreds of thousands
or, by some reports, millions, of Hispanics were clawing for entry by any means,
legal or illegal?

Lolita Lebron, Puerto Rican nationalist leader, being led to
a police car by two officers following her arrest in the shooting of five congressmen in the House of Representatives,
1954. Courtesy of the Library of Congress, cph 3c25396.

On March 1, 1954, another group of Puerto Rican nationalists punctuated their
point. Spraying the U.S. House of Representatives with gunfire from a visitors gal-
lery, they wounded five congressmen. Most Americans rejected any claim Congress
was "the body responsible for the military intervention of the United States in
Puerto Rico for more than fifty years," as Puerto Rican nationalists declared.[47]

The image of the United States' suppressing independence or human rights
was simply foreign to most Americans. Some saw the Puerto Rican attacks as
communist-inspired. They accepted the attacks with other conspiracy theories
citing communists as the source of unrest among U.S. racial minorities. Most
Americans, certainly most whites, scorned any image of the United States as
other than benevolent. They rejected charges of discrimination in actions such
as "Operation Wetback."

The Immigration and Naturalization Service (INS) dragnet launched in June
1954 aimed to deport hundreds of thousands of alleged undocumented persons to
Mexico. The roundup recalled the 1930s "Mexican Repatriation" that deported
or "voluntarily repatriated" to Mexico perhaps as many as 2 million persons of

Mexican ancestry, although approximately 1.2 million were native-born U.S. citizens.[48]

The U.S. Supreme Court in May 1954 acknowledged systemic discrimination against Mexican Americans and other Hispanics. It noted their peculiar racialized status. Officially categorized as "whites," they were routinely segregated like nonwhites. The Court pronounced its finding in reviewing Mexican American Pete Hernández's appeal of his indictment and conviction for murder. The record indisputably showed Texas treated Mexican Americans as "a distinct class." It had by its "laws, as written or as applied, singled out that class for different treatment not based on some reasonable classification." And in doing so, "the guarantees of the Constitution have been violated," Chief Justice Earl Warren emphasized for the unanimous Court.[49]

The Court's *Hernandez* ruling recognized equal protection claims the League of United Latin American Citizens (LULAC) and other Hispanics had long pushed. Reversing long practice, however, required more than court decisions. So Hispanics increasingly exercised their muscle in the direction of effective political mobilization.

Hispanics in the 1950s sat with little direct, substantive official representation. Despite their significant numbers in localities, particularly in California and the Southwest, they had only a weak voice, if any, in public councils. Their underrepresentation was historic. In most places, it was simply nonrepresentation. Like blacks and other nonwhites, Hispanics found that entrenched structures of power shut them out.

In some areas, Hispanics suffered worse discrimination than any other group. On average, they earned lower wages than anyone else. Reflecting their varied backgrounds, distinct groups among Hispanics occupied different rungs on the wage ladder. Cuban men did best. They alone among Hispanics earned more than black males. Mexicans earned least. Age, education (including English fluency), region, and economic sector affected earnings. Beyond all other factors, discrimination stood steadfast. The distance between European-featured Cubans and darker, Indian-featured Mexicans illustrated American preferences.

Both color and culture made a difference. Caribbean Hispanics, such as Puerto Ricans and Cubans, struggled with multiple minority effects. Race, religion, heritage, language, ethnicity, and class all distinguished them. Whether stuck in developing urban barrios or in rural areas, Hispanics faced restricted access to services. Systemic discrimination especially limited their educational opportunities. To the degree schooling laid the basis for life achievement, such limited access cut off Hispanic prospects.

Growing numbers throughout the 1950s and beyond shifted Hispanics' life situations, structural relations, and even group references. The term *Hispanic*, itself, began giving way. The historic pointer to Spain and European origins had long since lost general accuracy. Fresh migrations marked directions from south of the United States. They signaled Latinos. Rising voices further insisted on more individual identities. Calls arose also among some to be known separately as Chicanos. New immigrants particularly resisted the old lumping. They increasingly demanded self-determined identities.

EUROPEAN AMERICANS

White Americans swaggered into the 1950s. The United States was number one in the world, and they were number one in the United States. They ruled the roost in the world's dominant military power with its atomic bombs, and they directed its world-dominant economic engine. U.S. production and consumption paced the world. Unprecedented abundance flowed throughout the nation. To much of the rest of the world, and at home, too, Americans appeared a people of plenty, an affluent society. And the color of that rich appearance was almost uniformly white.

America's position was not entirely soothing. The nation's shining success belied emotional and moral turmoil. Its skyrocketing wealth did not reach everywhere. The stark contrast of private opulence and public poverty usually appeared in its traditional nonwhite image. That produced sore spots. Nonwhites' agitation over inequality rubbed many whites raw. More than nonwhites stood without equitable shares. As most Americans were white, most poor Americans also were white. Being left behind made many poor whites edgy. It aroused their needs to distinguish themselves. For many that meant distancing themselves from nonwhites, especially blacks.

The distancing effect compounded residential segregation. White Americans with means headed for the suburbs in the 1950s. They left U.S. cities mostly to less fortunate whites and to nonwhites. That was particularly so in the nation's industrial centers. The World War II boom in the 1940s had expanded urban populations. It especially attracted nonwhites. In the 1950s, notably in the Northeast and Midwest, center cities remained places to work, but they became less and less places for whites to live, shop, or socialize. Urban neighborhoods changed color and character. As nonwhites moved in, whites moved out. No group surpassed blacks as blockbusters. Few whites willingly lived in neighborhoods with any sizable number of blacks.

Suburbs seemed havens. They grew initially as residences for a homogenous white middle-class. Their traditional character acted as a beacon in the 1950s. Drawing to their exclusivity those who could afford it, suburbs sheltered a range of whites. Leaving the city allowed them to leave nonwhites elsewhere. If they grudgingly had to accept them where they worked, they did not have to where they lived. They could simply avoid where nonwhites lived. And they did so, rolling by in relative privacy as automobiles replaced old streetcars and trolleys as the primary means to and from work.

Suburbs offered social and spatial distance only for a relative few. Some blue-collar settlements sprouted. Old ethnic enclaves persisted. Elsewhere in the 1950s, whites found their old arm's length distance with nonwhites shrinking uncomfortably. Southern cities came to symbolize the growing tensions of the times. From Atlanta to Baltimore, Baton Rouge, Birmingham, Houston, Jackson, Little Rock, Montgomery, Richmond, Selma, St. Louis, and places in between, the South in the 1950s became the violent center for clashing visions of U.S. race relations.

Schools rather than homes sat as the ignition point for eruptions over whites' privileged exclusivity. Feeling blacks insistently encroaching, many southern whites already had their resistance up in the 1950s. Challenges to school segregation escalated their anger. Touching children, as it did, the issue reached tender emotions. That helped make the U.S. Supreme Court's May 1954 decision in *Brown v. Board of Education* so explosive.

Outlawing traditional southern separation of white children from black children in public schools disturbed many whites whose core beliefs rested on racial distance. Kentucky's *Louisville Courier Journal* described the *Brown* decision as "'a mortal blow' to Old South dogma." The lily-white University of Virginia's *Cavalier Daily* declared, "we feel that the people of the South are justified in their bitterness concerning this decision. To many people," the student newspaper explained, "this decision is contrary to a way of life and violates the way in which they have thought since 1619."[50]

Many southern whites simply rebuffed racial change. They dismissed federal court-ordered school desegregation. To resisters, the U.S. Supreme Court's 1955 implementation order in *Brown II* for "all deliberate speed" meant standing fast.

And they were quick also to hold the line elsewhere. They refused blacks equal access everywhere. They vowed segregation forever. It would become no lost cause, if they could help it. They persisted with their old-line "separate," fully understanding it was not "equal." If segregation left blacks, or other nonwhites, without effective access to public facilities so be it. If blacks and others could not vote, or hold certain jobs, or live in certain places that was nothing more than the nature of things. Segregationists declared themselves unwilling to change.

Many southern whites savaged blacks. In coded language smacking of the 1800s, they denounced blacks who protested segregation as "uppity," "pushy," and "forgetting their place." They raged also at the federal government. Their massive resistance spilled beyond the 1950s. The issue reached the core of how they saw themselves. It was about who they thought they were. Views of race formed their individual and collective identities. Race was a natural basis of community in their self-centered vision.

In the view of many whites in the South and throughout America, race relations flowed from nature and culture. They turned on personal values. They were community matters. If race relations were governmental in any way, they were local. At most, they were matters for states. The federal government had no proper role in race relations, resistive whites decreed. They denounced intervention from the nation's capital as interference. They particularly vilified the Supreme Court.

Members of Congress led the damnation. "We regard the decision of the Supreme Court in the school cases as clear abuse of judicial power," declared the Southern Manifesto of March 1956. In all, 19 senators and 81 representatives signed the resolution. They pledged themselves "to use all lawful means to bring about a reversal of this decision which is contrary to the Constitution and to prevent the use of force in its implementation." They counseled against "disorder and lawless acts."[51]

Arkansas's Governor Orval Faubus, its legislature, and other state officials in September 1957 blatantly defied U.S. law. They forcefully blocked black students from attending previously all-white public schools in Little Rock. Their defiance forced President Dwight D. Eisenhower, against his instincts and erstwhile judgment, to order U.S. 101st Airborne troops to protect the first black students to attend the Arkansas capital's Central High School.

In and out of schools, whites battled desegregation throughout the 1950s and beyond. They fought over parks and other public facilities, including local and interstate transportation. They clashed over eating places, amusements, and neighborhoods. Their battle lines seemingly stretched in all directions. Their resistance characterized their views of race relations.

Many saw race relations as a zero-sum game. And it was more than black-and-white. In their view, it was whites against nonwhites. They spurned American Indians, Asian Americans, and Hispanic Americans, too. Reviving nativism, many also opposed immigrants. Some saw their fight as that of true Americans against all others. They denounced the desegregation push as part of a communist-inspired conspiracy to corrupt the character of America.

LAW AND GOVERNMENT

Changing race relations marked deep tensions in U.S. law and government during the 1950s. Following momentum from the 1940s, nonwhites pressed forward with increasing insistence during the decade. They protested being relegated to second-class citizenship or being denied access to citizenship at all. Their protest focused on public policies. It centered on what government was doing or not doing. It put U.S. law itself on trial.

While his successor, Dwight D. Eisenhower, shied from race issues, President Harry S Truman put issues of racial inequity onto the national agenda before leaving office in 1953. Congress generally rebuffed his leadership. Its influential southern contingent filibustered or otherwise blocked civil rights initiatives throughout much of the decade. Congress exercised its own initiatives on race-related issues, however, often negatively.

The Indian termination policy was a prime example of congressional retrenchment. Beginning in August 1953, Congress moved to sever Indians' federal status. It initiated an end to federal recognition of Indian tribes and groups. It laid siege against tribal sovereignty. It cut funding for traditional federal Indian programs. It pushed to dismiss Indians from American public life or at least from being what many perceived as a federal problem.

Last couple to be married under public law 717, which made possible more than 1,300 G.I.–Japanese marriages, 1951. Courtesy of the Library of Congress, cph 3b32331.

Congress retrenched immigration policy. The Displaced Persons Act of 1950 extended post-World War II narrow openings in immigration. It accommodated 200,000 refugees and other displaced persons. Congress allowed entry to another 200,000 in 1953 and more in later years, responding to events such as the failed 1956 Hungarian Revolution and Fidel Castro's 1959 Cuban Revolution. The refugee total reached 600,000 during the decade. Overwhelmingly, most granted entry were Europeans. Only in 1953 did Congress extend refugee status to non-Europeans, largely in response to the Korean War (1950–1953).

Congress in the 1950s finally rescinded its pre-World War II ban against Asian immigrants. It further lifted the bar against Asians becoming naturalized U.S. citizens. Yet anti-Asian bias persisted in immigration law. The 1952 McCarran-Walter Immigration and Nationality Act reiterated the 1924 quota system. It divided the world into zones and allotted racialized quotas. It counted ancestry and appearance, not necessarily the place from which persons entered America. The act offered only token quotas for Asians. The paltry annual allowance of 105 ethnic Chinese immigrants worldwide well illustrated the contemptibly small numbers. Congress did allow entry of so-called Asian war brides. So Asian wives and children of U.S. citizens gained entry without quota restrictions.

Significantly, the 1952 act imposed no quota on immigrants born in the Western Hemisphere. Yet the federal government hardly welcomed immigrants from south of the border. In fact, the Immigration and Naturalization Service (INS) launched "Operation Wetback" in June 1954 to drive many Hispanics out of America. The dragnet operated largely in California, Texas, Arizona, and New Mexico. The ostensible targets were illegal immigrants; however, anyone who appeared Mexican or Latino fell under suspicion.

The INS claimed its 1954 sweep removed 1.3 million persons. As in the so-called Mexican Repatriation during the Great Depression of the 1930s, tens of thousands of those expelled by fear or force were American-born, U.S. citizens. The move hardly halted the chain migration of undocumented workers from south of the border. U.S. officials appeared to recognize the fact. They appeared to act more in a political show than to actually stop the cross-border traffic. Powerful interests, particularly western agri-businesses, greatly profited from cheap labor illegals provided. So long as jobs beckoned, immigrants would continue to come however they could.

Immigration, whether illegal or legal, proved a growing issue in the 1950s. It significantly affected race relations as it focused attention again on recurring questions of American identity. Whom to admit and how many were big questions. Answers varied sharply. Some persisted in advocating an old vision of America as a white man's land. They favored admitting only, or mostly, northern and western Europeans. Others shunned all immigrants, preferring a nation of native-born Americans. Still others suggested some immigrants were incapable of becoming American.

Nevada U.S. Senator Patrick A. McCarran articulated several restrictionist themes. A prime mover on immigration law during the 1950s, he argued that "we have in the United States today hard-core, indigestible blocs which have not become integrated into the American way of life, but which, on the contrary are its deadly enemies."[52] He moved to bar entry as much as possible. Moreover, the 1952 act bearing McCarran's name authorized federal agents to deport aliens and even naturalized citizens for "subversive activities."[53] The mix of ideology and immigration brimmed with issues of identity. It spilled over against those colored as politically and culturally undesirable.

Contested immigration policy reflected rampant fears of change. Indeed, the nation seemed to be battling schizophrenia. Part clung to an oppressive orthodoxy. Its conservative stance turned from painful realities toward idealized traditional relations. It sought to turn from an increasingly colorful America to a pale past. Nonwhites resisted such retrenchment. Blacks especially lost patience with segregation that by law and practice relegated them to the nation's rear.

Changing law and practice to accommodate blacks' and other nonwhites' demands for equal treatment did more than roil the nation's vaunted social serenity.

Neither President Eisenhower nor the Congress championed such change, however. For most of the 1950s America's executive and legislative branches stood firmly for the racial status quo. In contrast, federal courts emerged in the forefront of changing race relations.

The Supreme Court found itself in the lead on the national stage. Following precedents developing particularly since the 1930s, the Court confronted segregation. Indeed, it opened the 1950s with three landmark decisions against racial discrimination. In *Sweatt v. Painter* and *McLaurin v. Oklahoma State Regents*, both treating public postgraduate schooling, the Court prohibited states from denying blacks benefits provided whites with the same educational qualifications. Such a denial based on race, Chief Justice Fred M. Vinson explained for a unanimous Court, violated the Fourteenth Amendment's Equal Protection Clause. On the same day, June 5, 1950, the unanimous Court struck down segregation in interstate transportation. In *Henderson v. United States*, Justice Harold H. Burton upheld the individual "right to be free from unreasonable discriminations."[54]

In its 1950 rulings that public services must be made available on equal terms to all in America, the Court shied away from confronting *Plessy v. Ferguson's* 1896 separate but equal doctrine. It simply emphasized the illegal lack of equality. The Court insisted U.S. law recognized neither color nor culture in protecting personal or political rights. Constitutional equal protection shielded all racialized groups. It reached beyond any simple black/white divide, the Court showed in May 1954.

In *Hernandez v. Texas*, the Court rebuked Texas's traditional discrimination against Mexican Americans. Texas law classified them as "white" but treated them as "a distinct class," Chief Justice Earl Warren noted. The state by its "laws, as written or as applied, singled out that class for different treatment not based on some reasonable classification," he explained. So Texas's discriminations against Mexican Americans created a situation in which "the guarantees of the Constitution have been violated," the Court ruled.[55]

The Court further demonstrated its commitment to equal protection exactly two weeks after deciding *Hernandez v. Texas*. On May 17, 1954, it issued its landmark *Brown v. Board of Education* ruling. Counted as one of the most influential decisions in U.S. history, it consolidated cases from four states—Delaware, Kansas, South Carolina, and Virginia. The unanimous opinion crashed the longstanding American convention of racially separate public schools. It focused on constitutional principles, not on measuring factors. The Court focused on no separate-but-equal issues. The answer to the constitutional questions in the Court's view lay elsewhere than in comparing buildings, curricula, teacher qualifications, or salaries.

The Court made public-school segregation itself the issue in its *Brown* decision. Chief Justice Warren pronounced the unanimous Court's ruling that "in the field of public education the doctrine of 'separate but equal' has no place. Separate educational facilities are inherently unequal."[56]

Virginia's *Richmond Times-Dispatch* declared the ruling "the most momentous decision in the interracial field since the Dred Scott case of 1857." In decreeing "school segregation unconstitutional, a long era came to an end," the *Dallas News* explained. "Whether we are better off for that, time alone will tell. It is the fact that must be faced. The effect will reach all interracial relations," the Texas daily predicted.[57]

Announcing so far-reaching a principle was one thing. Implementing it was another. The Court recognized sundry practical problems. For a year it continued deliberation on remedies. In May 1955, in what became known as *Brown II*, the Court directed resolution to the locally based federal district courts. Acknowledging the need for time to adjust, it ordered progress "with all deliberate speed" toward operating affected "public schools on a racially nondiscriminatory basis."[58] Yet the Court clearly underestimated the massive resistance that sprang up against school desegregation.

Many refused to yield to the principle that "racial discrimination in public education is unconstitutional," as the Court directed in May 1955.[59] Southern segregationist leaders preached defiance. Virginia U.S. Senator and former governor Harry F. Byrd Sr. insisted on states' rights to resist unconstitutional federal actions, such as he considered the *Brown* rulings to be.

Subscribing to Byrd's defiance, the Virginia General Assembly prohibited state funding for any racially integrated school. Other southern congressmen joined Byrd. A total of 19 senators and 81 representatives from 11 southern states jointly issued a "Southern Manifesto" denouncing the Supreme Court. They titled it a "Declaration of Constitutional Principles." It labeled the *Brown* desegregation order a "clear abuse of judicial power."[60] South Carolina U.S. Senator Strom Thurmond pledged to "use every lawful means" to resist the Court ruling. "We are free morally and legally to oppose the decision. We must fight it to the end," he declared on the Senate floor.[61]

Resistance leaders publicly counseled calm. Their manifesto urged supporters to "scrupulously refrain from disorder and lawless acts." Yet violence was frequent as segregationists took to the streets to block implementation of federal court desegregation rulings. They organized so-called white citizens councils across the South. They rioted at the University of Alabama in Tuscaloosa to block court-ordered desegregation there. The university yielded to pressure from infuriated whites in March 1956 by expelling the black student, Autherine Lucy, it had admitted weeks earlier under court order.

Arkansas Governor Orval Faubus on September 4, 1957, called out National Guard troops to block nine black students from attending Little Rock Central High School. Television images of soldiers in arms blocking six girls and three boys from entering a school shocked the sensibilities of many worldwide. The outcry pushed President Eisenhower to warn Faubus against interfering further with federal court orders. The governor yielded and removed the state troops, but white mobs replaced them. On September 24, President Eisenhower reluctantly ordered the U.S. Army's 101st Airborne Division to Little Rock to secure the black students' safety at Central High.

Confrontation subsided in the face of armed troops. Off the streets, however, constitutional challenges persisted. Like the Virginia General Assembly, the

Arkansas State Legislature at Governor Faubus's urging refused to yield to the federal courts. Arkansas's white officials closed public schools rather than desegregate. Virginia districts had done the same. All-white private schools sprang up to accommodate displaced students. Blacks and many poor students sat without schooling.

The U.S. Supreme Court convened in special term in 1958 with the direct defiance to federal court orders under consideration. In *Cooper v. Aaron* (1958), the Court firmly reiterated that obeying federal court rulings was not optional. It was not a matter of opinion. It was a matter of obeying the U.S. Constitution, and that duty embraced everyone, the Court reminded. It pointedly addressed Governor Faubus and the Arkansas legislature. "No state legislator or executive or judicial officer can war against the Constitution without violating his undertaking to support it," the chief justice emphasized in rehearsing simple principles of U.S. law.[62]

"The Constitution created a government dedicated to equal justice under law. The Fourteenth Amendment embodied and emphasized that ideal," Chief Justice Warren explained. "State support of segregated schools through any arrangement, management, funds, or property cannot be squared with the Amendment's command that no State shall deny to any person within its jurisdiction the equal protection of the laws," he concluded.[63]

The Court's decisions implementing *Brown* hardly finished segregation. In fact, the Court pointedly restricted its ruling to public school. It left *Plessy*'s separate but equal doctrine untouched in several significant points. For example, it left untouched legal bans on interracial sex and marriage. As the 1950s case of *Naim v. Naim* illustrated, states remained free to discriminate by race in their laws determining who might marry whom. *Naim* also illustrated segregation's reach beyond any simple black/white dichotomy.

Segregation relegated all nonwhites to subordinate status. Virginia's Supreme Court of Appeals reiterated the point in June 1955 in voiding a union between Chinese American Ham Say Naim and the white Ruby Elaine Naim. Upholding the state's anti-miscegenation laws, the court repeated its traditional finding. "The preservation of racial integrity is the unquestioned policy of this State, and that it is sound and wholesome, cannot be gainsaid," Virginia's highest court held. The policy was "for the peace and happiness of the colored race, as well as of the white," the court insisted. "More than half of the States of the Union have miscegenation statutes," it noted.[64] Although offered multiple opportunities to reverse the *Naim* decision, the U.S. Supreme Court in November 1955 let it stand. Not until 1967 in *Loving v. Virginia* would the nation's highest court declare anti-miscegenation statutes unconstitutional, confirming marriage as a matter of personal choice not state-imposed racial dictates.

Still, race relations pressures built. By 1955 U.S. public policy had reversed its traditional favoring of segregation. The U.S. Supreme Court's refreshing view of equal protection doctrine, as exemplified in its *Brown* rulings, opened developments against public discrimination in an increasing number of sites. The Court's November 1955 rulings in *Mayor and Council of Baltimore City v. Dawson* and

Holmes v. City of Atlanta further expressed personal rights of equal access to public facilities. The two rulings outlawed racial segregation in public parks, play-
grounds, and golf courses.

The 381-day Montgomery Bus Boycott quickened desegregation challenges
and resistance. The action followed Rosa Parks's refusal, on December 1, 1955,
to yield her seat to a white on a public bus in Alabama's capital. City and state
segregation laws required blacks to give up their seats to whites on command.
Parks knew the law. She willfully disobeyed it, and she was hardly the first black
woman to do so.

Tired of unequal treatment, blacks organized a showdown on Parks's arrest.
The local Women's Political Council urged blacks not to ride Montgomery city
buses beginning on Monday, December 5. The freshly installed, 26-year-old
pastor of Montgomery's Dexter Avenue Baptist Church, the Reverend Martin
Luther King Jr., became the primary spokesperson for the boycott that lasted until
December 20, 1956.

A class-action lawsuit accompanied the boycott. Four black women—Aurelia
S. Browder, Susie McDonald, Claudette Colvin, and Mary Louise Smith—sued
the Montgomery city bus company, city and state commissioners overseeing
buses, individual bus drivers, and the city police chief. For themselves and other
blacks, the four complained segregation on public buses violated U.S. constitutional protections.

On June 5, 1956, U.S. Circuit Judge Richard T. Rives and District Judge Frank
Johnson, sitting on a three-judge federal panel, agreed with the complaint.[65] District Judge Seybourn H. Lynne dissented. In his mind, *Plessy v. Ferguson* remained
controlling law. On November 13, 1956, the Supreme Court affirmed the majority decision. So the Montgomery boycott won in fact and in law.

Growing black agitation and resistance televised worldwide forced federal response beyond the courts. Put on the spot, President Eisenhower urged cautious
accommodation to desegregation. His conservative leadership supplied several
notable results. None were entirely his doing, but his administration contributed. During his eight years (1953–1961), desegregation of the armed forces
proceeded, D.C. public schools desegregated, and nondiscrimination in federal
hiring and contracting advanced. Most notably, responding to Eisenhower's domestic initiatives, Congress in September 1957 enacted the first federal civil
rights statute since 1875.

In line with Eisenhower's pushing symbols more than substance in the area of
civil rights, the 1957 act was more a sop than a solution. It aimed to show moder-
ate federal concern focused almost exclusively on securing and protecting voting
rights. Its narrowness reflected political realities. Southern senators threatened
to filibuster any robust measures. Simply getting Congress to pass the act was a
milestone achievement.

Although limited, the act advanced the cause. It added an assistant attorney
general in the Department of Justice and enhanced judicial powers and criminal
penalties for civil rights violations. Most significantly, it established a temporary,

six-member investigative civil rights commission to study and report to the president on federal law and policy. Sixty days after so reporting, the commission was to cease, but subsequent pressures transformed it into an enduring watchdog.

Powerful southerners supported the 1957 act as a cap. They hoped it would quell spreading agitation. By then, however, escalating confrontation was spilling more and more into America's streets. On all sides, people had surged beyond local and national political leaders. Grassroots organizing mushroomed, especially among southern blacks. Patience was no longer likely. Times of polite moderation were past. Deep societal changes were revolutionizing race relations. On buses, at eateries, and other sites of day-to-day interaction, new days had dawned. No elite personal politics, trading horses or whatever else, promised to reclaim shifted power. People across America were rising up over racial inequities, and they were forcing law and government to follow as the 1950s closed.

MEDIA AND MASS COMMUNICATIONS

Television was the mass medium of the 1950s. Indeed, the decade launched what commentators have labeled the "Age of Television." TV grew during the decade from a rarity into a commonplace. About 14,000 U.S. households had a TV in 1947. The number soared to six million by 1950. That averaged a set for about one-in-six of the nation's 38.8 million family households. By 1960 the nation boasted 60 million TVs. Nine-in-ten of America's 44.9 million family households then had at least one set. The device altered the pattern and perception of American life.

Television became no mere household appliance. It morphed into an organizational node. It became Americans' primary information provider and opinion shaper. It became the U.S. societal connections center. It advanced in the 1950s to dominate mass communications, media, and culture. It seduced with continuous, fresh, and irresistible images. It invited Americans to see themselves, to see others, and to see themselves as others saw them.

More than beamed electronic bits, television transferred the locus of community control. Command over what was appropriate for whom to see began retreating from nearby behind-the-scene elites to remote behind-the-screen decision makers. Television made the local national and the national local. Increasingly little in U.S. life remained beyond TV lights. Much appeared different as the world shrank to on-screen images.

Television put U.S. race relations on a world stage not seen before. It made visible to millions systemic behavior clearly contradicting the professed creed of American liberal equality. More than simply highlighting the nonwhite/white gap, television exhibited repressive segregation for personal and public scrutiny. Nationwide viewers could see scenes for themselves. They could judge what was happening. The images before their eyes became driving realities. If seeing was believing, many white Americans came—some for the first time—to understand the ugly realities of U.S. apartheid. What they saw on television made denial difficult, if not impossible.

As the 1950s developed, anti-segregation protests became challenging, eye-catching spectacles. Television carried them as visual imperatives. The images caught a public eye unable to turn away. The moving sights and sounds seized attention. They shook old understandings and shifted political and social sensibilities. Television promoted a fresh public process of remote participation. It created something of an interactive audience. It became a primary protest tool. Indeed, getting the protest story out, more and more came to mean getting the protest story on television.

Race relations became a consuming topic in the 1950s. News media in the North especially focused on racial protest with blacks in the lead. Particularly outside the South, whites viewed ugly racial events such as 14-year-old Chicagoan Emmett Till's 1955 Mississippi lynching or the 1955–1956 bus boycott in Montgomery, Alabama, as not possibly being in America. Most distanced themselves from stark southern segregation. In the South itself, local slants differed. More and more, they turned inward. TV's unblinking eye left open few other directions.

As a national medium, television tended to spoil homegrown illusions. It let few stay self-contained. Its producers and programmers had no more insights necessarily than their counterparts in radio and print media. Whatever the medium, U.S. coverage of the 1950s segregation crisis appeared almost as foreign news. It was clearly news the mainstream media did not well understand. Their newsrooms and other facilities were, after all, mostly segregated white bastions. Their reporting often was without insight. Yet the medium of TV itself offered clearer and deeper perceptions of the nation's segregation. The pictures produced their own effects.

Television connected Americans in an enlarged national community. In focusing on the segregation crisis, TV and other media quickened hoary arguments about the nation's character and commitments. The questions of America's political constitution resembled the 1850s. They carried the rumblings of a new civil war. Could the South stand apart with its own social system and rules? Television pushed beyond local standards. It collapsed regional and sectional perceptions.

Television projected national ideals. Its imagined America loomed almost colorless. It shunned overt racial bias. Indeed, its idealized community brooked no intolerance. It was at least self-conscious about recognizing and respecting differences. So, for example, the Columbia Broadcasting System (CBS) yielded reluctantly in 1953 to persistent black protests and canceled its hit, all-black cast TV series *Amos 'n' Andy* after three seasons. Criticized for demeaning blacks with stereotypes, the show was nevertheless one of the few places blacks regularly appeared in 1950s television.

Throughout the decade, the National Association for the Advancement of Colored People (NAACP) and other organizations bitterly protested the absence of nonwhites in TV's regular programming. The NAACP declared that "the absence of Negro performers on television denotes a denial of the Negro citizen's place in American life."[66] The Coordinating Council for Negro Performers (CCNP) launched repeated campaigns in the 1950s to get blacks on television. The CCNP urged supporters to write letters and visit broadcasters, placement agencies, and advertisers to insist on TV including nonwhites.

Breaking through what some came to call the "Glass Curtain" remained difficult. TV networks seldom spotlighted nonwhites. They appeared interested mostly in carrying only comedic racial minorities and then only at the margins. Nonwhites could be sidekicks but not much more of substance. When they appeared at all, they usually were in the background.

"Tonto" on *The Lone Ranger* illustrated the character. Canadian Mohawk Jay Silverheels played the role. The faithful companion of the white hero seldom emerged from the shadows on one of TVs most popular westerns. Yet at least he was there. He was identified and identifiable on the series, which aired from 1949 to 1957.

Not infrequently TV westerns hardly paused on American Indians. They stood in the distance or they rode to the attack—usually losing. They seldom came into

Jay Silverheels as Tonto and Clayton Moore as the Lone Ranger, on ABC's *The Lone Ranger*, which ran from 1949–1957. © ABC. Courtesy of ABC and Photofest.

focus as acknowledged personalities. The half-hour series *Broken Arrow* proved the exception. Aired from 1956 to 1958 and syndicated as *Cochise,* the program featured the Chiricahua Apache chief in the 1870s Southwest. The show provided perhaps U.S. television's only prolonged, positive spotlight on American Indians.

The Syrian-born American Michael Ansara played Cochise. He, himself, complained of the stiff limits imposed on the character. "Cochise could do one of two things," Ansara recalled in a 1960s *TV Guide* magazine interview. He could "stand with his arms folded, looking noble; or stand with his arms at his side, looking noble."[67] Despite being the title character, Cochise was not the real lead of the show. That role went to his white blood-brother, the Indian agent Tom Jeffords. The Indians themselves were more or less façades.

Asian Americans were almost wholly absent on U.S. television in the 1950s. The 39-episode *The New Adventures of Charlie Chan* came closest to offering a glimpse. Aired in 1957–1958, the independently syndicated series carried little of Asian American substance. The New York City-born Irish American J. Carrol Naish portrayed the inscrutable and wily Chinese American detective in yellow-face. The stereotyped dialect and settings simulated little of the dimensions and diversity of Chinese American or other Asian American communities. The criminal mastermind at the other end of the Asian crime scene appeared briefly in 1956 in the short-lived series *Adventures of Dr. Fu Manchu.* Hop Sing appeared in 1959 as the family Chinese American cook on the long-running National Broadcasting Company (NBC) series *Bonanza* (1959–1973). Played by veteran American-born actor Victor Sen Yung, the character continued the servant stereotype. Nevertheless, he was one of the few Asian American presences on 1950s U.S. television.

Hispanic Americans fared little better. "Ricky Ricardo" was TV's chief Latino presence in 1950s U.S. television. Cuban-born Desi Arnaz played the second-fiddle character against his real-life wife Lucille Ball. Their *I Love Lucy* (1951–1957) and its successor *The Lucy-Desi Comedy Hour* (1957–1960) ran as one of the most popular programs in TV history. Mimicking his real-life persona as a Latin-rhythm band leader, Arnaz played foil and little more on the live audience sitcom. He was simply another guy struggling to cope with his always-trying wife and big-city life on New York's East 68th Street. Indeed, the Ricardos appeared as just another striving couple on the showbiz margins. They were colorful, but little, if anything, of any American minority flickered in their act.

Not surprisingly, 1950s U.S. television struggled most with blacks. Programmers appeared willing to broadcast blacks regularly only in demeaning, comedic roles such as those in *Amos 'n' Andy* or *Beulah.* Special programming did provide some black presence. Performers such as jazz trumpeter Louis Armstrong and the versatile singer-dancer-instrumentalist Sammy Davis Jr. got occasional spots. NBC in January 1955 carried the 27-year-old black soprano sensation Leontyne Price in a one-shot televised spectacular. It featured her as celebrated fictional singer Floria Tosca. Price triumphed in the title role in the adaptation of Italian Giacomo Puccini's three-act quasi-tragic opera that had premiered in

Italy in 1900. The gospel star Mahalia Jackson also crashed the curtain. Chicago CBS affiliate WBBM-TV provided her an occasional half-hour show beginning in March 1955. But talk of expanding it nationally proved fruitless.

Racial prejudice simply blocked black TV appearances. Indeed, some southern stations refused to carry NBC's 1955 production of *Tosca* with Leontyne Price. The torrid interracial love scenes were apparently too much for some viewers. Yet Laurel, Mississippi, made special arrangements to receive *Tosca*. The hometown folk were eager to see Price, their local girl who made good.

Other black performers suffered bans as public villains. For example, television programmers shunned the phenomenal Paul Robeson. Just as Hollywood's big screen had in the 1940s, TV's small screen blacklisted the magnetic and multitalented baritone. He appeared simply too much for many U.S. audiences. Indeed, his prodigious talents and achievements appeared to provoke resentment rather than adulation among some white Americans.

Robeson was a four-letter collegiate athlete and twice a first-team All-America football player. A *Phi Beta Kappa* graduate, he was valedictorian at Rutgers University in his native New Jersey. He graduated from Columbia Law School in the same

Paul Robeson as seen in *Tales of Manhattan* (1942). © 20th Century Fox. Courtesy of 20th Century Fox/Photofest.

1923 class as future U.S. Supreme Court Justice William O. Douglas. He became an international star of stage and screen. His concert basso became legendary, as did his performances as Shakespeare's Othello and Eugene O'Neill's Emperor Jones.

Robeson's communist sympathies made him more than *persona non grata* among those fearful of so-called un-American activities. NBC-TV refused to allow him to appear in March 1950 on its *Today with Mrs. Roosevelt* program. The weekly series former First Lady Eleanor Roosevelt hosted discussed contemporary domestic and international problems. The then 51-year-old, well-traveled, and knowledgeable Robeson was more than qualified for a spot. His canceled appearance was in no way an issue of the show's character. It was about Robeson's being who he was. A network spokesman reportedly declared the Promethean black would never appear on NBC, period.

The black press persistently bemoaned that "the available talent of regularly scheduled television personalities is lily-white," as the *Chicago Defender* put it in a March 1955 editorial. "We love television but there is something seriously wrong with such an important and rapidly growing industry which only finds a guest room in its house for the darker brother," the editorial complained.[68]

While blacks lamented the dearth of their appearances on television, some whites complained blacks were overrepresented. Alabama's daily *Birmingham News* radio and TV editor Roger Thames stirred the issue in 1956. "Are there too many Negroes on TV?" he asked snidely. "I believe that we of the South and maybe of the nation, are so interested in race matters that some of us may magnify out of true proportion the extent of participation by Negroes in TV," Thames explained. If "anybody thinks there are too many Negroes on a particular show, write the sponsors of that show and protest," he urged.[69]

Thames openly confirmed his campaign was backlash. Whites had a right to complain, he insisted, "because the NAACP is spending a lot of time in TV production offices demanding more and more participation by Negroes in television." Thames suggested further it was okay for racial prejudice to drive such protests. "Of course I am prejudiced, just as other Southern-born and bred people are prejudice," he confessed.[70]

Television was the frontline in U.S. media struggles over race. Yet it was only part of the battle. TV took over American households in the 1950s, but it did not completely displace other media. Radio, for example, found new strengths. It flourished internationally as a primary cold war weapon. The Voice of America, started in 1942 to produce World War II propaganda, expanded its broadcasts under the U.S. Information Agency (USIA). Founded in 1950, Radio Free Europe/Radio Liberty joined the propaganda wars. It boasted a mission "to promote democratic values and institutions by disseminating factual information and ideas."[71]

U.S. race relations became crucial in overseas broadcast wars. Communists attacked U.S. treatment of racial minorities. They viewed blacks especially as America's vulnerable underbelly. Criticisms of U.S. apartheid made America defensive. As President Harry S Truman persistently repeated before leaving office in 1953, the Cold War made race central in America's democratic image. It made civil rights a national security issue.

Enemies abroad awaited any false U.S. move. Thus President Dwight D. Eisenhower found his hand forced in September 1957. Arkansas Governor Orval Faubus and the bulk of the state's administration stood defiant against federal court-ordered school desegregation. Governor Faubus, in fact, called out the Arkansas National Guard to block black children from entering previously all-white public schools in the state's capital city. The Texas-born Eisenhower sympathized with his fellow southern whites. Barely two months before the Little Rock crisis, the president had declared, "I cannot imagine any set of circumstances that would ever induce me to send federal troops . . . into any area to enforce the orders of a federal court."[72] With the world listening and watching, however, sending in federal troops was exactly what Eisenhower was forced to do. He had to vindicate federal authority and save face in the global eye.

Positioning on race was more than a matter of international relations. The battle for hearts and minds engrossed U.S. media at home. While focus fell more and more on television, radio persisted as an important player. Its growing reach since the 1930s positioned it as a truly mass medium. If radio could not match television in spectacle, it compensated in volume. Radio was everywhere. In 1950 more than 95 percent of U.S. households had at least one radio. And it was not merely at home. Radio was at work, on the way to work, at eateries and bars. It had a pervasiveness television yet lacked. It provided the decade's soundtrack.

Radio's more repetitive message fit an important niche. Its news and commentary especially attracted attention as vehicles for influence and persuasion, a phenomenon corporations had noticed and exploited since the 1930s. They made radio a major component in corporate public relations. The medium gave advertisers a voice that print lacked. And it cost considerably less than TV, which had first topped radio in advertising revenues in 1949.

Industrial giants such as chemicals producer DuPont and automakers General Motors and Ford tooted their corporate horns on radio. So did smaller concerns. Sponsors backed shows to confirm and improve their status in U.S. society. They wanted to position themselves as good citizens. That made them sensitive to race issues.

Most advertisers wanted nonwhites' business. They were not in business to turn away dollars. They could not survive without whites, however. They danced a fine line. They reached for new nonwhite customers while trying to hold fast to old white ones. Their advertising sold ideology. It peddled corporate perspectives. With those ideologies and perspectives came worldviews. In the absence of visuals, radio messages were more subtle in some ways and more direct in others. They easily inserted notions for daily discourse.

Radio was itself segregated, however. It broadcast primarily to whites. It offered relatively few nonwhite voices. That was the overwhelming audience and direction from the first, when KDKA in Pittsburgh, Pennsylvania, pioneered U.S. mass communication radio in its debut on November 2, 1920. Reaching white ethnics and nonwhite minorities challenged early programmers. Sporadic non-English broadcasting satisfied some needs. Special formatting satisfied others. So-called black appeal radio was one such special format. Some-time *Chicago Defender* correspondent Jack L. Cooper pioneered it with his "The All Negro Hour" on WSBC in Chicago in 1929.

Getting blacks and other nonwhites into the radio demographic was one thing. Getting them into radio as owner-operators was another. The 1950s were the first decade of U.S. black radio ownership. WERD-AM aired its 900-watts in Atlanta, Georgia, on October 4, 1949, as the nation's first black-owned radio station. KPRS/KPRT-AM aired in Kansas City, Missouri, in 1951. WCHB in Inkster, Michigan, aired in November 1956 as the first black-owned station built from the ground up rather than acquired by purchase. Its sister WCHD-FM (which became WJZZ-FM in Detroit) aired in 1960.

No significant numbers of U.S. minority broadcast owners emerged until well after the 1950s. The Heftel network started in the 1960s. Moving from Hawaii to Los Angeles, California, it developed into the Hispanic Broadcasting Corporation (HBC). It aimed to own and program top performing Spanish-language radio stations in the 15 largest Spanish-language U.S. radio markets. Similarly, the Multicultural Radio Broadcasting Inc. (MRBI) would later emerge (1982) as the largest Asian-American owned media group. Even at their post-1950s peak, however, racial minorities remained marginal operators as U.S. broadcasters. They never owned or operated as much as 2 percent of the nation's full power commercial radio stations. Television station ownership was even more paltry.

Minority publishers in the 1950s had far more impact than minority broadcasters. The black press continued to lead in influence as minority media and mass communication sentinels and opinion-makers. Almost every community had its contributors. Spanish-language and other non-English newspapers revived with immigration in the 1950s. The flow of Puerto Ricans into New York City, for example, lifted *El Diario de Nueva York* into a significant voice. In Florida, the *Diario Las Américas* in Miami developed into a sustained voice from its founding in 1953.

Various weeklies, often short-lived, serviced Spanish-language communities throughout California and also in Chicago. The San Francisco-based Japanese-English *Hokubei Mainichi* (translated as "North America Daily"), begun in 1948 to reconnect dislocated internment camp victims, developed in the 1950s to convey community-specific news for Japanese Americans throughout California. Other Asian American papers, largely in California and in New York City, also contributed their community focus.

These publications existed primarily as community resources. They functioned also as chroniclers, creating a public record. Government officials and others dependent on the public eye took notice. Often unwelcome and usually derided, minority media did yeoman's service in reporting local detail and developments other media generally skipped. They persisted with unpleasant news. They gave voice to minority complaints and concerns. Their presence made a difference in community response to race relations developments. They pushed behind-the-scenes community management into the public eye. Community leaders could no longer simply arrange their visions for public harmony behind private closed doors. The 1953 Baton Rouge bus boycott illustrated the shifting paradigm. Behind-the-scenes negotiations necessarily continued, of course. But the substance and shape for negotiations developed more and more in the media and in the streets. Elites had to scramble to be seen leading, rather than following, their communities.

Minority publishers let interested readers know some of the thinking outside the mainstream. They operated, however, mostly on a one-way street. Their readers came from their own communities. Almost no crossover occurred. As in the sad scenario of broader U.S. race relations, direct exchange was limited. Few whites read any minority press. Nor did they have significant conversations with non-whites. They knew little personally beyond what they saw on television, heard on the radio, or read. Few had any sense of the nation's bubbling racial volcano.

In his *Chicago Defender* column "Adventures in Race Relations," Enoc P. Waters Jr. repeatedly returned to the theme of white Americans' being clueless about the real issues of race relations. Few whites, for example, sensed the "deep-seeded bitterness over the stubborn refusal of the whites who wield the power to grant Negroes the respect due them as human beings and the rights due them as citizens," Waters noted in January 1959.[73]

The black press and other minority publishers responded to white curiosity about nonwhites' identities, intentions, and desires. The seldom articulated but persistent white question appeared to be, "What is it minorities want?" That was the clear frame of the question for blacks as they pushed in the forefront of the 1950s anti-segregation protests. Many whites appeared to await some answer they could accept.

Elevated to the national spotlight during the 1955–1956 Montgomery Bus Boycott, the fresh Reverend Martin Luther King Jr.—just passing 30 years old when the decade ended—articulated answers many found acceptable. He increasingly became a media mainstay after the January 1956 bombing of his home in Alabama's capital city where he pastored the Dexter Avenue Baptist Church. Covering such shocking spectacles, mainstream outlets advanced significantly on the race relations front in the 1950s. Almost necessarily they had to advance. Intensifying protests forced them forward. Yet most approached only the periphery. They struggled to grasp nonwhites' stories. Getting to the explosive depths of U.S. race relations awaited another decade.

CULTURAL SCENE

Television was the dominant development on the U.S. cultural scene in the 1950s. It reprogrammed America. TV adventures, comedy, drama, musical variety, news, science fiction, soap operas, sports, and other programming distinctively rearranged American life. The revolution was not so much televised as

Martin Luther King Jr. (right), on the speakers' platform at the Prayer Pilgrimage for Freedom in Washington, D.C., May 17, 1957. He sits with (right to left) Rev. Thomas Kilgore, A. Philip Randolph, and Roy Wilkins. Courtesy of the Library of Congress, LC-USZ62-125026.

television was the revolution. TV brought drastic and far-reaching change to the 150.7 million Americans in 1950 and more to the 179.3 million by 1960.

Television's development accompanied tremendous U.S. demographic expansion and shifts. TV became sitter and caregiver for children called "the baby boom." The nation's largest birth cohort delivered 76 million children between 1946 and 1964. From 3.3 million in 1946, U.S. births peaked at 4.3 million in 1957 and 1961. The U.S. Census marked the boom as closing with 4.0 million births in 1964. The horde of young drove change in a growing and moving America.

Early baby boomers set an especially emotional backdrop for race relations. They became substantive and symbolic bodies over whom race and culture wars intensified during the 1950s. Understandably held dear, their growing presence escalated the desegregation crisis. Indeed, their enlarged numbers deepened stakes everywhere in American life. Boomers became tied, at least rhetorically, to almost every major life decision. They sat centered in various personal, political, and social calculus of where adults chose to live, work, and play. Their going to school or preparing to go to school heated concerns about where and with whom they would be in school. That compounded concerns and consequences of the

U.S. Supreme Court's public-school desegregation decisions following *Brown v. Board of Education* in 1954.

U.S. schools stood as primary cultural sites in the 1950s, as ever. To change them proposed to transform basic elements of American life. And one basic element was their color. Despite any popular and political rhetoric to the contrary, America's schools operated as racial isolates. That was their traditional and persistent character nationwide.

School location mattered little. Nor did educational models matter much. Teachers and students tended to be of a single color inside any U.S. school. That was so in the fading little red rural schoolhouse. It was so in the self-important urban and ex-urban preparatory academy. It was so, too, in the increasingly crowded city school. The pattern was not regional. It existed north and south, east and west. It was national. It was the American way in primary and secondary education.

Despite all rhetoric, American schools tended to be no democratic, egalitarian, integrated, or level training grounds. Schools perpetuated their surrounding society. They acted as community chaperones. Usually guardians of existing values, they supervised and separated their young charges. And race was a primary separator.

Americans everywhere understood schools' importance. That made schools primary battle sites. Schools stood as strategic high ground commanding entrances to much of America's riches. They were almost magical places. They certainly had transformative potential. They were not equal, however. They tended to be better and worse, richer and poorer. They tended to be white and nonwhite.

Segregation by law or by practice kept America's schools separate and unequal. Segregation did more than deprive nonwhites of equal educational opportunities. It usually denied them any quality schooling. That was clearest with blacks, but they were hardly alone in being underserved. American Indians and Hispanic Americans also suffered peculiarly. Those whose first language was not English faced multiple drawbacks. The nation's public schools simply did not work effectively for all students.

Getting quality education for nonwhite students was the impetus for the U.S. Supreme Court's landmark 1954 *Brown* decision. Moving to desegregating America's public schools was no simple matter, however. It touched core cultural values. Segregationists lambasted it as threatening to destroy a way of life. They were right. So much tied into schools. Throughout the 1950s, the nation struggled with its self-images and its projections. Desegregation forced America to take a hard look at what it was and what it was to become.

Television news helped prod popular and political considerations. But general TV programming contributed little to diversity. It tended to simulate a society where race and class did not exist or were invisible. TV's common 1950s set pieces projected placid white wholesomeness. They were homogenized. The 1957–1958 Columbia Broadcasting System (CBS) family situation comedy *Leave It to Beaver* exemplified the essential characteristics. Theodore "Beaver" Cleaver romped in idealized Mayfield. The community was a pristine, lily white ex-urban model of America. Few difficulties intruded. So-called problems arose simply from Beaver's being impish. His stay-at-home mother, June, and his accountant father, Ward, appeared flawless. Even Beaver's older brother, Wally, appeared unflawed. The Cleavers were not even a stereotype. They were figments. They were simply unreal. So was much of the contemporary social setting 1950s' American TV presented.

Even when television offered "real" people, the family-oriented programming remained unreal. TVs longest-running sitcom well illustrated the typical programming's insubstantial social dimensions. The 14-year run of *The Adventures of Ozzie and Harriet* (1952–1966) featured the Nelsons as themselves. Parents Ozzie and Harriet were not the almost always semiformal clad Ward and June Cleaver. Nor were their sons, David and Ricky, Wally or the Beaver. Yet normal Nelson family life revealed them in public and private as exemplars of an unruffled domestic ideology of comfortable conformity. Their lives lacked more than color.

Outside of news, television often appeared to deny contemporary reality. Its programming in many ways was a sham. The late 1950s quiz show scandals revealed aspects of the fraud. The pioneering 1955 $64,000 Question fascinated viewers with its cash-focused suspense, and the mania spawned imitators. By the 1957–1958 season, TV was airing 22 quiz and game shows. The success invited scrutiny. New York grand jury and congressional investigations in 1958 sniffed at TV deception. Hard looks pushed the National Broadcasting Company (NBC) in October 1958 to cancel its leading quiz show, *Twenty-One*. CBS canceled the *$64,000 Question* in November. Programmers had manipulated the games to concoct a particular American character. They did much the same in other programming.

TV's 1950s sitcoms particularly projected idealized social constructs. They routinely proffered white, prosperous, upwardly mobile, stable, two-parent-two-child families living in single-family detached homes. Social trends were creeping fast from any such American reality. Disintegration was haunting American families. The divorce rate was creeping up. Poverty was rising. So was urban crowding. TV barely hinted at the disconcerting momentum. *Make Room for Daddy* (1953–1957) nodded at part of the trends. Transitioning to *The Danny Thomas Show* in 1956, it shifted to a single-parent family. Yet the urban, widower, male-headed household remained atypical. And America's nonwhite population remained nowhere in sight.

Television concepts, formula, and images seemed to crave and cling to convention in the 1950s. Other cultural media proved more daring. Particularly, the big screen, stage, and literature did more to challenge cultural assumptions and patterns of U.S. race relations. American Indians, for example, got a bit more play on the 1950s big screen than on TV. The 1950 film *Apache Chief* focused on Indians. It depicted a good-evil struggle. Protagonist Young Eagle was the good Indian. Protector of whites, he pursued peace. His rival Black Wolf was the renegade white-killer. Good won, of course. That was to say, the whites were saved—and, by implication, the Indians, too. *Broken Arrow* (1950) also showed a sympathetic side of Indians, with its partial focus on Apache chief Cochise. The popular 1956–1958 TV series of the same title spun off from it.

The 1951 film *Tomahawk* presented a notably accurate historical view of whites' dispossessing Black Hills Sioux after an 1866 gold discovery. Still, the film focused not on Indians but on the white hero, frontier scout Jim Bridger. It also offered a bit of interracial sex. Bridger's Cherokee wife, Monahseetah, guided his sensitivities. Bostonian Susan Cabot played Monahseetah in redface. The film did feature two actual Indians. Sioux Chief American Horse and Comanche Chief Bad Bear both appeared but were uncredited.

The 1955 film *Apache Woman* probed Western anti-Indian racism. Halfbreed Anne LeBeau was the title character, but the film's focus followed a white man, government agent Rex Muffet. He sought the source of attacks on the unspecified western town's whites. They blamed marauding Apaches. And there was an Indian villain, Anne's brother Armand LeBeau. Interracial romance between Anne and Rex sparked further interest, although her being half-white lessened miscegenation tensions.

White men's coupling with nonwhite women seemed to raise relatively few eyebrows. Nonwhite men's imposing themselves on white women, however, produced outrage. That was an underlying theme in the 1956 epic John Ford/John Wayne classic *The Searchers*. It was a white-girl captivity story. Yet the horror of her plight played a distant second fiddle to the personality study of her troubled principal rescuer. The Indian-hating ex-Confederate Ethan Edwards doggedly trekked five years from Texas to the Canadian border. Revenge, not rescue, loomed as his goal. He aimed to kill the Comanche raiders who slew his family and took his niece, Debbie Edwards.

The Searchers paired racial identity with the irrationality of racism. Ethan Edwards emerged over the film's 119 minutes as at least crazed. Tormented by a love-hate struggle, he no longer clearly saw the correct thing for him to do. He avenged the original transgression and reclaimed the girl. His seeming success turned haunting, however. With her in hand, he appeared to deem her dead after five years with red men. She lost her identity in his eyes. She was no longer the little white girl on whom he doted. She had become a squaw. She was a marked woman beyond saving. Ethan considered death alone would release and redeem her. The movie pressed his questions on the audience. Could the rescued Debbie live as a white woman after being with Indian men? Did being with them make her Indian? Was being dead truly better than being red?

The Searchers raised troubling questions in the 1950s. Indian identity proved easier for American audiences to deal with than black identity. The American dilemma cast for Debbie Edwards paled against the troubled predicament of mixed black identity. The old saga of "passing" returned. The problem came with persons who looked white but were black by legal and social measures. Perching on that cutting edge posed an ugly and unhappy predicament. It was most often a woman's story. It was a different kind of captivity narrative. The much-heralded 1959 version of *Imitation of Life* revisited the hoary theme.

The plot counterposed multiple parallels of two mother-daughter pairs. Aspiring white stage actress Lora Meredith and her daughter Suzie led the focus. Their black maid Annie Johnson and her daughter Sarah Jane followed. Neither mother had a husband. Both scratched to make ends meet. Their contrasting suffering and success displayed much in the complicated discourse of race and a woman's place in America.

Heartache and shame befell the blacks. Blocked from being accepted for their talents, both Johnsons were heartsick. Mother Annie acquiesced to the black/white divide. Daughter Sarah Jane rejected it, and with it herself and her mother. White to all appearances, she tried "passing." Her sobering end suggested the impossibility of contesting racial contingencies. There was no overcoming race. That appeared the movie's most prominent message. It suggested also that blacks could not be happy if they tried to leave their assigned social place.

Racial violence erupting from blacks' being out of place appeared prominently in film throughout the decade. The 1950 *No Way Out* turned on raw racism. The film reversed common color-coded class positions. It featured an upper-middle-class black in conflict with lowlife whites. In his first major film role, Sidney Poitier portrayed the black physician Luther Brooks. He faced recalcitrant white patients Ray and John Biddle. The brothers needed emergency care after being shot in a foiled gas station robbery. Ray flatly rejected the black doctor's care. John was in no condition to refuse. When John died despite Dr. Brooks's heroic efforts, Ray vowed revenge. Deluded by his racism, he believed the black doctor purposely killed his brother.

No Way Out projected desegregation problems. Entrenched racism among whites and nonwhites would not end easily, the film suggested. Violence lurked, no matter the best intentions. Evil appeared set inevitably to triumph over good in racial matters. Even in the face of dire need, segregationists on both sides of the color line would not surrender. Against such dire prospects, everyday drama appeared almost escapist entertainment. The 1954 all-black cast musical *Carmen Jones* illustrated the contrast.

Set in the segregated world of an all-black U.S. Army camp, although it ventured to the black Mecca of Chicago, *Carmen Jones* replayed a romance of besotted, unrequited love. It was an old story. Revising French composer Georges Bizet's 1875 opera *Carmen*, it significantly gave major work to black performers such as Dorothy Dandridge, Harry Belafonte, Brock Peters, Pearl Bailey, Max Roach, and Diahann Carroll. That was quite a contribution. Dandridge emerged from the film as a certified American sex symbol and the first black nominated for an Academy of Motion Picture Arts and Sciences "Oscar" award as best actress.

The messages in 1950s American movies treating race tended to deliver a disconcerting conservatism. Filmmakers reached out to touch hot themes but invariably drew back from upsetting convention. *Island in the Sun* (1957) exemplified the reach and result. In the film, white beauty Joan Fontaine openly lusted after black Sidney Poitier. Potential miscegenation drove the plot, but it sank in hoary racist orthodoxy.

The film distanced the scene from U.S. viewers, setting itself on a fictional West Indian island. It was as if the action could not occur in America. The black man-white woman sex climaxed in a kiss. Even that created consternation and commotion at some U.S. showings. Perversely, death befell the black man seemingly for simply touching a white woman sexually. Yet in a parallel subplot, black beauty Dorothy Dandridge not only embraced, but married, a white English civil servant. Such portrayals reinforced segregation's duplicitous, racist and gendered standards. There was no ridicule. The results appeared as ordained realities.

Boldly titled *The Defiant Ones*, the 1958 film reached across the black/white divide to racial conciliation. Sidney Poitier and Tony Curtis portrayed a black and white pair of convicts (Noah Cullen and Joker Jackson) chained together. They escaped a crashed prison truck. Linked as they were, each hotheaded and unmanageable, the pair learned their survival depended on cooperating. Their developing respect and fellowship projected a hopeful note into an intensifying national argument over desegregation. It clearly contrasted with the 1950 *No Way Out*.

Hollywood at least engaged blacks and whites in domestic scenes in the 1950s. The industry struggled with Asian Americans. It usually proved bigger on scenic Asian locales than on substantive Asian images. And it seemed unable to locate Asian Americans. It ordinarily left Asians in Asia or elsewhere outside the United States. It rarely pictured native-born, homegrown Asian Americans. Stereotypes, subordinated characters, and actors in yellowface persisted.

The 1950 film *Oriental Evil* illustrated the point. Set in postwar Japan, it offered roles for several Japanese actors such as Noritomu Moriaji and Tadaichi Hirakawa. They remained background, however. They paraded as stereotypes. The low-budget mystery's focus fell on a white woman's quest to clear her dead brother's name of drug-trafficking allegations while she was romantically pursued by a shady white ex-serviceman. Only the fateful mysteries of the Orient saved the heroine, but not by Asian actors.

South Pacific (1958) was a scenic extravaganza. Aside from the island backdrop, however, U.S. Navy nurse Nellie Forbush's musical enchanted evenings offered few notes on native peoples. Yet a sexual subtheme stirred. A U.S. Marine lieutenant fell in love with a native islander girl, as Hollywood repeated the exotic sex theme.

The 1952 *Japanese War Bride* scaled notable heights. It pictured an Asian in America, and it forthrightly confronted U.S. racism. The film hit both anti-Japanese hatred and miscegenation. Wounded Korean War veteran Jim Sterling met and married Japanese nurse Tae Shimizu (portrayed by China-born Japanese actress and singer Yoshiko "Shirley" Yamaguchi). Their love bridged their gaps. Coming to California from Japan, however, the couple did not live happily ever after. Sterling's Salinas Valley family, friends, and neighbors shunned his wife and worked to break up the marriage. The birth of the couple's son became no larger happy event. Seeing the fruit of miscegenation only further maddened the racists. The movie unabashedly depicted ugly intolerance.

The 1955 film *Love Is a Many-Splendored Thing* also pursued interracial romance between Asians and whites. It presented the conventional pattern of a white man and nonwhite woman. On the eve of the Korean War (1950–1953), married U.S. news correspondent Mark Elliott coupled with widowed Eurasian physician Han Suyin (played in yellowface by Jennifer Jones). Their adultery and miscegenation apparently doomed their love. It appeared an error. Portraying Elliott, actor William Holden tagged the film's moral: "A great many mistakes are made in the name of loneliness," he said. The two had no future.

Sayonara (1957) repeated the ill-fated scenario in part. U.S. "ace" fighter pilot Major Lloyd Gruver bucked the system. Stationed in Japan during the Korean War, he fell in love with Japanese theater performer Hana-ogi. He saw the dismal fate racist military rules imposed on such couples. His plane crew chief wed a Japanese woman. The brass refused to recognize the marriage. They ordered the chief back to the United States and denied permission for his pregnant wife to accompany him. The distraught couple, refusing to be parted, committed suicide. That sealed Gruver's resolve. The movie twisted the ending of the James A. Michener novel on which it was based. Gruver said "*sayonara*" (goodbye or farewell) to Hana-ogi in the novel, leaving her behind in Japan. The film had him say "*sayonara*" to the racist system, determined to hold fast to his love.

Interracial sex stirred audiences cheaply, yet 1950s' Hollywood managed also to slip in some cross-cultural understanding—even if as comedy. The 1956 *Teahouse of the August Moon* wryly satirized the wisdom of a *pax Americana* that imposed U.S. means and mores on the world. Part of the underlying story also contrasted bureaucracy with democracy, as command decisions fell to popular will.

In post-World War II Japan, inept U.S. Army Captain Fishby dutifully clutched his orders to build a school to Americanize the Okinawa village of Tobiki. The villagers had different ideas. They wanted a teahouse, and in the comedy, they win. A young geisha called Lotus Blossom helped assimilate Captain Fishby to local customs, desires, and mores. Although the cast featured several Japanese actors (notably, Machiko Kyô in the role of Lotus Blossom), Nebraska-born white rising-star Marlon Brando played in yellowface the lead Japanese character, the wily interpreter Sakini.

The height of Hollywood's 1950s attention to Asian Americans may well have been *Go for Broke!* It featured native-born, home-grown Asian Americans—although not in the United States. The 1951 film notably focused on the U.S. Army's 442nd Regiment. Heroic far beyond any call of duty, the Japanese American unit fought desperate battles in Europe against both Nazi enemies and American bigots. The Nisei reflected the struggle blacks pilloried in their "Double V Campaign" for democracy abroad and at home. The movie ran with a documentary truth.

Hollywood's 1950s hits on race relations mostly reflected rich pickings from novels and plays. The bulk for the big screen came from adapting materials. *Imitation of Life*, for instance, was a remake of a 1934 film based on Fannie Hurst's 1933 novel of the same name. *Carmen Jones* (1954) adapted Oscar Hammerstein II's

1943 Broadway musical. In turn, it adapted Georges Bizet's 1875 opera based on French dramatist Prosper Mérimée's 1845 novella *Carmen*.

Some ideas emerged directly for the big screen. *The Defiant Ones* (1958), for example, was Harold Jacob Smith's original screenplay. The scripts for *Apache Chief* (1950), *No Way out* (1950), *Oriental Evil* (1950), *Go for Broke!* (1951), *Japanese War Bride* (1952), and *Apache Woman* (1955) were also original screenplays. That reflected in part that materials thought suitable on Asians and American Indians were not so readily available in any pipeline.

Materials treating Indians tended to be fresher. The original scripts for westerns showed that. So did *Tomahawk* (1951), adapted from Daniel Jarrett's short story, and *The Searchers* (1956), adapted from Alan Le May's 1954 novel. Hollywood's 1950s treatments of Asians also exhibited more contemporary material. Vern J. Sneider's 1951 novel, *The Teahouse of the August Moon*, provided the basis for the movie. The 1952 novel *A Many-Splendoured Thing* by Han Suyin (a pseudonym for Eurasian physician Elizabeth Comber) was the basis for the similarly titled 1955 film. *South Pacific* (1958) developed from the Richard Rodgers and Oscar Hammerstein Broadway smash that won the 1950 Pulitzer Prize for Drama. The story came from James A. Michener's 1948 Pulitzer Prize for Fiction winner, *Tales of the South Pacific*.

Hollywood loved spectacles, particularly in the 1950s. It pushed the wide, panorama view to distinguish itself from television. Techniques such as Cinemascope, Cinerama, and VistaVision produced magic not available at home. The industry hoped to wow viewers into theaters. While venturesome in technique, however, film remained socially conservative. If a few movies shocked, most steered clear of racial controversy. Spokespersons frequently retreated to claims the industry's business was entertainment not education. Hollywood offered some studies in character and realism, but advancing racial conciliation was a political agenda item not an entertainment value.

Hollywood was not beyond politics, of course. It often packaged indirect messages. Its 1950s science fiction barrage of alien invasions captured both cold war fears and white nightmares of nonwhites moving into the neighborhood. Fifties' films subtly exhibited populist politics, but they seldom screened nonwhite protests. When nonwhites, particularly blacks, got out of their traditional socially determined space, they seldom succeeded on screen. Apparently such visions were not even escapist entertainment. Hollywood considered such images would not attract moviegoers who were overwhelmingly whites. And while it speculated on what nonwhites might want to see, the industry in the 1950s was not ready to offer much. It continued to cater to whites' tastes.

More of a hunger for nonconformity growled in U.S. literature in the 1950s. It sought its own assurances more in questioning than in accepting convention. The bicoastal Bohemian literary and social movement called the beat generation or beat movement well illustrated the mode and mood. It percolated in and spilled out from New York City's Greenwich Village and in California from Los Angeles's Venice West and San Francisco's North Beach.

Beatniks attacked "square" society. Poetry early delivered their clear shrill tone. *Howl,* New York poet Allen Ginsberg's 1956 evocative and raunchy collection, offered a beatnik banner. Poet Lawrence Ferlinghetti's City Lights Bookstore, started in 1953 in San Francisco, provided a home for its wanderers' readings. Novelists joined the outpouring. Notably, Jack Kerouac followed his *The Town and the City* (1950) with the classic beat novel, *On the Road* (1957).

Most often beatniks were self-absorbed. They preached personal freedom. In dress and manner they reached back to the streets. They made poverty chic. They attacked materialism and insensitivity. They made jazz more than music. It became the sound of hip society, the language of a "now" generation. In pushing against traditional American frameworks, beatniks broadened the bridge for popular reception of expanding protest from blacks and other nonwhites and marginalized groups.

Beatniks did not treat race as such. Nor did much mainstream literature in the 1950s. Highbrow works, represented in part by Pulitzer Prize winners, reached back in U.S. history. A. B. Guthrie Jr.'s 1950 fiction winner, *The Way West;* Conrad Richter's 1951 winner, *The Town;* MacKinlay Kantor's 1956 winner, *Andersonville;* and Robert Lewis Taylor's 1959 winner, *The Travels of Jaimie McPheeters* exemplified the focus. John Patrick's 1954 drama winner, *The Teahouse of the August Moon,* alone among Pulitzer winners ventured to treat American cultural contacts with others.

Bestsellers of the decade also seldom ventured far from U.S. domestic scenes. They almost nowhere approached race relations. Several bestsellers at least glimpsed non-American scenes. Most notable was John Gunther's 1955 nonfiction bestseller *Inside Africa,* a 960-page sketch of Earth's second largest continent. In his 1956 bestseller, *The Tribe That Lost Its Head,* novelist Nicholas Monsarrat narrated problems of destabilization and violence in Africa. Finnish historical novelist Mika Waltari's 1951 bestseller, *The Wanderer,* introduced readers to tensions between Christianity and Islam in sixteenth-century Europe. His 785-page *The Egyptian,* a 1954 bestseller, recreated life during the ancient dynasties.

Kon-Tiki, Norwegian ethnographer and adventurer Thor Heyerdahl's 1950 work, carried readers on a raft attempt to validate pre-Colombian contacts between Polynesia and South America. The documentary film (also titled *Kon Tiki*) of Heyerdahl's expedition won a 1951 Academy Award. His 1958 nonfiction bestseller *Aku-Aku: The Secret of Easter Island* further extended his contact explorations. James A. Michener also mined the Pacific scene with two 1950s fiction bestsellers *Return to Paradise* (1951) and *Hawaii* (1959). So did James Jones in his 1953 bestseller, *From Here to Eternity.*

U.S. readers showed slight, if any, inclination to embrace on a popular level literature treating race. Perhaps they found it too disturbing. Especially when it sought to unsettle traditional racial perceptions and perspectives, literature treating American race relations received more polite nods than eager page-turning in the 1950s. Ralph Ellison's 1952 novel, *Invisible Man,* illustrated the cool popular approval of a masterwork on black identity and American racial constructs. Critics acclaimed the work. It won the 1953 National Book Award and made Ellison a lifelong recognized literary figure. Yet his socially invisible and unnamed contemporary black first-person protagonist's unapologetic review and renunciation of failed U.S. racial reform struck too close to home to make his work popular. Indeed, it represented a rejection of popular values.

More easily consumed, apparently, were more distant racial settings. Kyle Onstott's 1957 bodice-ripper novel *Mandingo*, for example, far outsold *Invisible Man*. It lacked any direct contemporary reach. It stayed in bygone days. Set in the 1830s, its sex and violence dramatized life on a fictional Alabama plantation called Falconhurst. Past slavery sat easier with readers than contemporary commentary on black stereotyping in white-dominated society. *Mandingo* reportedly sold 9.5 million copies over the years. It became the first volume in a trilogy with *Drum* (1962) and *Master of Falconhurst* (1964). *Mandingo* also became a movie (1975). *Invisible Man* simply became a literary classic. Treated in classrooms and at cocktail parties, it enjoyed no mass audience as *Mandingo* did. The film tie-in keyed popularity. Much literature filtered to American mass audiences mostly through movies, after all.

The thrust of the civil rights movement gave rise to a black urban realism. After *Invisible Man*, the signal event in the genre was expatriate James Baldwin's 1953 semiautobiographical first, and perhaps best, novel, *Go Tell It on the Mountain*. Set in New York City's Harlem, its 14-year-old protagonist opened his black family to full view. He emphasized his tortured relations with his father. Further, he exhibited a spiritual awakening and quest for independence that signaled aggressive, fresh black attitudes. Baldwin made clear his political commentary as an outspoken civil rights advocate in his 1955 essays, *Notes of a Native Son*. His 1956 novel, *Giovanni's Room*, struck another first, openly treating black homosexuality.

Baldwin marked the challenge of a new day. His 1955 stage drama, *The Amen Corner*, with its urban black family's spiritual yearning and unrest, fit with the rising work of other black dramatists. William Blackwell Branch's 1951 one-act, *A Medal for Willie*, focused on contemporary bigotry. It laid out relations in a southern town where black parents received their son's posthumous award for bravery during World War II. Branch's 1954 play, *In Splendid Error*, also deftly displayed rising civil rights themes. It reached out to discomfort middle-class white consciences. Using the American penchant to more easily accept dead blacks than lives ones, Branch staged a historical fiction featuring black abolitionists Frederick Douglass and Harriet Tubman and white John Brown. Their work for liberty-and-justice-for-all laid implicit claim on any socially aware audience. It paralleled past and present to personalize explosive 1950s racial issues.

Louis Peterson's *Take a Giant Step* (1953) brought issues north, focusing on a black teenager's confronting his identity and his environment in New England. Alice Childress's Obie Award-winning melodrama, *Trouble in Mind* (1955), scathingly revisited a black lynching in the South. Loften Mitchell's *A Land Beyond the River* (1957) and Lorraine Hansberry's *A Raisin in the Sun* (1959) rounded out the

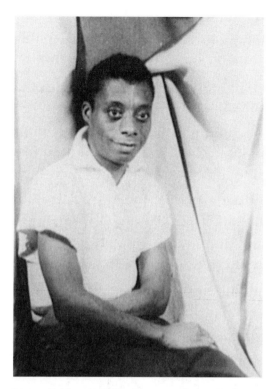

James Baldwin, 1955. Photograph by Carl Van Vechten. Courtesy of the Library of Congress, LC-USZ62-42481.

demonstration during the decade that opened Broadway and American theater more broadly to dramas blacks wrote and acted in and which focused on them.

The 1957 musical *West Side Story*, developed from Arthur Laurents's 1956 book, recognized Hispanics as an urban reality of the 1950s. It replayed the star-crossed lovers classic English playwright William Shakespeare canonized in *Romeo and Juliet*. Set in New York's Manhattan, Puerto Rican and Irish and Italian teenagers squared off for turf in juvenile delinquent gangs, the Sharks and the Jets. Identity and other cultural and social issues surfaced in the drama, but they were not centered. Nor was there much spotlighting elsewhere of other than whites in 1950s' U.S. theater.

Musical novelties offered a few glimpses of Asian American connections, but from afar and without domestic links. The Rogers and Hammerstein musical play *South Pacific*, with its 1958 film version, illustrated the approach. So did the 1953 prize-winning play *The Teahouse of the August Moon*. Rogers and Hammerstein's 1958 *Flower Drum Song* produced a domestic scene focused on illegal immigrant Mei Li in San Francisco's Chinatown. Native American theater also struggled for emergence and discovery. Pushing beyond being a media hand-me-down was, however, not a success of the 1950s. Like both Hispanic American and Asian American English-language theater, the Native American stage developed in later decades. The screen, not the stage, remained its primary venue—such as it was.

Away from reflected images of big and little screens, race relations in the 1950s advanced in American culture in the more direct, head-to-head world of sports. Media contributed, of course. Biographical sports films such as *The Jackie Robinson Story* (1950), *The Harlem Globetrotters* (1951), and *The Joe Louis Story* (1953) carried entertainment with social value. Simultaneously exhibiting America's racist barriers and prodigious nonwhite talents, such films gently suggested social benefits lay in desegregation. Yet to some the films perversely proved no need for social change as nonwhites with talent and drive could rise by their own means to reach the American Dream.

In fact, more and more in the 1950s' world of American sports and entertainment, nonwhites were rising to public acclaim. Multitalented Althea Gibson exemplified nonwhite athletes' grabbing success when opportunity opened. In August

Althea Gibson at Wimbledon, 1957. Courtesy of the Library of Congress, cph 3b26900.

1950, she became the first black to play tennis in the U.S. Championships. She won in 1957, becoming the United States Tennis Association's first black champion. She repeated in 1958. She was also the first black champion at the French Open, where she won singles in 1956, and at Wimbledon in England where she won singles in 1957 and 1958. She was also a repeat grand slam doubles champion.

In the 1950s, a rising stream of blacks followed Jackie Robinson and Larry Doby's 1947 introduction in Major League Baseball (MLB). Latinos also came. Venezuelan-born shortstop Alfonso "Chico" Carrasquel of the Chicago White Sox in 1951 became the first Hispanic American player in MLB's All-Star Game. Hitting .341 in 1954, Mexican-born Cleveland Indian second baseman Roberto "Beto" Avila became the first Hispanic American to win a MLB batting championship. In 1956 Venezuelan-born shortstop Luis Aparicio of the Baltimore Orioles became the first Hispanic American named MLB Rookie of the Year.

The National Football League (NFL) got less attention than MLB for integrating. But in 1946, the year *before* Jackie Robinson played for the Brooklyn Dodgers, Kenny Washington and Woody Strode suited up for the Rams, just relocated from Cleveland, Ohio, to Los Angeles, California. Cleveland Browns Marion Motley and Bill Willis joined them as the first blacks to play in the NFL; 29 other blacks joined the NFL by 1950. Marion Motley led the NFL in rushing in 1950, and during the decade, 143 blacks played in the league.

The color line fell also in the National Basketball Association (NBA). In 1950 Nathaniel "Sweetwater" Clifton joined the New York Knicks, Chuck Cooper joined the Boston Celtics, and Earl Lloyd played for the Washington Capitols. In 1953, 6'6" Don Barksdale became the first black to play in the NBA All-Star game; in 1948 he had been the first black to play for the U.S. Olympic basketball team.

The National Hockey League (NHL) signed its first black player—the Canadian Willie O'Ree—in January 1958. Although blind in one eye, he proved he could play with the best. In September 1959, William Wright became the first black U.S. Golf Association champion, winning the U.S. Amateur Public Links title in Colorado Springs.

As the 1950s ended, nonwhites had pushed from invisibility in almost every aspect of U.S. life. With blacks in the forefront as one-tenth of the U.S. population, racial minorities had come with growing public force to insist on American culture's recognizing and respecting who they were. And they were getting improved public reception.

Along with screen images and feats on playing fields, the sounds of the 1950s produced racial fusion. Crossovers integrated American music. The issue was reaching mass white audiences with other than traditional European sounds. Rhythm and blues, often known simply as R&B, made headway in the 1940s. Its thumping beats and suggestive lyrics left record producers leery about its having any reception in middle-class white America. But in the 1950s white musicians picked up and toned down the style. Pat Boone, Gale Storm, and the Fontane Sisters, for example, made pop covers of R&B hits. Record producers discovered an almost insatiable new audience for R&B and its spin off into rock 'n' roll. White teenagers consumed the fresh music as the sound of their rebellion. Radio blared it as so-called disc jockeys rode the harmonies hard on their shows. Dick Clark's *American Bandstand* ABC-TV show, starting in 1957, gave the sound a national showcase.

Elvis Presley personified the movement. The Mississippi-born, poor Memphis boy mixed white hillbilly and black blues with personal flamboyance. He dominated the hit charts by the late 1950s. His 1956 threesome of "Heartbreak Hotel," "Don't Be Cruel," and "Love Me Tender" and his 1957 "All Shook Up" soared. His TV appearances, especially on CBS's Sunday night *Ed Sullivan Show,* drew unprecedented audiences. Scrambling for part of the growing craze, music producers opened their arms to black artists such as Bo Diddly, Fats Domino, Chuck Berry, and Little Richard. A more soulful sound also brought enlarged audiences to Sam Cooke, Ray Charles, James Brown, Jackie Wilson, and Otis Redding, for example. In January 1959, Berry Gordy Jr. established what would become Motown records in Detroit, Michigan. Featuring first the Miracles with William "Smokey" Robinson, Motown grew in coming decades as the soundtrack of the baby boomer generation.

On a cooler side, jazz also grew. Its improvisation infusing African rhythms in European harmonies had become increasingly popular in the 1940s. Trumpeter Louis "Satchmo" Armstrong and pianist-composer-bandleader Edward Kennedy "Duke" Ellington, for example, evolved and expanded jazz for broadening audiences. Its syncopated rhythms drew together blues and ragtime in polyphonic ensembles. From small jazz clubs in New York City's Harlem and Greenwich Village and also in northern California, varying forms of jazz reached out even more widely in the 1950s. Trumpeter-composer Miles Davis soared in the crossover. Dizzy Gillespie, Charlie "Bird" Parker, Thelonious Monk, the Modern Jazz Quartet, Gerry Mulligan, Dave Brubeck, and a host of others added to jazz as a popular American music form.

Latin sounds more and more mixed into popular American music as well in the 1950s. Latin dance fads were particularly big. The cha-cha-cha became a craze. So did the mambo and rumba. Catalan-Cuban bandleader Xavier Cugat, the "king of rhumba," for earlier generations of Americans gave way in the 1950s to a new generation of dance hall conductors. Puerto Ricans Tito Puente and Eddie Palmieri became new kings. Reigning from New York clubs, they played to flocking subjects.

Perhaps even larger for Latinos in the 1950s crossover of musical forms was Ritchie Valens. The California-born Chicano singer-guitarist became a teenage heartthrob. He joined scrubbed whites such as Frankie Avalon, Bobby Rydell, and Fabian. He sparked a Latin pop explosion in the doo-wop generation. His 1959 hit "La Bamba" took on a life of its own after an airplane crash in February 1959 killed Valens along with rock 'n' roll singer Buddy Holly. Their dying together symbolized something of the cultural connections in the 1950s that had moved beyond segregation by race to reach fresh American popularity. That marked the decade as an important moment in changing U.S. race relations.

Ritchie Valens. Courtesy of Photofest.

INFLUENTIAL THEORIES AND VIEWS ON RACE RELATIONS

America found itself in the 1950s dealing more and more with practical re-alities in race relations. It showed less interest in general theory. It craved ideas for immediate solutions. With blacks marching in the forefront as 10 percent of the U.S. population in 1950, parades of nonwhites demonstrated the nation's pressing racial problems throughout the decade. Most of the influential views and theories on U.S. race relations that rose to popular recognition searched for solutions that could be put into immediate practice. The pressing questions of the decade facing the segregation problem were "What" and "How"?

Two broad sources of views and theories emerged. One came from scholars and social commentators. The other came from sidewalks and streets. Social scientists predominated among the scholars who became expert guides to past patterns and to designs to improve future race relations. Swedish political economist Gun-nar Myrdal's 1944 *An American Dilemma: The Negro Problem and Modern Democracy* became a semisacred writing in the 1950s. The 1,500-page, multiyear study the Carnegie Corporation of New York funded painfully detailed patterns and problems of U.S. race relations. The 1954 Supreme Court decision in *Brown v. Board of Education* cited the Myrdal work. In its footnote 11, Chief Justice Earl Warren's opinion for the unanimous Court significantly referenced several social science works. Most came from psychologists. He cited them as "modern authority" for a finding that public school segregation "has a detrimental effect upon the colored children."[74]

Black psychologist Kenneth B. Clark led Chief Justice Warren's cited experts. A Columbia University-trained Ph.D. (the first ever black doctorate there in psychology), Clark gained prominent attention for his 1950 White House conference presentation on the effect of prejudice and discrimination on personality development. He emerged in the 1950s as a leading contributor to civil rights. He testified repeatedly as an expert witness in litigation.

A well-respected scholar, Clark was also a dedicated activist who rejected halfway measures. To counter the effects of racism, he early advocated "policies and programs which are directed at the roots and foundations of the motivational pattern of a people." He pressed for "a sudden, dramatic, and honest reversal of the present exploitation and humiliation." He fully recognized the breadth of such an undertaking. "In order to achieve such an end it would be necessary for the officers of the legislative and executive branches of our government to attack the problem with zeal, honesty, and definiteness. It would be necessary to utilize every medium of propaganda and education—moving pictures, radio, newspapers and magazines," he had advised in the 1940s in writing on reversing anti-Negro attitudes in the United States.[75]

An unapologetic militant, Clark urged his fellow social scientists in the 1950s to engage in hands-on desegregation work. "[T]he social and psychological sciences are at present on the threshold of making direct and significant contributions to the progress of a rapidly changing society," he noted. He called for scholars to join reform efforts. He fully appreciated the need for unbiased research and reporting of findings. Indeed, he insisted on uncompromising intellectual honesty and exhorted social scientists to "assume the responsibility of developing their own safeguards." He believed true scholarship transcended the world of ideas and entered the world of action. Scholarship in his view was not some pie in the sky. It had practical utility. He unceasingly advocated "the direct use of social science findings in the process of social change."[76]

Clark's approach reflected what some commentators and critics called "social engineering." It was a hotly contested view in the 1950s, and not then alone. Its perspective was not new. The basic approach had been argued since the Scientific Revolution in Enlightenment Europe in the 1600s and 1700s. The discovery of physical laws in nature prompted many to adopt the view that scientifically discoverable laws controlled both natural environments and social environments. If that were so, people could apply such laws to produce desired outcomes. They could design improved human societies. They could use scientific knowledge to solve human problems such as race relations. That was what Clark advocated.

The Austrian-born philosopher Karl Popper had helped popularize the term *social engineering* with his influential 1945 book *The Open Society and Its Enemies*.

Teaching at England's London School of Economics, Popper's views on social and political philosophy enjoyed significant influence. Like Clark, he advocated hands-on, socially conscious scholarship. "The only course open to the social sciences is . . . to tackle the practical problems of our time with the help of the theoretical methods which are fundamentally the same in *all* sciences," Popper wrote. "A social technology is needed which can be tested by social engineering," he insisted. "The social engineer believes that man is the master of his own destiny, and that in accordance with our aims we can influence or change the history of man just as we have changed the face of the earth," he boldly declared.[77]

Popper had many critics, as did social engineering, itself. Most critics conceded natural laws existed and governed human affairs. That was not the issue. The character and changeability of such laws were what was contested. Critics contended that *immutable* natural laws determined social relations and results. They rejected the premise that societies rested simply on changeable, human-made normative laws.

Echoing the hoary sounds of pro-slavery rhetoric, some pro-segregationist critics of social engineering insisted divine or natural law ordained white superiority and nonwhite inferiority. They viewed race relations as unvariable. In their eyes American apartheid was unalterable. White supremacy and racial segregation existed as the divine or natural order of things. No human intervention could change the nature of the races or their relations, such critics insisted.

Value conflicts obviously separated the contrasting views of social engineering. Social positioning had much to do with perspectives. An easy divide separated haves from have-nots. The halves tended to conservatism. Understandably, they wanted to keep what they had. They liked what they had. Moreover, many white segregationist psychologically needed what they had. Their social distance from nonwhites defined their value. Indeed, it defined their identity. Segregation defined the world they knew. They feared change. Improving the lot of nonwhites was not on their agenda. Or, if it appeared, it had low priority. They hardly saw it reflecting any common good or general welfare. Desegregation was pointless, wrenching change from their perspective. It was "contrary to a way of life and violates the way in which they have thought since 1619," the then lily-white University of Virginia's student *Cavalier Daily* declared in May 1954 in responding to the U.S. Supreme Court's *Brown* decision.[78]

Segregationists denounced desegregation as trying to turn the world upside down. Many invoked pseudoscience to support their views. They conjured their own visions of natural law. They early lambasted the *Brown* decision as deviating from law of every kind and level. *New York Times* reporter James Reston captured the point of such criticism the day after the *Brown* decision. The head of his story read "A Sociological Decision; Court Founded Its Segregation Ruling on Hearts and Minds Rather Than Laws."[79]

Critics were not simply southern whites. Segregation had nationwide support, and desegregation had nationwide detractors. Carleton Putnam emerged in the late 1950s, for example, touting what he called "race and reason."[80] The U.S.

airline pioneer, then living in McLean, Virginia, was the scion of a distinguished white New England revolutionary war family. His publicized "Yankee view" staunchly defended racial segregation as a commonsense, logical, and scientifically based social arrangement. He would come to denounce desegregation as "thoroughly infected with the equalitarian virus."[81]

Desegregation promised disaster, Putnam prophesied. It bucked the natural order. Or, at least, it tried to. It aimed to put blacks where they did not belong. It hoisted them into positions they could not keep. What Putnam would call innate "inequalities of intellect" limited blacks to where they sat in segregation.[82] There was no changing their position. It resulted from who they were, and there was no changing that.

America's social character rested on recognizing racial differences, Putnam and his ilk insisted. In their view, ignoring immutable distinctions promised only frustration and resentment. It would lessen standards and reduce the general quality of U.S. life. It would lead to violence, especially in larger cities where blacks and whites crowding together and competing for social space and place would increase, not decrease, racial antagonisms. Putnam forecast only dismal days if desegregation proceeded.

Putnam's rusty rhetoric of race-based intelligence seemed perennial. Evolutionist Charles Darwin's polymath cousin Francis Galton's 1884 *Hereditary Genius* elevated such conceptions of race and intelligence to modern heights. Nothing appeared able to banish notions of innate racial differences. Audrey M. Shuey fueled the 1950s debate on racial intelligence. Chairman of the department of psychology at Randolph Macon Woman's College in Lynchburg, Virginia, she published a study in 1958 titled *The Testing of Negro Intelligence*. Her work reviewed results from nearly 300 published psychometric studies done almost exclusively in the United States between 1913 and 1957. She concluded that the accepted facts "all point to the presence of some native differences between Negroes and whites as determined by intelligence tests."[83]

That differences existed in America between whites and nonwhites, especially between whites and blacks, was incontestable. The causes, extent, and consequences of the differences were, however, much contested. Debate raged over the influence of cultural and environmental factors and over blacks' character and capacity to improve. The theme pushed discourse in diverse directions. It drove some back to arguments for and against American Negro slavery as background for understanding racial problems in the 1950s. The 1957 reissue of Gilbert H. Barnes's 1933 book *The Anti-Slavery Impulse*, for example, aimed apparently to remind readers of the problem of the "peculiar institution" and the need to eradicate it.

A generation of history writers had crested at depicting slavery as almost innocuous. Orville W. Taylor's 1958 *Negro Slavery in Arkansas* was a late example of the approach. Black historian Edgar A. Toppin took to task this scion of slaveholders' matter-of-fact "manifold defense of slavery."[84] But Taylor was hardly alone. Revisiting the advent and aftermath of the Civil War—which some sought to sanitize under the title "the War between the States"—came in fact and fiction.

More than a few untrained hands raised the question *Why the Civil War*, as Austrian-born chemist and inventor Otto Eisenschiml titled his 1958 book. Professionals were hard at work, too. Princeton University history professor Robert A. Lively's 1957 *Fiction Fights the Civil War* reviewed nearly 400 novels on the apparently unending sectional conflict. Bruce Catton's *A Stillness at Appomattox*, the closing volume of his Civil War trilogy, won the 1954 Pulitzer Prize for History. MacKinlay Kantor's *Andersonville* won the 1956 Pulitzer Prize for Fiction. Neither tales of ghastly battles nor prison camp horrors carried much about slavery as a cause of the war or of slaves' emancipation as a consequence.

Lingering projections of happy slaves mixed in the 1950s with comments about how blacks were better off under segregation. Apartheid kept blacks where they belonged, as slavery had, segregationists asserted. Adhering to such views some saw the error of forced emancipation being repeated in forced desegregation. In line with Carleton Putnam's later comments, Carolina journalist and radio and television commentator Waldemar E. Debnam cursed desegregation as a harbinger of what he termed "mongrelization" in his 1955 book, *Then My Old Kentucky Home, Good Night!*[85] He roundly criticized the *Brown* decision as wrongly reasoning to disastrous results. Blacks simply could not be put on the same footing as whites, Debnam and his cohort insisted.

Relatively few white commentators or scholars challenged the apparent, accepted wisdom of black inferiority. Instead, they disagreed primarily on the causes, character, and effects of such inferiority. They divided over the roles of nature and nurture. Some simply held blacks naturally lacked the essential or substantive attributes to be treated the same as whites. Others suggested blacks suffered from correctable pathologies. Psychologist Bertram P. Karon in his 1958 work, *The Negro Personality*, explained "many of the 'characteristics of the Negro' are merely those of lower class people in general, as compared with the middle class; being poorer, less educated, more 'loose' sexually, and more interested in present pleasures than in long-term goals."[86] Negroes could be "cured" of such characteristics. Given correct conditioning, they could abandon their deviations, the later longtime professor at Michigan State University suggested.

Historian Kenneth M. Stampp stirred much reaction in 1956 with his first major book, *The Peculiar Institution: Slavery in the Ante-Bellum South*. With sweeping revision, he offered in his preface that "innately American slaves were merely ordinary human beings, that innately Negroes *are*, after all, only white men with black skins, nothing more, nothing less."[87] Many rejected out-of-hand his claim that no essential difference separated blacks and whites. Others challenged such claims as ahistorical or undocumented anthropological or sociological assumptions. Nevertheless, as a reviewer in the 1958 *Journal of Economic History* noted, Stampp's work was "an important chapter in historical revisionism which takes on special significance at this time when racism and States'-rights doctrines are enjoying a resurgence in various sections of the South."[88]

Attacking paternalism and highlighting slavery's deprivations, Stampp accented slavery's moral tragedy. He did not conclude that slavery crippled blacks, however. Rather, he rendered slaves as characteristically unaffected by their generations of institutionalization. Injecting his views of social psychology into understanding slaves, historian Stanley Elkins's 1959 *Slavery: A Problem in American Institutional and Intellectual Life* challenged Stampp. The cheerful, childish, submissive slave was a character to be reckoned with to understand not only slavery, but blacks' current condition, Elkins insisted.

Where Stampp attacked and dismissed paternalism, Elkins sought to explain its influence on slaves. He claimed slaveholders wielded an "absolute power" that infantilized slaves. It created in the slave a "relationship with his master [that] was one of utter dependence and childlike attachment," Elkins asserted.[89] And that was not simply a past problem of slavery. It lingered to explain at least in part blacks' post-slavery performance.

American Negro slavery created "Sambo," Elkins argued. That was no simple black caricature. Sambo was an actual and unique character. He was "the typical plantation slave," Elkins insisted. Sambo was "docile but irresponsible, loyal but lazy, humble but chronically given to lying and stealing; his behavior was full of infantile silliness and his talk inflated with childish exaggeration," Elkins argued.[90] Here was a source of the pathologies, or at least the symptoms of black "deviance" psychologist Bertram P. Karon and others described.

Whether slavery mattered or not was itself a distinct question in the 1950s. Rather than focus on the past, many Americans preferred to focus on the present and future. Most nonblack Americans considered they had nothing to do with slavery. It was long over in their minds. They argued for Americans to put slavery behind them and move on. Blacks especially needed to put slavery behind themselves and move on, the view continued.

Blacks, themselves, urged breaking with the past and moving on. To them that meant ending segregation, which they saw as the residue of slavery. Many blacks and nonblacks agreed racial confusion, hatred, and separation stemmed from conditioning and learning. Indeed, prominent attention during the 1950s focused on conditioning and learning as essential to racial prejudice. Gerhard Saenger's *The Social Psychology of Prejudice* (1953) and Gordon Allport's *The Nature of Prejudice* (1954) both attributed discrimination largely to social atmosphere, to peer pressure.

Discrimination was something of a self-fulfilling prophecy for social distance in Saenger's and Allport's views. To break the cycle required bold legal and social action. As with the Supreme Court's *Brown* decision, however, the emerging social science literature proved better at explaining *why* change was needed. It did less well in specifying *what* change was needed. At best the scholarly source of views and theories offered elegant critiques of segregation as an entrenched social system. It proved less practical in directing desegregation. It skirted or provided only general outlines for what was the most effective process to undo white domination and nonwhites subordination.

The most immediate answers to desegregation questions came from the second broad source of racial views and theories in the 1950s—the sidewalks and streets.

Desegregation progressed during the decade by dint of practical, popular pressures. People on the sidewalks and in the streets pushed and pulled. A herky-jerky accommodation resulted. The Baton Rouge Bus Boycott of 1953 signaled the pattern. The Montgomery Bus Boycott of 1955–1956 confirmed it.

A growing people's movement against segregation and racial inequities shifted American perspectives and thinking in the 1950s. From mobilizing for local action, desegregation protesters enlarged their social and political context and impact throughout the decade. Expanding mass demonstrations extended protest networks. They relayed urgency for change throughout the nation. Television projected the urgency. It made the urgency personal to viewers. It made them participants. One way or another, media focus on the desegregation struggle shifted attitudes.

Desegregation protesters were not alone. Pro-segregationists mounted massive resistance. It was not an exclusive southern phenomenon. At least 2,000 Illinois whites, for example, massed in August 1953 to block a black family from living in the Chicago Housing Authority's Trumbull Park Homes. Brick- and stone-throwing whites rioted for neighborhood racial homogeneity. Whites in localities throughout the North resisted desegregation. They balked at changing their racially exclusive residential, schooling, and social patterns no less than southern whites. The main sectional difference was the South's segregation by law.

Significant numbers of whites across sections shared their racial recalcitrance. Some saw themselves as counterrevolutionaries. In their view desegregation represented radicalism. It sought to overthrow decades, if not centuries, of tradition. It sought to impose an invidious egalitarianism. It threatened standards of living. It ignored values. It tended to level social relations to a lowest common denominator in the views of such resisters.

Critics of what became capitalized in the South as "Massive Resistance" often too easily dismissed such protest as futile fighting against ineluctable tides. But the tides flowed to and fro. Change was clearly afoot in the 1950s. Where it would go was not so clear. America at the end of the decade was not what it had been at the beginning of the decade. "This world is white no longer, and it never will be white again," boldly declared 31-year-old black writer James Baldwin in his 1955 collection of essays, *Notes of a Native Son*.[91]

What America would be was very much in question. Desegregation, which some shifted to integration, violently refreshened America's search for identity. The nation's distinctive color-coded cast was under siege. Its collective character appeared tottering. It was being shaken by people in the streets, as millions watched on television. Blacks and other desegregation protesters acted with no elaborately formulated grand design or theory. They pressed immediate, practical issues. Blacks wanted equal access to public buses. With other nonwhites, they wanted their children to have quality public schooling. They wanted to vote and have their votes counted. They were demanding no complex remedies in their view. They were demanding an end to racial inequities.

The protesters' very presence and persistence generated social change. They challenged local and national public will. The novice pastor of the Dexter

Avenue Baptist Church in Montgomery, Alabama, caught the tenor of the moment. Thrust into the spotlight during the 1955–1956 bus boycott, the Reverend Martin Luther King Jr. challenged the nation. "Where Do We Go from Here?" he queried in the long concluding chapter of his 1958 book *Stride toward Freedom*.

A genuine people's movement confronted the United States, King indicated. "The Montgomery story would have taken place if the leaders of the protest had never been born," he wrote.[92] The issues of the day were not influential theories. They turned on practical realities. "We have no alternative but to protest," King had declared in his first public statement during the bus boycott. "For many years we have shown an amazing patience. We have sometimes given our white brothers the feeling that we liked the way we were being treated," he explained. "But we come here tonight to be saved from that patience that makes us patient with anything less than freedom and justice."[93] That was the influential view of U.S. race relations as the 1950s closed.

RESOURCE GUIDE

SUGGESTED READINGS

General and Cultural

Branch, Taylor. *Parting the Waters: America in the King Years, 1954–1963*. New York: Simon and Schuster, 1988.

Early, Gerald Lyn. *One Nation under a Groove: Motown and American Culture*. Ann Arbor: University of Michigan Press, 2004.

Gillon, Stephen M. *The American Paradox: A History of the United States since 1945*. Boston: Houghton Mifflin Company, 2003.

Halberstam, David. *The Fifties*. New York: Villard, 1993.

Hixton, Walter L. *Parting the Curtain: Propaganda, Culture, and the Cold War*. New York: St. Martin's Press, 1997.

Kallen, Stuart A. *The 1950s: America's Decades*. San Diego, CA: Greenhaven Press, 2000.

MacDonald, J. Fred. *Blacks and White TV: Afro-Americans in Television since 1948*. Chicago: Nelson-Hall, 1983.

MacDonald, J. Fred. *One Nation under Television*. New York: Pantheon, 1990.

Marling, Karal Ann. *As Seen on TV: The Visual Culture of Everyday Life in the 1950s*. Cambridge: Harvard University Press, 1994.

Miller, Douglas T., and Marion Nowak. *The Fifties: The Way We Really Were*. Garden City, NY: Doubleday, 1975.

Stone, I. F. *The Haunted Fifties, 1953–1963: A Nonconformist History of Our Times*. Boston: Little, Brown, 1963.

Szatmary, David P. *Rockin' in Time: A Social History of Rock and Roll*. Englewood Cliffs, NJ: Prentice-Hall, 1987.

Waller, Don. *The Motown Story*. New York: C. Scribner, 1985.

Ward, Brian. *Radio and the Struggle for Civil Rights in the South.* Gainesville: University Press of Florida, 2004.

Williams, Juan. *Eyes on the Prize: America's Civil Rights Years, 1954–1965.* New York: Viking Press, 1987.

Wills, Charles A. *America in the 1950s: Decades of American History.* New York: Chelsea House, 2005.

Woll, Allen L., and Randall M. Miller. *Ethnic and Racial Images in American Film and Television: Historical Essays and Bibliography.* New York: Garland, 1987.

African Americans

Burk, Robert Fredrick. *The Eisenhower Administration and Black Civil Rights.* Knoxville: University of Tennessee Press, 1984.

Kluger, Richard. *Simple Justice: The History of Brown v. Board of Education and Black America's Struggle for Equality.* New York: Knopf, 1976.

Patterson, James T. Brown v. Board of Education: *A Civil Rights Milestone and Its Troubled Legacy.* New York: Oxford University Press, 2001.

American Indians

Fixico, Donald L. *Termination and Relocation: Federal Indian Policy 1945–1960.* Albuquerque: University of New Mexico Press, 1986.

Philip, Kenneth R. *Termination Revisited: American Indians on the Trail to Self-Determination, 1933–1953.* Lincoln: University of Nebraska Press, 1999.

Valandra, Edward Charles. *Not without Our Consent: Lakota Resistance to Termination, 1950–59.* Urbana: University of Illinois Press, 2006.

Asian Americans

Bascara, Victor. *Model-Minority Imperialism.* Minneapolis: University of Minnesota Press, 2006.

Chen, Tina. *Double Agency: Acts of Impersonation in Asian American Literature and Culture.* Stanford: Stanford University Press, 2005.

Chung, Hye Seung. *Hollywood Asian: Philip Ahn and the Politics of Cross-Ethnic Performance.* Philadelphia: Temple University Press, 2006.

de Jesús, Melinda L., ed. *Pinay Power: Peminist Critical Theory: Theorizing the Filipina/American Experience.* New York: Routledge, 2005.

Hurh, Won Moo. *The Korean Americans.* Westport, CT: Greenwood Press, 1998.

Koshy, Susan. *Sexual Naturalization: Asian Americans and Miscegenation.* Stanford: Stanford University Press, 2004.

Lee, Jennifer, and Min Zhou, eds. *Asian American Youth: Culture, Identity, and Ethnicity.* New York: Routledge, 2004.

Tiongson, Antonio T. Jr., Edgardo V. Gutierrez, and Ricardo V. Gutierrez, eds. *Positively No Filipinos Allowed: Building Communities and Discourse.* Philadelphia: Temple University Press, 2006.

Zhao, Xiaojian. *Remaking Chinese America: Immigration, Family, and Community, 1940–1965.* New Brunswick, NJ: Rutgers University Press, 2002.

European Americans

Bartley, Numan. *The Rise of Massive Resistance*. Baton Rouge: Louisiana State University Press, 1969.

Feldman, Glenn, ed. *Before Brown: Civil Rights and White Backlash in the Modern South*. Tuscaloosa: University of Alabama Press, 2004.

Hirsch, Arnold R. "Massive Resistance in the Urban North: Trumbull Park, Chicago, 1953–1966." *Journal of American History* 82, no. 2 (September 1995): 522–550.

Kruse, Kevin Michael. *White Flight: Atlanta and the Making of Modern Conservatism*. Princeton, NJ: Princeton University Press, 2005.

Lassiter, Matthew D., and Andrew B. Lewis, eds. *The Moderates' Dilemma: Massive Resistance to School Desegregation in Virginia*. Charlottesville: University Press of Virginia, 1998.

Lewis, George. *Massive Resistance: The White Response to the Civil Rights Movement*. New York: Oxford University Press, 2006.

Moye, J. Todd. *Let the People Decide: Black Freedom and White Resistance Movements in Sunflower County, Mississippi, 1945–1986*. Chapel Hill: University of North Carolina Press, 2004.

Muse, Benjamin. *Virginia's Massive Resistance*. Bloomington: Indiana University Press, 1961.

Webb, Clive, ed. *Massive Resistance: Southern Opposition to the Second Reconstruction*. New York: Oxford University Press, 2005.

Wilhoit, Francis M. *The Politics of Massive Resistance*. New York: George Braziller, 1973.

Hispanic Americans

Acuña, Rodolfo F. *Sometimes There Is No Other Side: Chicanos and the Myth of Equality*. Notre Dame, IN: University of Notre Dame Press, 1998.

Aranda, Elizabeth M. *Emotional Bridges to Puerto Rico: Migration, Return Migration, and the Struggles of Incorporation*. Lanham, MD: Rowman & Littlefield, 2007.

Cervantez, Ernesto E. *Once upon the 1950s*. Bethel, CT: Rutledge Books, 1997.

Duignan, Peter J., and Lewis H. Gann. *The Spanish Speakers in the United States: A History*. Rev. ed. Lanham, MD: University Press of America, 1998.

García, Juan Ramon. *Operation Wetback: The Mass Deportation of Mexican Undocumented Workers in 1954*. Westport, CT: Greenwood Press, 1980.

Gracia, Jorge J. E., and Pablo De Greiff, eds. *Hispanics/Latinos in the United States: Ethnicity, Race, and Rights*. New York: Routledge, 2000.

Kaplowitz, Craig Allan. *LULAC, Mexican Americans, and National Policy*. College Station: Texas A & M University Press, 2005.

Márquez, Benjamin. *LULAC: The Evolution of a Mexican American Political Organization*. Austin: University of Texas Press, 1993.

Moquin, Wayne, ed. *A Documentary History of the Mexican Americans*. New York: Praeger Publishers, 1971.

Negrón-Muntaner, Frances, and Ramón Grosfo. *Puerto Rican Jam: Rethinking Colonialism and Nationalism*. Minneapolis: University of Minnesota Press, 1997.

Olivas, Michael A. ed. *Colored Men and Hombres Aquí: Hernández v. Texas and the Emergence of Mexican American Lawyering*. Houston, TX: Arte Publico Press, 2006.

Rosales, Francisco A. *Testimonio: A Documentary History of the Mexican-American Struggle for Civil Rights*. San Antonio, TX: Arte Publico Press, 2000.

United States-Puerto Rico Commission on the Status of Puerto Rico. *Status of Puerto Rico: Selected Background Studies, Prepared for the United States-Puerto Rico Commission on the Status of Puerto Rico.* Washington, DC: GPO, 1966; reprint, New York: Arno Press, 1975.

Public Policy

Gardner, Michael R. *Harry Truman and Civil Rights: Moral Courage and Political Risks.* Carbondale: Southern Illinois University Press, 2002.

Pauley, Garth E. *The Modern Presidency & Civil Rights: Rhetoric on Race from Roosevelt to Nixon.* College Station: Texas A&M University Press, 2001.

Plummer, Brenda Gayle, ed. *Window on Freedom: Race, Civil Rights, and Foreign Affairs, 1945–1988.* Chapel Hill: University of North Carolina Press, 2003.

Powell, Colin L. *President Truman and the Desegregation of the Armed Forces: A 50th Anniversary View of Executive Order 9981.* Washington, DC: National Legal Center for the Public Interest, 1998.

Shull, Steven A. *American Civil Rights Policy from Truman to Clinton: The Role of Presidential Leadership.* Armonk, NY: M.E. Sharpe, 1999.

Wexler, Sanford. *The Civil Rights Movement: An Eyewitness History.* New York: Facts on File, 1993.

FILMS AND VIDEOS

DISCovering Multicultural America: African Americans, Hispanic Americans, Asian Americans, Native Americans. Detroit MI: Gale Research, 1996. CD-Rom interactive multimedia.

Eyes on the Prize: America's Civil Rights Years. Produced and directed by Judith Vecchione. ca. 360 min. Blackside, Inc. 1986. 6 videocassettes.

The Ground beneath Our Feet: Virginia's History since the Civil War. Episode 3—*Massive Resistance.* 60 min. Produced by George H. Gilliam. Central Virginia Public Television (CVPTV), 2000.

Signpost to Freedom: The 1953 Baton Rouge Bus Boycott. Produced and directed by Christina Melton and C.E. Richards. 57 min. Louisiana Public Broadcasting, 2005. TV documentary.

WEB SITES

The Advertiser Co., "The Story of the Montgomery Bus Boycott." http://www.montgomeryboycott.com/.

The Brown Foundation for Educational Equity, Excellence and Research. http://brownvboard.org/foundation/.

Library of Congress, "African American Odyssey: The Civil Rights Era." http://memory.loc.gov/ammem/aaohtml/exhibit/aopart9.html.

Milwaukee Public Museum, "Menominee Termination and Restoration." http://www.mpm.edu/wirp/ICW-97.html.

National Park Service, "Brown v. Board of Education National Historic Site, Kansas." www.nps.gov/brvb/.

Presidential Task Force on Asian Americans / Northern Illinois University, "Landmarks in Asian American History." http://www3.niu.edu/ptaa/history.htm.

Seattle Civil Rights and Labor History Project, "Asian Americans and Seattle's Civil Rights History." http://depts.washington.edu/civilr/Asian%20Americans.htm.

Southwest Indian Relief Council, "Termination Policy 1953–1968." http://www.nrcpro grams.org/site/PageServer?pagename=swirc_hist_terminationpolicy.

University of Michigan Library's *Brown v. Board of Education* Digital Archive. http://www.lib.umich.edu/exhibits/brownarchive/.

Virginia Historical Society, "The Civil Rights Movement in Virginia: Massive Resistance." http://www.vahistorical.org/civilrights/massiveresistance.htm.

NOTES

1. H.R. Con. Res. 108, 67 Stat. B 132 (1953).
2. Editorial, "Trouble for the Indians," *Washington Post*, August 12, 1953, 10.
3. Editorial, "Flexible Indian Policy," *Washington Post*, November 2, 1953, 8.
4. H.R. Con. Res. 108, 67 Stat. B 132 (1953).
5. "Trouble for the Indians," 10.
6. John Collier, "Indian Rule," *Washington Post*, August 12, 1953, 10.
7. Collier, "Indian Rule," 10.
8. "Trouble for the Indians," 10.
9. Editorial, "Veto Called for," *New York Times*, August 27, 1954, 20.
10. "Veto Called for," 20.
11. *Brown v. Board of Education*, 347 U.S. 483, 495 (1954).
12. *Plessy v. Ferguson*, 163 U.S. 537, 540 (1896).
13. *Brown*, 347 U.S. 483, 493.
14. *Cumming v. Richmond County Board of Education*, 175 U.S. 528, 545 (1899).
15. *Cumming*, 175 U.S. 528, 545.
16. *Roberts v. City of Boston*, 59 Mass. 198, 210 (1850).
17. *Brown*, 347 U.S. at 493.
18. *Brown*, 347 U.S. at 493.
19. *Brown*, 347 U.S. at 495.
20. *Brown*, 347 U.S. at 495.
21. Gladwin Hill, "Southwest Winks at 'Wetback' Jobs," *New York Times*, March 28, 1951, 31; John Dillin, "How Eisenhower Solved Illegal Border Crossings from Mexico," *Christian Science Monitor*, July 6, 2006, 20.
22. Bill Dredge, "Wetbacks Herded at Nogales Camp: 1187 Wait in Blistering Heat for Long Leg of the Journey Home," *Los Angeles Times*, June 20, 1954, 1A.
23. "150,000 'Wetbacks' Taken in Round-Up," *New York Times*, July 30, 1954, 7.
24. Gladwin Hill, "700 on Coast Open 'Wetback' Drive; Mobile Task Forces Round Up Border Jumpers in Test of New Federal Strategy," *New York Times*, June 18, 1954, 14.
25. Hill, "700 on Coast Open 'Wetback' Drive," 14.
26. Dredge, "Wetbacks Herded at Nogales Camp," 1A.
27. See "Apology Act for the 1930s Mexican Repatriation Program," Cal. Gov. Code §§ 8720–8721 (a)-(c).

28. "Horde Departs for Native Soil," *Los Angeles Times*, April 24, 1931, 1.

29. Success Story: Congressman-Elect to Visit Native India," *Los Angeles Times*, November 9, 1956, 22.

30. Totton J. Anderson, "The 1956 Election in California," *Western Political Quarterly* 10, no. 1 (March 1957): 106.

31. 1913 Cal. Stat. chap. 113 (May 19, 1913); 1 Cal. Gen. Laws, Act 261 (Deering 1944, 1945 Supp.).

32. California State Board of Control, *California and the Orientals* (Sacramento: California State Printing Office, 1920); Karen Leonard, "Punjabi Farmers and California's Alien Land Law," *Agricultural History* 59, no. 4 (October 1985): 550 n5.

33. *United States v. Bhagat Singh Thind*, 261 U.S. 204, 215 (1923).

34. The quotation from the Eisenhower Diary, July 20, 1953, appears in Michael S. Mayer, "With Much Deliberation and Some Speed: Eisenhower and the *Brown* Decision," *Journal of Southern History* 52, no. 1 (February 1986): 49.

35. *Brown v. Board of Education*, 347 U.S. 483, 495 (1954).

36. *Signpost to Freedom: The 1953 Baton Rouge Bus Boycott*, Christina Melton, prod. Louisiana Public Broadcasting (LPB) 2005, DVD.

37. Editorial, "Flexible Indian Policy," *Washington Post*, November 2, 1953, 8.

38. President Andrew Jackson, First Annual Address to Congress, December 6, 1829, in *A Compilation of the Messages and Papers of the Presidents, 1789–1897* (New York: Bureau of National Literature, 1897), 999–1001.

39. Jackson, First Annual Address, 1000.

40. Jackson, First Annual Address, 1000.

41. Donald Fixico, *Termination and Relocation: Federal Indian Policy 1945–1960* (Albuquerque: University of New Mexico Press, 1986), 98.

42. Success Story: Congressman-Elect to Visit Native India," *Los Angeles Times*, November 9, 1956, 22.

43. "Hawaii Legislators Pledge Rights Aid: First Senator of Asian Ancestry is Millionaire," *Chicago Defender*, August 15, 1959, 21.

44. "Hawaii Legislators Pledge Rights Aid," 21.

45. Chalmers M. Roberts and Alfred E. Lewis, "Plotters Felled by Blazing Guns at Blair House; Third Man Held; Police Slay Assassin at Truman's Door," *Washington Post*, March 2, 1950, 1.

46. "October 26 Set as Death Date: Sentence Pronounced for His Killing of White House Guard," *Washington Post*, April 7, 1951, B1.

47. Peter Kihss, "'Sublime Heroism' Cited in Shooting: Puerto Rico Nationalist Party Leader Calls Attack New Demand for Freedom," *New York Times*, March 3, 1954, 14.

48. See "Apology Act for the 1930s Mexican Repatriation Program," Cal. Gov. Code §§ 8720–8721 (a)-(c).

49. *Hernandez v. Texas*, 347 U.S. 475, 478 (1954).

50. "Editorial Excerpts From the Nation's Press on Segregation Ruling," *New York Times*, May 18, 1954, 19, quoting Kentucky's *Louisville Courier Journal* and the University of Virginia (Charlottesville) *Daily Cavalier*.

51. 102 *Cong. Rec.* 4459–4460 (March 12, 1956).

52. 99 Cong. Rec. 1518 (March 2, 1953) (statement of Sen. McCarran).

53. Immigration and Nationality Act of 1952 (McCarran-Walter Act), 66 Stat. 163, Pub. L. No. 82–414, 241–250.

54. *Henderson v. United States*, 339 U.S. 816, 824 (1950).

55. *Hernandez v. Texas*, 347 U.S. 475, 478 (1954).

56. *Brown v. Board of Education*, 347 U.S. 483, 495 (1954).

57. *Richmond Times-Dispatch* and *Dallas News*, quoted in "Editorial Excerpts From the Nation's Press on Segregation Ruling," *New York Times*, May 18, 1954, 19.

58. *Brown v. Board of Education (Brown II)*, 349 U.S. 294, 301 (1955).

59. *Brown II*, 298.

60. 102 Cong. Rec. 4459–4460 (March 12, 1956).

61. Robert E. Baker, "Anti-Court Manifesto Stirs Row; Senate Fireworks Follow Attack by Southerners on Desegregation Manifesto against Supreme Court Sets Off Fireworks in the Senate," *Washington Post*, March 13, 1956, 1.

62. *Cooper v. Aaron*, 358 U.S. 1, 18 (1958).

63. *Cooper v. Aaron*, at 18–20.

64. *Naim v. Naim*, 197 Va. 80, 83, quoting with approval *Wood v. Commonwealth*, 159 Va. 963, 965, 166 S.E. 477 (1932).

65. *Gayle v. Browder*, 142 F. Supp. 707, 717 (D.C.M.D. Ala. 1956).

66. "Launch Drive to Aid Sepia TV Hopefuls," *Chicago Defender*, September 3, 1955, 7.

67. Alex McNeil, *Total Television: A Comprehensive Guide to Programming from 1948 to the Present*, 3rd ed. (New York: Penguin Books, 1991), 111, quoting 1960 *TV Guide* magazine interview.

68. "Our Opinions: TV Ain't the Thing," *Chicago Defender*, March 19, 1955, 9.

69. "Dixie Scribe Suggests Readers Protest Sepias on TV," *Chicago Defender*, August 14, 1956, 14.

70. "Dixie Scribe Suggest Readers Protest Sepias on TV," 14.

71. Arch Puddington, *Broadcasting Freedom: The Cold War Triumph of Radio Free Europe and Radio Liberty* (Lexington: University Press of Kentucky, 2000), 3.

72. James W. Vander Zanden, "The Impact of Little Rock," *Journal of Educational Sociology* 35, no. 8 (April 1962): 382.

73. Enoc P. Waters Jr., "Adventures in Race Relations," *Chicago Defender*, January 3, 1959, 10.

74. *Brown v. Board of Education*, 374 U.S. 483, 494.

75. Kenneth B. Clark, "Morale of the Negro on the Home Front: World Wars I and II," *Journal of Negro Education* 12, no. 3 (Summer 1943): 428.

76. Kenneth B. Clark, "The Social Scientist as an Expert Witness in Civil Rights Litigation," *Social Problems* 1, no. 1 (June 1953): 10.

77. Karl R. Popper, *The Open Society and Its Enemies*, 2 vols. (London: G. Routledge & Sons, 1945), 2:210, 1:17; William H. Tolman, *Social Engineering: A Record of Things Done by American Industrialists Employing Upwards of One and One-Half Million People* (New York: McGraw Publishing, 1909), developed the phrase "social engineering" to describe applying social sciences for industrial betterment. Steel magnate Andrew Carnegie wrote an introduction for Tolman's work.

78. "Editorial Excerpts from the Nation's Press on Segregation Ruling," *New York Times*, May 18, 1954, 19.

79. *New York Times*, May 18, 1954, 14.

80. Carleton Putnam, *Race and Reason: A Yankee View* (Washington, DC: Public Affairs Press, 1961), codified for wider distribution Putnam's thinking announced in the 1950s.

81. Carleton Putnam, "Letters: Culture and Race," *Science* 135, no. 3507 (March 16, 1962): 967.

82. Putnam, 967.

83. Audrey M. Shuey, *The Testing of Negro Intelligence* (Lynchburg, VA: J.P. Bell, 1958), 318.

84. Edgar A. Toppin, Review of *Negro Slavery in Arkansas* by Orville W. Taylor, *Journal of Negro History* 44, no. 2 (April 1959): 178.

85. Waldemar E. Debnam, *Then My Old Kentucky Home, Good Night!* (Raleigh, NC: NP, 1955), vii.

86. Bertram P. Karon, *The Negro Personality* (New York: Springer, 1958), 31.

87. Kenneth M. Stampp, *The Peculiar Institution* (New York: Knopf, 1956), vii.

88. Richard B. Morris, Review of *The Peculiar Institution: Slavery in the Ante-Bellum South* by Kenneth M. Stampp, *Journal of Economic History* 18, no. 1 (March 1958): 89.

89. Stanley Elkins, *Slavery: A Problem in American Institutional and Intellectual Life* (Chicago: University of Chicago Press, 1959), 82.

90. Elkins, 82.

91. James Baldwin, *Notes of a Native Son* (Boston: Beacon Press, 1955), 175.

92. Martin Luther King Jr., *Stride toward Freedom: The Montgomery Story* (New York: Harper & Brothers, 1958), 69.

93. Quoted in Stephen B. Oates, *Let the Trumpet Sound: The Life of Martin Luther King, Jr.* (New York: Harper & Row, 1982), 70.

Selected Bibliography

Acuña, Rudolfo. *Community under Siege: A Chronicle of Chicanos East of the Los Angeles River, 1945–1975*. Los Angeles: Chicano Studies Research Center, 1984.

Almaguer, Tomás. *Racial Faultlines: The Historical Origins of White Supremacy in California*. Berkeley: University of California Press, 1994.

Anderson, Carol Elaine. *Eyes off the Prize: The United Nations and the African American Struggle for Human Rights, 1944–1955*. New York: Cambridge University Press, 2003.

Avakian, Monique. *Atlas of Asian-American History*. New York: Facts on File, 2002.

Barger, W. K., and Ernesto M. Reza. *The Farm Labor Movement in the Midwest: Social Change and Adaptation among Migrant Farmworkers*. Austin: University of Texas Press, 1994.

Bayor, Ronald H., ed. *The Columbia Documentary History of Race and Ethnicity in America*. New York: Columbia University Press, 2004.

Bender, Steven W. *Greasers and Gringos: Latinos, Law, and the American Imagination*. New ed. New York: New York University Press, 2005.

Bernardi, Daniel, ed. *Classic Hollywood, Classic Whiteness*. Minneapolis: University of Minnesota Press, 2001.

Bernstein, Allison. *American Indians and World War II: Toward a New Era in Indian Affairs*. Norman: University of Oklahoma Press, 1991.

Bogle, Don. *Toms, Coons, Mulattoes, Mammies & Bucks: An Interpretive History of Blacks in American Films*. New York: Viking Press, 1973.

Bolt, Christine. *American Indian Policy and American Reform: Case Studies of the Campaign to Assimilate the American Indians*. Boston: Allen & Unwin, 1987.

Brooks, Roy L. et al. *Civil Rights Litigation: Cases and Perspectives*. 2nd ed. Durham, NC: Carolina Academic Press, 2000.

Browning, Harley L., and Rodolfo O. De La Garza. *Mexican Immigrants and Mexican Americans: An Evolving Relation*. Austin: University of Texas Press, 1986.

Buchanan, Paul D. *Race Relations in the United States: A Chronology, 1896–2005*. Jefferson, NC: McFarland & Co., 2005.

Burt, Larry W. *Tribalism in Crisis: Federal Indian Policy, 1953–1961*. Albuquerque: University of New Mexico Press, 1982.

Camarillo, Albert. *Latinos in the United States: A Historical Bibliography*. Santa Barbara, CA: ABC-Clio, 1986.

Capeci, Dominic J. Jr. *Race Relations in Wartime Detroit: The Sojourner Truth Housing Controversy of 1942*. Philadelphia: Temple University Press, 1984.

Castaneda, Alejandra. *The Politics of Citizenship of Mexican Migrants*. New York: LFB Scholarly Publishing, 2006.

Christian, Karen. *Show and Tell: Identity as Performance in U.S. Latina/o Fiction*. Albuquerque: University of New Mexico Press, 1997.

Clark, Christine, and James O'Donnell. *Becoming and Unbecoming White: Owning and Disowning a Racial Identity*. Westport, CT: Bergin & Garvey, 1999.

Collier-Thomas, Bettye, and V. P. Franklin. *Sisters in the Struggle: African-American Women in the Civil Rights-Black Power Movement*. New York: New York University Press, 2001.

Conniff, Michael L., and Thomas J. Davis. *Africans in the Americas: A History of the Black Diaspora*. Reprint ed. Caldwell, NJ: Blackburn Press, 2002.

Cooper, Paulette. *Growing up Puerto Rican*. New York: Arbor House, 1972.

Daniels, Roger. *Concentration Camps USA: Japanese America and World War II*. New York: Holt, Reinhardt and Winston, 1972.

Darby, William. *Necessary American Fictions: Popular Literature of the 1950s*. Bowling Green, OH: Bowling Green State University Popular Press, 1987.

Davis, Thomas J. *Race Relations in America*. Westport, CT: Greenwood Press, 2006.

De la Garza, Rodolfo O. et al. *Latino Voices: Mexican, Puerto Rican & Cuban Perspectives on American Politics*. Boulder, CO: Westview Press, 1992.

De la Garza, Rodolfo O. et al. *The Mexican American Experience: An Interdisciplinary Anthology*. Austin: University of Texas Press, 1985.

Deloria, Philip J. *Playing Indian*. New Haven, CT: Yale University Press, 1998.

Dixon, Wheeler Winston. *American Cinema of the 1940s: Themes and Variations*. New Brunswick, NJ: Rutgers University Press, 2005.

Donovan, Robert J., and Ray Scherer. *Unsilent Revolution: Television News and American Public Life*. New York: Cambridge University Press, 1992.

Dudziak, Mary L. *Cold War Civil Rights: Race and the Image of American Democracy*. Princeton: Princeton University Press, 2000.

Enciso, Carmen E. *Hispanic Americans in Congress, 1822–1995*. Washington, DC: GPO, 1995.

Erenberg, Lewis A., and Susan E. Hirsch. *The War in American Culture: Society and Consciousness during World War II*. New ed. Chicago: University of Chicago Press, 1996.

Espiritu, Yen Le. *Asian American Panethnicity: Bridging Institutions and Identities*. Philadelphia: Temple University Press, 1992.

Espiritu, Yen Le. *Asian American Women and Men: Labor, Laws and Love*. Thousand Oaks, CA: Sage Publications, 1997.

Fixico, Donald L. *Termination and Relocation: Federal Indian Policy 1945–1960*. Albuquerque: University of New Mexico Press, 1986.

Foster, David William, ed. *Sourcebook of Hispanic Culture in the United States*. Chicago: American Library Association, 1982.

Francis, Charles E. *The Tuskegee Airmen: The Men Who Changed a Nation*. Boston: Braden, 1993.

Frankenberg, Ruth. *White Women, Race Matters: The Social Construction of Whiteness*. Minneapolis: University of Minnesota Press, 1993.

Friedman, Ian C. *Latino Athletes*. New York: Facts on File, 2007.

Gardner, Audrie, and Anne Loftis. *The Great Betrayal: The Evacuation of the Japanese-Americans during World War II*. New York: Macmillan, 1969.

Gardner, Martha. *The Qualities of a Citizen: Women, Immigration, and Citizenship*. Princeton: Princeton University Press, 2005.

Garza-Falcon, Leticia M. *Gente Decente: A Borderlands Response to the Rhetoric of Domination*. Austin: University of Texas Press, 1998.

Gourley, Catherine. *Rosie and Mrs. America: Perceptions of Women in the 1930s and 1940s*. Minneapolis: Twenty-First Century Books, 2007.

Gracia, Jorge J. E. *Hispanic/Latino Identity: A Philosophical Perspective*. Malden, MA: Blackwell, 2000.

Gutiérrez, David G. *Walls and Mirrors: Mexican Americans, Mexican Immigrants, and the Politics of Ethnicity*. Berkeley: University of California Press, 1995.

Halberstam, David. *The Fifties*. New York: Villard Books, 1993.

Hanke, Ken. *Charlie Chan at the Movies: History, Filmography, and Criticism*. Jefferson, NC: McFarland, 1989.

Hay, Samuel A. *African American Theatre: An Historical and Critical Analysis*. New York: Cambridge University Press, 1994.

Healey, Joseph F., and Eileen O'Brien, eds. *Race, Ethnicity, and Gender: Selected Readings*. Thousand Oaks, CA: Pine Forge Press, 2004.

Hero, Rodney E. *Latinos and the U.S. Political System: Two-Tiered Pluralism*. Philadelphia: Temple University Press, 1992.

Hirsch, Arnold R. *Making the Second Ghetto: Race and Housing in Chicago, 1940–1960*. New York: Cambridge University Press, 1983.

Hune, Shirley. *Pacific Migration to the United States: Trends and Themes in Historical and Sociological Literature*. Washington, DC: Research Institute on Immigration and Ethnic Studies, Smithsonian Institution, 1977.

Jenkins, McKay. *The South in Black and White: Race, Sex, and Literature in the 1940s*. Chapel Hill: University of North Carolina Press, 1999.

Kanellos, Nicolás, and Claudio Esteva-Fabregat, eds. *Handbook of Hispanic Cultures in the United States*. Houston: Arte Público Press, 1993.

Kim, Hyung-Chan. *Dictionary of Asian American History*. Westport, CT: Greenwood Press, 1986.

Kim, Hyung-Chan, ed. *Asian Americans and the Supreme Court: A Documentary History*. Westport, CT: Greenwood Press, 1992.

Koppes, Clayton R., and Gregory D. Black. *Hollywood Goes to War: How Politics, Profits, and Propaganda Shaped World War II Movies*. New York: Free Press, 1987.

Krenn, Michael L. *Black Diplomacy: African Americans and the State Department, 1945–1969*, 1999.

Lee, Stacey J. *Unraveling the "Model Minority" Stereotype: Listening to Asian American Youth*. New York: Teachers College Press, 1996.

Lhamon, W. T. Jr. *Deliberate Speed: The Origins of a Cultural Style in the American 1950s*. Rev. ed. Cambridge, MA: Harvard University Press, 1990.

Lipsitz, George. *Rainbow at Midnight: Labor and Culture in the 1940s*. Urbana: University of Illinois Press, 1994.

Mack, Raymond W. *Prejudice and Race Relations*. Chicago: Quadrangle Books, 1970.

Martinez Wood, Jamie. *Latino Writers and Journalists*. New York: Facts on File, 2007.

Meier, Kenneth J., and Joseph Stewart Jr. *The Politics of Hispanic Education*. Albany: State University of New York Press, 1991.

Miller, Patricia B., and David K. Wiggins, eds. *Sport and the Color Line: Black Athletes and Race Relations in Twentieth-Century America*. New York: Routledge, 2004.

Moran, Rachel F. *The Regulation of Race and Romance*. Chicago: University of Chicago Press, 2001.

Morrison, Toni. *Playing in the Dark: Whiteness and the Literary Imagination.* Cambridge, MA: Harvard University Press, 1992.

Nelson, Emmanuel S., ed. *Asian American Novelists: A Bio-Bibliographical Critical Sourcebook.* Westport, CT: Greenwood Press, 2000.

Niiya, Brian, ed. *Encyclopedia of Japanese American History: An A-to-Z Reference from 1868 to the Present.* New York: Facts on File, 2001.

North, Michael. *The Dialect of Modernism: Race, Language, and Twentieth-Century Literature.* New York: Oxford University Press, 1994.

Novas, Himilce, and Lan Cao. *Everything You Need to Know about Asian American History.* Rev. ed. New York: Plume, 2004.

Okihiro, Gary Y. *The Columbia Guide to Asian American History.* New York: Columbia University Press, 2001.

Olivas, Michael A., ed. *Colored Men and Hombres Aquí: Hernández v. Texas and the Emergence of Mexican American Lawyering.* Houston, TX: Arte Publico Press, 2006.

Ono, Kent A., ed. *A Companion to Asian American Studies.* Malden, MA: Blackwell, 2005.

Padilla, Felix M. *Latino Ethnic Consciousness: The Case of Mexican Americans and Puerto Ricans in Chicago.* Notre Dame: University of Notre Dame Press, 1985.

Philip, Kenneth R. *Termination Revisited: American Indians on the Trail to Self-Determination, 1933–1953.* Lincoln: University of Nebraska Press, 1999.

Reed, Merl E. *Seed Time for the Modern Civil Rights Movement: The President's Committee on Fair Employment Practice, 1941–1946.* Baton Rouge: Louisiana State University Press, 1991.

Rodriguez, Clara E. *Latin Looks: Images of Latinas and Latinos in the U.S. Media.* Boulder, CO: Westview, 1997.

Rollins, Peter C., ed. *The Columbia Companion to American History on Film: How the Movies Have Portrayed the American Past.* New York: Columbia University Press, 2007.

Rosales, Francisco A. *Chicano!: The History of the Mexican American Civil Rights Movement.* 2nd rev. ed. Houston: Arte Publico Press, 1997.

Rosales, Francisco A. *Testimonio: A Documentary History of the Mexican-American Struggle for Civil Rights.* Houston: Arte Publico Press, 2000.

Ruiz, Vicki L. *From Out of the Shadows: Mexican Women in Twentieth-Century America.* New York: Oxford University Press, 1999.

Sable, Martin H. *Mexican and Mexican-American Agricultural Labor in the United States: An International Bibliography.* New York: Haworth Press, 1987.

Sanchez, George J. *Becoming Mexican American: Ethnicity, Culture, and Identity in Chicano Los Angeles, 1900–1945.* New York: Oxford University Press, 1993.

Schultz, Jeffrey D. *Hispanic Americans and Native Americans.* Phoenix, AZ: Oryx Press, 2000.

Scott, Joseph W. *The Black Revolts: Racial Stratification in the U.S.A.* Cambridge, MA: Schenkman, 1976.

Simpson, Caroline Chung. *An Absent Presence: Japanese Americans in Post-War American Culture, 1945–1960.* Durham: Duke University Press, 2001.

Sleeper, Jim. *The Closest of Strangers: Liberalism and the Politics of Race in New York.* New York: W. W. Norton, 1990.

Sollors, Werner. *Beyond Ethnicity: Consent and Descent in American Culture.* New York: Oxford University Press, 1986.

Sonneborn, Liz. *Chronology of American Indian History: The Trail of the Wind.* New York: Facts on File, 2006.

Southern, David W. *Gunnar Myrdal and Black-White Relations: The Use and Abuse of* An American Dilemma, *1944–1969*. Baton Rouge: Louisiana State University Press, 1987.

Stanley, Harold W. *Voter Mobilization and the Politics of Race: The South and Universal Suffrage, 1952–1984*. New York: Praeger, 1987.

Svingen, Orlan J. "Jim Crow, Indian Style." *American Indian Quarterly* 11, no. 4 (Autumn 1987): 275–286.

Takaki, Ronald. *Strangers from a Different Shore: A History of Asian Americans*. Boston: Back Bay Books/Little, Brown, 1998.

Takaki, Ronald, Rebecca Stefoff, and Carol Takaki. *Democracy and Race: Asian Americans and World War II*. New York: Chelsea House, 1994.

Theoharis, Jeanne, and Komozi Woodard. *Freedom North: Black Freedom Struggles Outside the South, 1940–1980*. New York: Palgrave Macmillan, 2003.

Wagenheim, Olga Jiménez de. *The Puerto Ricans: A Documentary History*. Princeton: M. Wiener Publishers, 1994.

Webb, Clive. *Massive Resistance: Southern Opposition to the Second Reconstruction*. New York: Oxford University Press, 2005.

Weyl, Nathaniel. *The Negro in American Culture*. New York, 1960.

Wong, Kevin Scott. *Americans First: Chinese Americans and the Second World War*. Cambridge: Harvard University Press, 2005.

Wu, Jean Yu-Wen Shen, and Min Song. *Asian American Studies: A Reader*. New Brunswick: Rutgers University Press, 2000.

Yin, Xiao-huang. *Chinese American Literature since the 1850s*. Urbana: University of Illinois Press, 2000.

Zahniser, Steven. *Mexican Migration to the United States: The Role of Migration Networks and Human Capital Accumulation*. New York: Routledge, 1999.

Zia, Helen. *Asian American Dreams: The Emergence of an American People*. New York: Farrar Straus Giroux, 2000.

Index

About the Author

THOMAS J. DAVIS teaches history at Arizona State University, Tempe.